PRAISE FOR *TRAVELS WITH HARLEY*

"A well-crafted memoir that captures the tone of our times yet embraces timeless elements that help define who we are, *Travels With Harley* is a treat to read. Holshek's experiences and reflections on what it means to be an American in these times are both penetrating and refreshing—an antidote to pessimism and a reminder of what makes life worth living."

—*General James N. Mattis, US Marine Corps (Ret.)*

"*Travels with Harley* could equally be titled *National Security and the Art of Motorcycle Maintenance.* Insightful and refreshing!"

—*Anne-Marie Slaughter, CEO, New America Foundation and author of* The Idea That Is America

"Colonel Chris Holshek had a long and distinguished career on the front lines of freedom for our nation. In this riveting personal memoir that is one part memory and one part impressions from the seat of his beloved Harley, he takes us through both his fascinating career and his impressions of the nation he defended so well. Ride strong, and read this book!"

—*Admiral James Stavridis, former NATO Supreme Allied Commander and dean of the Fletcher School at Tufts University*

"If this book doesn't make you want to grab a helmet and jump on a motorcycle to rediscover America, you need to check your pulse. Holshek's exquisite observations give us the big, bold and beautiful as well as the bumpy and burdensome of the American identity. *Travels with Harley* is nothing short of brilliant—a modern philosophic classic comparable in depth to Thoreau's *Walden.*"

—*Dr. Lisa Schirch, professor of peacebuilding, Eastern Mennonite University, and author of* The Little Book of Strategic Peacebuilding

"Chris Holshek has written a brilliant account of his journey through our great land. His reflections, life lessons, and interpretations of his experiences are true gems that are well worth the read. He has captured the meaning of his lifelong service to our Nation and to the real nature of our greatness."

—*General Anthony C. Zinni, US Marine Corps (Ret.) and author of* Before the First Shots are Fired

"Always thoughtful and often profound, Chris Holshek's observations are also exhilarating and inspiring. He is both a lucid historian and an entertaining chronicler of his travels. However, his crowning achievement is his ability to editorialize on it all insightfully and controversially, making *Travels with Harley* an entertaining and educational read."

—*Robert V. Sicina, executive in residence at the American University Kogod School of Business and former president of American Express Bank Ltd.*

"*Travels with Harley* is far more than a travelogue or a memoir. It is also a voyage of civil–military discovery that addresses the most critical lessons of Vietnam, Iraq, and Afghanistan. At the end it is clear that real peace means finding a level of national and community stability that can meet the psychological as well as physical needs of people everywhere."

—*Anthony H. Cordesman, Burke Chair in Strategy, Center for Strategic and International Studies*

"*Travels with Harley* takes you on an intimate ride on America's history as well as its highways, where you get a real opportunity to reflect on where this great country has been, and more importantly, where it is going."

—*Rick Wolff, senior executive editor, Houghton Mifflin Harcourt Publishing, and Host of WFAN New York Radio's* The Sports Edge

"This book bowled me over! Holshek's bracing and thought-provoking reflections are required for anyone wanting to understand the deep complexity of the United States. In a powerful voice leavened with humor and irony, we can feel the wind as he discovers America anew, weaving together how history, geography, and culture have shaped our understanding of ourselves and the rest of the world. His ruminations on service, dignity, freedom, and peace, war, and the state of our nation are at once wise and challenging. A wonderful read!"

—*Melanie Greenberg, president and CEO, The Alliance for Peacebuilding*

"A must-read for those thinking about the future direction of America and what they can do about it."

—*Kristin Lord, former executive vice president of the US Institute of Peace and former executive vice president and director of studies, Center for a New American Security*

"I have no doubt that *Travels with Harley* will touch hearts at a global level and enrich all who read it. You are in for a real treat."

—*Major General Muhammad Tahir, Pakistan Army (Ret.)*

"Through his travelogue, Chris Holshek offers us a unique perspective on where we are as a nation. This once-in-a-lifetime story is vital and compelling, even for those who never will climb on a Harley."

—*Jordan Ryan, vice president, Peace Programs, the Carter Center*

TRAVELS
WITH
HARLEY

Tom,

Thank you for your

service, then and now!

TRAVELS
WITH
HARLEY

JOURNEYS IN SEARCH OF
PERSONAL AND NATIONAL IDENTITY

CHRISTOPHER HOLSHEK

INKSHARES

Published by Inkshares, Inc., San Francisco, California
www.inkshares.com

Edited by Jaimee Garbacik and Girl Friday Productions, designed by Girl Friday
Productions
www.girlfridayproductions.com

Cover design by Marc Cohen

ISBN: 9781941758373
e-ISBN: 9781941758380
Library of Congress Control Number: 2015939059

First edition

Printed in the United States of America

For Rosa, the angel of my better nature, and all who have journeyed to find themselves in the service of their fellow human beings

CONTENTS

FOREWORD

In early 2010, Chris Holshek, an Army Civil Affairs colonel nearing the end of his military career and possessing a great wealth of relevant experience, joined the Project on National Security Reform (PNSR), a transpartisan organization in Washington, DC, then working to modernize and improve the ways and means the United States employs in the twenty-first century to "secure the blessings of liberty for ourselves and our posterity."

Chris believed so strongly in PNSR's cause that he remained as a senior associate after his retirement from the Army and until PNSR disbanded two years later.

Beyond his energy and enthusiasm, Chris displayed the rare ability to think outside the box. He often reminded us, however, through his rare civil–military perspective of seeing how policy works (or doesn't work) on the ground, that it was really about understanding the box that America is in already. To reform a dangerously outdated national security system, he looked beyond the need to forge a new consensus among US leaders and citizens. He saw the need to revise the idea of *national security* itself. The concept needed to become much broader, to include untraditional dimensions such as economics, law enforcement, health, trade, and the environment. And it needed to become more inclusive, taking a whole-of-nation approach to benefit from all of the capacities of this great country.

When Chris announced his plan to mark his Army retirement with a motorcycle trip around the United States to help him think about what his impressive career had taught him about being an American in the world, we urged him to share his impressions with us and others. The journal of his trip, *Two Wheels and Two Questions*, afforded an opportunity for many to gain the benefit of Chris's insights and discoveries as he traveled beyond the Washington Beltway to sense how Americans viewed their future. Now, again at the urging of many friends and colleagues, Chris is carrying forth his work and insights in this book.

Most of us merely witness history, and only a few find themselves in history books. Yet many, mostly unknown, people move us in small yet significant ways along the path of human destiny. In the major transformation efforts in which I have been involved, among them the Goldwater-Nichols Defense Reorganization Act described in *Victory on the Potomac*, many dedicated people worked behind the scenes to achieve the required changes. Chris is one of these unsung movers of history, as his contributions and leadership have demonstrated throughout his civil–military career, at PNSR, and right up to this day.

In helping us frame the great nationwide discussion now taking place about our future, Chris makes a valuable contribution through his realistic sense of his country's role in the world, gained through years of experience in numerous places. In many ways, the whole-of-government, whole-of-nation, and even whole-of-world perspectives so desperately needed in our national leadership are instinctive to people like Chris because he has lived and worked them years before we ever coined these terms. His twists of phrase in this book reflect the twists and turns of the experiences and insights of someone who represents a treasured minority of collaborative national security and peacebuilding professionals—a minority that we hope will grow to become more mainstream as we go forward into the twenty-first century.

As our paths crossed at PNSR, Chris had likewise come to learn that the dysfunction in Washington is so immense and entrenched that it cannot reform itself. Our performance shortfalls go beyond party or persuasion, and change requires participation from all corners and walks of life in America. Change in great societies, after all, comes from the bottom up more than the top down. Or, as PNSR came to phrase it, "It takes a nation to fix a government."

This is why Chris's call to a new and refreshed sense of citizenship and service that thinks globally and acts locally is so vital to the future peace, prosperity, and security of the United States and the world to which it is increasingly connected.

For those who are concerned about America's future, this book is essential reading. It contains profound insights and wisdom from an experienced and knowledgeable practitioner who has thought deeply about the idea, as well as the reality, of America. Taking this journey with Chris provides a rich, thought-provoking education. You won't want to miss it.

James R. Locher III
Former President and CEO
Project on National Security Reform

INTRODUCTION

This book came into the world much as its author did—unexpectedly but not at all unwanted.

In May 2010, I took my new Harley-Davidson Dyna Wide Glide, black and chrome with orange flames on the fuel tank, over eight thousand miles around the continental United States from and back to the Washington, DC, area to mark the end of three decades of civil–military service inside (and sometimes outside) the US Army as a Civil Affairs officer. On my last day in the military I wanted to be where it all started—at New Mexico Military Institute—closing one chapter in order to open another. This kind of closure is particularly difficult for people in the military: When you live a life of service, you never stop serving. To continue serving my country from inside the Washington Beltway, I felt I had to see the country outside of it but realized I hadn't seen much of America, having spent twenty of my service years abroad. "I thought I'd take a look around the place," I began to tell people.

In many ways, it was also an azimuth check—a reference to a starting point, as in land navigation and orienteering—to see where I had come from, what directions I had taken, and where I might be going. It was also a voyage of (re)discovery of the land of my identity. Like many veterans, as Elizabeth Samet explained in *No Man's Land*, I took to the road seeking intelligibility that only an adventure like this can enable. "The road has all the answers," as one rider put it. "The road is a

promise fulfilled." In my own lifetime, I often took roads less traveled—
but that, as Robert Frost said, "has made all the difference."

In a nod to *Travels with Charley*—John Steinbeck's account about
his own cross-country venture in a pickup camper with his dog—this
book is an account of my own multilayered journey. As Steinbeck did
when he drove around "a galaxy of states" in search of America at the
time of my birth, I likewise learned that you can experience America
only on a personal level. "A journey is a person in itself; no two are alike,"
he wrote. "We find after years of struggle that we do not take a trip; a
trip takes us." Often, the longest of journeys circles back to the place
where it all started, where the traveler discovers something that was
there all along but awaited validation by experience. Joseph Campbell,
America's greatest mythologist, called this the "heroic cycle"—a going
out, an illumination, and a return with a higher level of understanding
about oneself and the world.

Not long after my ride began, serendipity set in—life being, as John
Lennon sang, "what happens to you while you're busy making other
plans." In other words, "no plan survives the first five minutes of con-
tact with the enemy," as they say in the Army. The first half took me
westward along a southern axis—from Virginia, through North and
South Carolina, Georgia, Alabama, Mississippi, Louisiana, Texas, and
then New Mexico. After I returned to where my career began at New
Mexico Military Institute, the trip became more and more ad hoc.
Bypassing the Grand Canyon in Arizona and after stopping in Las
Vegas, I rolled into Simi Valley, California.

Then came a deviation more apt for my time than Steinbeck's. At
the behest of George Mason University, I flew back to Washington to
take a dozen graduate students on a field trip to Liberia. After resuming my ride up the California coast and back into Nevada, my mental
as well as physical wanderings spread out in the vast, open spaces of
Utah, Idaho, Wyoming, Montana, and South Dakota. Then the circles
they opened began to close through Iowa, Missouri, Indiana, Kentucky,
and finally West Virginia.

You can read about a country all you want, but until you've gone
out and seen it, met some of its people, and traveled its roads, you
haven't experienced it. This I knew from traveling abroad first. "Go to

foreign countries," Goethe advised, "and you will get to know the good things one possesses at home." One thing about most Americans is that they have little to no clue how lucky they are. But that, I also discovered from this trip, is a conclusion each American must come to in his or her own way and time.

America is a rich and rough country. Its breathtaking scenery belies the fierce challenges of an environment that has helped shape a national character forged in struggle. Other than on foot or horseback, you can only get a feel for its elemental freedoms and dangers on a motorcycle. Riding a motorcycle is a more active form of travel than aiming an automobile. "You're in the scene, not just watching it anymore, and the sense of presence is overwhelming," explained Robert Pirsig in his classic *Zen and the Art of Motorcycle Maintenance*. This is impossible in a sport-utility vehicle or a pickup truck. They are vestiges of our romanticization of rugged individualism and personal mobility, which is really why they sell more than they should. But you can't be a rugged individualist in an SUV, a motor home, or even a present-day version of Steinbeck's "Rocinante." Most never leave pavement and are as well appointed as luxury sedans.

Besides, the authenticity of any character-defining experience is in its discomforts and dangers. "You've got to go out on a limb sometimes because that's where the fruit is," said Will Rogers. Adversity, after all, is self-introduction; the adventure you get is not always the one you want but ultimately the one you need. As I was riding along, meditating in motion, I wondered what all the people talking and texting found to be so important as to distract them from the real world they're oblivious to in the cocoons of their cars, insulated from the nature they pine for but only as voyeurs.

For many, the idea of adventure is now a video game on a smartphone or a TV "reality" series—virtual and vicarious but invalidated and superficial. The gaggle of gadgets to satisfy our shortening attention spans deprives us of environmental association and detaches us further from our surroundings, reinforcing a mind-set of willful ignorance. The world becomes the things we view it through; but it's not the world itself. Such is also the downside of social media—we are connected to other human beings but, again, vicariously. And in our alienation from the world around us, we become strangers to our-selves. As in Iraq, I never used a GPS on this trip. Instead, I got up in the morning, studied the map, read the road signs and the lay of the land, and stopped and asked real persons for suggestions, if not directions.

Even how we earn our daily bread is now automated and abstracted. Most of us labor in air-conditioned offices and never get dirt on our hands. When I first worked in Washington at the age of twenty, I noticed the contrast between the hands-on blue-collar work I had just done as a teenager—raising a roof, laying out a patio deck, or baling wagonloads of hay—and the white-collar office work of an incoming century in the form of images on screens. Even most of our money has become invisible. In the course of my career, war has also become figu-rative. We fight wars against tactics like terrorism using drones driven by joysticks and see cyberwarfare as an existential threat. It's hard to comprehend the value or impact of something you can't get your hands on, or something that's communal but not personally felt.

Even old age and death—the greatest of democratizers—remain puritanically secluded in America. The mass exodus away from the land and an agricultural existence and toward a more urban lifestyle means that we've antiseptically left death and the natural world behind us. We park our geriatrics in assisted-living centers and bury our dead in well-manicured cemeteries. In contrast, while stationed in Europe I visited Vienna's Zentralfriedhof, where many of the great compos-ers are interred, and saw joggers, skaters and skateboarders, lovers, playing children, and strolling people. For Native Americans, death is an inseparable part of natural life, not an evil to overcome. But their immigrant successors today deny death or even old age, making it hard to embrace the journey of life. (Similarly, singular among peoples are Americans' convoluted attitudes about sex—in contrast to their accla-mation of violence. There are more guns and porn in the United States than most other countries combined.)

All these things, however, aren't problems to be fixed but pro-cesses to be managed. To do that, you need to know who you are and what you're about—to center yourself around values rooted in real-ity. That requires a trip more than a tool. Having a sense of personal and communal identity provides a moral compass that helps one face today's complex and dynamic world, navigate the fog of uncertainty, and weather the storms of change. But that doesn't come passively by watching a television, computer, or smartphone screen. Nor is it inconsequential.

Technology is liberating in that it helps us gain power over space and time, but at the risk of personal and social alienation. Technology is morally neutral, and it doesn't give us identity—we find out who we really are in the field of action and in personal interface, not on Facebook or Twitter, which are just bigger nets to cast. Instant communication and information overload flattens our decision cycles, squeezing out time to process things and make up our own minds about what we value. So we either simply react to all the stimuli, like mice in a Skinner box, or allow others to process it for us—then wonder why we can't make sense of things.

Our consciousness and innate moral compass, however, help us to realize the responsibilities such power necessitates. Without them, technology becomes a monster, supplanting rather than supplementing our humanity. "Conscience is the soul of freedom," Thomas Merton tells us in *No Man Is an Island*. "Without conscience, freedom never knows what to do with itself." This is why rights cannot exist without responsibilities, and why art helps us make sense of things by giving them context. True moderation strikes a synergy between art and science, contemplation and action, feeling and thinking. The founders of the nation called this human faculty to bring these things together and transcend them "reason."

The yearning for authenticity and a genuine sense of connection with nature and other persons may be why motorcycle sales are rising. More than cars, motorcycles are appropriate metaphors of the elemental American quest for freedom in individual and social mobility. Through their demand for self-discipline, they also allow both the mind and the body to wander and find balance—you have time to do a lot of thinking while riding for hours over long stretches of landscape. As bikers say, "Four wheels move the body, but two wheels move the soul." As the veterans in Samet's *No Man's Land* did, I returned home from my road adventure feeling that the interactions with those I met along the way, brief and singular as they were, "constituted real and honest connections, animated by generosity, solidarity, and a healthy curiosity."

There are many reasons to take a journey, but chief among them is to learn. Travel is a form of education and education a form of travel—one is a physical activity leading to contemplative change and the other a mental journey inspiring a new undertaking. A journey, after all, is a movement between states of being, or a transition. "Traveling with patience is allowing time to rule and shape our lives," Pope Francis told us in *His Life in His Own Words*. "To travel in patience means accepting that life is a continuous learning experience." So, as I have done all my life, I set out like Odysseus that spring morning in search of something greater than myself, knowing that to complete Campbell's heroic cycle, the process of bringing to expression what I gleaned from that experience still lay ahead.

Not long after I published my initial findings for the Project on National Security Reform (PNSR), I realized, as my thoughts evolved in the *Huffington Post*, *Foreign Policy*, and other places, that I was tapping into a much larger and more enduring national conversation. Over time, and at the suggestion of many, the call to that phase of the journey became irresistible. I felt obligated to write this book much as artists are artists not because they want to be but because they have to be, or else they will be less than themselves—incomplete until they finish their work. Like for the many whose insights I quote in this book, my own adventure led to discoveries unforeseen by those who went before me. Yet my experience and that which I've learned would have been impossible without their findings. Just as Steinbeck's book inspired me, this "motorcycle diary" is my own contribution to a conversation this country desperately needs to have.

Every one of us, in every generation, must take our own journey to learn what it means to be a member of our community and a citizen not only of our country but of the larger world that technology and trade are hooking us up with, within and beyond the horizons of our lifetime. If we don't find our own identity, it will be provided for us. "In the animal kingdom, the rule is eat or be eaten," explained renowned psychiatrist Thomas Szasz. "In the human kingdom, [it is] define or be defined."

The choices we make along the way of that journey reveal the true nature of our character. "Character," David Brooks advised us in *The*

Road to Character, "is not innate or automatic. You have to build it with effort and artistry." By taking that personal journey, we change ourselves and the concentric circles of the communities and countries to which we claim to belong. It is only through service to others and personal engagement within and beyond the known worlds of our communities and our nation that we can gain a true sense of ourselves, refresh our own sense of a connective national identity, transcendent of social divisions, and keep them both balanced and strong.

As I finished this manuscript, that revelation made it evident that there was still a lot of unfinished business. More than one veteran's story of what he learned about being an American in today's world, this book has, in turn, become a call to action for those who have lived a life of service to complete their mission by passing the baton of citizenship and leadership. As I explained to the organizers of the annual Rolling Thunder ride, "It's great we veterans get together every year, three or four hundred thousand of us, in Washington, and remember something larger than ourselves and thank each other for our service. But what happens after we die? What have we done to help the next generation understand about service and sacrifice, which we find second nature, so they can serve their country, even if not in uniform or overseas, to ensure its greatness?"

The book you are about to read is also a platform for a multimedia campaign that includes more cross-country rides as well as discussions in schools, town halls, and other places to facilitate intergenerational, intervocational, and intercommunal dialogue. Among the organizations joining the campaign's coalition of partners, the Freedoms Foundation—dedicated to helping American youth learn more about citizenship—is partnering with me to help incite this quiet riot. In turn, a portion of what you paid to read these lines is a donation to the Foundation's great cause, and I encourage you to join or contribute to any member(s) of the coalition or other like groups. You can find out more on associated websites and social media using *Travels with Harley*, *National Service Ride*, or my name as keywords.

Thanks for riding with me. And as soldiers say before going into combat: See you on the high ground.

CHAPTER 1

SOUTH CAROLINA: "PLEASE" AND "THANK YOU"

I got off to a good start on Cinco de Mayo, which is Spanish for "Fifth of May." The holiday was initially intended to commemorate the Mexican army's unlikely victory over invading French forces at *El Día de la Batalla de Puebla* on May 5, 1862. It gradually evolved into a commemoration of the cause of freedom, mainly by Southerners, at the time of the American Civil War. Mexican Americans now observe Cinco de Mayo as a day of heritage and pride. For the gringos, it seems to be a cause to party more than for those south of the border, where Mexico's Independence Day, September 16, is the most important national holiday.

I didn't begin my journey with all this in mind. Like a lot of coincidences I'm sure many other people find themselves in, it just worked out that way.

As I headed out on the highway from Alexandria, just across the river from the nation's capital, the early-morning air was cool and sweet but warmed considerably as the day wore on. Sometimes the first step of the longest journey is not so small—in this case, it was 532 miles. Congestion on Interstate 95 was surprisingly light at first, but that didn't last long. Virginia, at least in the northern vicinities, appears to be a state in constant search of a traffic jam. No matter what time of day, it seems to take longer to get to Richmond than it did for General Grant.

After sailing past the high-tech hub of Raleigh–Durham on Interstate 85, I hit Charlotte, North Carolina, by midafternoon. As billboards left and right told me either how much God loves me or that the adult superstore was just a few exits away, the traffic thickened on the multilane stretch through Greenville, South Carolina. Some were probably getting out of work at the BMW factory, now a landmark for a generation in the newly industrialized South.

After Greenville, I steered my Dyna Wide Glide southwest toward Central, South Carolina, along Route 123. As I snaked along the lushly wooded Upstate region on Six Mile Highway past the waterways feeding the Seneca River and nearby Lake Keowee, I noticed more new McMansions—large, luxurious single-family homes bought on the cheapest of credit—than last time I had been there just after the Iraq War. Many of the area's inhabitants are displaced northerners, among them "halfbacks" tired of living in overdeveloped Florida but able only to bring themselves to repatriate halfway back. *Halfback* also alludes to the South's love of (American) football, the most universal of religions there.

Central, exactly midway between Atlanta and Charlotte, is the home of retired Chief Master Sergeant Harold Randolph Manley, who served thirty-five years in the US Air Force, including tours in Vietnam, where he had seen more than his fair share of bad scenes. Uncle Randy was my father's Air Force buddy when he met my aunt Ann, my mother's younger sister, in England in the late 1950s. While my father, John, married my mother, Audrey, in England, Uncle Randy and Aunt Ann exchanged their vows on this side of the pond. They lived with us for a while in Highland Mills, in what I call "the Deep South of New York," where I grew up, near West Point and Stewart Air Base. As a toddler, I used to wait anxiously for Uncle Randy to return from the base, often refusing to eat until he came home.

By then, my father had left the Air Force, but Uncle Randy stayed on, rewarded with tours of duty in Vietnam, where he saw "Charlie" (slang for Viet Cong guerrillas) often come "over the wire" (barriers edging the camps) or send in children as suicide bombers. Throughout the tumultuous 1960s, we waited as a family for his return, each day anxiously watching the first televised war to somehow feel more connected to him. Over twenty years later, Uncle Randy retired to the farm that has belonged to his family for generations, comprised of hay fields and two or three dozen beef cattle.

Vietnam and its legacy loomed large in the years that spanned my military career. One of the last pieces of advice the Army Civil Affairs battalion I commanded in Iraq got when we returned in early 2004 was to remember to thank a Vietnam veteran for his service. I took the chance to do this in public a few years later when an Army buddy, Lieutenant Colonel Chuck Nettleship, asked me to appear on a panel on national strategy and security issues at his alma mater, Norwich University in Vermont. During the question-and-answer session, a Marine who had seen action in Vietnam had his question addressed by the other three panelists. Then it was my turn.

Looking straight at him, I said, "Before I answer your question, sir, I want to thank you for your service. The only difference between you and me is that I was fortunate enough to come home to a grateful nation. You were not. And yet your cause was no more or less noble. For that reason, your heroism is greater than mine. So, again, thank you for your service."

The whole place broke out in a standing ovation. I took that reaction as another sign that despite public opposition to the war in Vietnam, the American public has since moved on and matured to understand the difference between those who make foreign policy and those who dispatch, as I've heard (retired) Marine Corps General James Mattis call it, its "last six hundred meters." I've come to learn that, although the politics, the cause, or the morality give such service a certain important quality or context, what makes a hero is the deed itself—an act of personal sacrifice for something that is larger than oneself. If we can consider, for example, General Robert E. Lee and many other brave and honorable people from the South who fought for what turned out to be the wrong cause to be heroes—as indeed they were—then you get my point.

Uncle Randy, who stands a bit shorter and lighter than yours truly, was my first role model—a person I chose to learn from and emulate. Another was retired Marine Lieutenant Colonel Coulter "Buddy"

Tillett, a native of Virginia Beach, who commanded a company in Vietnam and then served in Somalia in the early 1990s before transitioning to the "service of peace" for another decade or so in at least a dozen United Nations field missions, including Eastern Slavonia, where we first met. In Iraq, I came upon Buddy after he barely survived the horrendous August 2003 truck bombing of the Canal Hotel outside Baghdad. He and I lost some good friends and colleagues that day, as we did a few years later in the Haiti earthquake. He is a personal hero and friend, and we share a passion for adventure and making a difference, Cuban cigars, single malt Scotch, and the New York Yankees.

Heroes, role models, and mentors come to us even if we aren't looking for them. We somehow set ourselves on a path that calls them to us. Whether personal or public, they help us shape our character and personality, and form our values and identity. An unexpected role model of late is Al Santoli, whose Vietnam memoir, *Everything We Had*, I read as a lieutenant and thought, "I would really like to meet this guy someday." More than thirty years later, a friend introduced us. Once a great soldier, he is now among the great peacebuilders of our time, having worked tirelessly since then through his nongovernmental organization (NGO), the Asia America Initiative—twice the hero, if you will.

I was fortunate to have some many heroes, role models, and mentors during especially my childhood. I took it somewhat for granted until much later on when, through my work overseas, I got to see how children and youth in broken societies are more vulnerable to extremist views. If they don't have a strong family or community structures, they get their identity from the street. It's not the gang you join—I eventually joined one—but what the gang stands for.

Among my earliest mentors was Dorothy Vassar, a friend and colleague of my mother. "Aunt Dot," half her heritage old New York Dutch and half German, was a widow with no children. She worked with my mother at Falkirk in Central Valley, New York, then a private psychiatric center and now a country club, and gravitated toward my family. Noticing my interest in the many books she had, she loaned or gave me some when my family couldn't afford them, and she also took me to the museums and other sites in "The City" to spark my intellectual growth. Another such guide was Salvatore Spezio, an Italian American who served as a Marine in the Pacific theater. As an officer at the local American Legion post, Sal nominated me in 1977 for New York Boys State—a weeklong summer camp focused on civics and government.

Then there were my teachers, among them Kevin McIntyre, an energetic Irish Catholic who was a biology teacher fresh out of the State University of New York at New Paltz. Kevin was among the first of my wrestling coaches and then tapped me to be the set designer and stage manager of the first musical performed at Washingtonville Senior High School. My social studies teacher, Joan Cashon, a perky, compact Italian American with a real zest for life, fanned my interest in history, geography, and current events.

All of my mentors embraced my unconventionality and dared me to be "exceptional" on my own terms. I'm still in touch with some of them today. They also made me think. Back when I was editor of the high school newspaper, I interviewed our principal, Herbert Fliegner, who started as a child soldier of sorts in the Hitler Youth and was pressed to defend Berlin. After a similar involuntary induction into the Young Pioneers of the Communist Party, in the Soviet zone, he escaped into West Germany, then emigrated to the United States and was soon drafted into the Army. In answer to a question on freedom of expression, including inflammatory newspaper articles and unapproved student protests, Mr. Fliegner leaned forward, peering at me over his spectacles. "Freedom is not license to just do what you want," he said in his Teutonic accent. "With each and every right comes an equal and concomitant responsibility. When you fail to assume those responsibilities, sooner or later you will forfeit the rights that go with them." Those words have stuck with me ever since.

Whether on a personal or collective level, the Second World War influenced every aspect of life in the late twentieth century. Be it my mother's family from Britain who survived the bombings or my paternal grandmother's family who survived the war in Germany, they all said the same thing: "You Americans have no idea how lucky you are. You don't know what war looks like." (Americans also know very little about war, even though US history, especially of late, is replete with it.)

For me, having grown up in a working-class family, the military was an obvious way to achieve two goals—get an education and see the world. During the Cold War, the military's VA loans and GI Bill made it possible for many—especially minorities—to enter the middle class. Patriotism, however, was less on my mind than the idea that I might have to kill someone someday. So I read books like John Keegan's *The Face of Battle* to get an idea of it. I volunteered at times in veterans' homes, listening to their stories, but asking them what killing was like seemed as intimate to me as asking an adult about sex. Somehow I knew: It's just something you don't ask a veteran—not even Uncle Randy. There are some things you have to find out for yourself.

Along with our experiences, we learn most about ourselves through others with whom we share those experiences. Like actors on a stage, heroes, role models, and mentors come and go and play varying roles in our lifelong play. Then we become one or the other ourselves, usually unexpectedly and sometimes without realizing it. Many of mine encouraged me to live an interesting life, to seek adventure well beyond the Empire State, and to learn more about myself by learning more about the world around me. Thus did others help this redheaded middle child with an overdeveloped sense of self-awareness to begin to form his own identity.

As a child and a teenager, I found adults far more interesting than kids my own age. Whether at family gatherings, on multifamily camping trips, or during public outings such as picnics and parades, I preferred to sit around and listen to others talk, especially to hear their stories, to the point of making a nuisance of myself. But I learned a lot from them.

I was lucky to have such a good start in life. As an adult, I have told my parents many times that if they've ever done anything right with me and my two sisters, Sheree and Susan, it's that they taught us to be self-responsible and to hold ourselves accountable for what we say and do (or don't do). My dad also taught me that although "both men and boys make mistakes, it's how well you learn from them that determines which one you are." In sports, he urged me to be a graceful winner by first learning how to lose gracefully—"There's no shame in failure if you've given it your best"—and to never quit. I can still see the last lines of Walter Wintle's poem plastered on the locker room wall, which I ritualistically read just before every home wrestling match:

Life's battles don't always go
To the stronger or faster man;
But soon or late the fellow who wins
Is the one who thinks he can.

My own upbringing was a process of reconciling dualities—being the middle child, the only son, and a bit "exceptional," as one teacher told me, although I preferred the word's less strident meaning. My father and mother were distinctly feeling and thinking types, respectively. Because I dared to be a bit different, I was the target of bullies. Playing the allegorical devil and angel on my shoulders, my Bronx-born dad told me to fight back while my British-born mother, stressing civility, advised me to not "lower myself to their level." Both were right in a way, but I had to resolve my internal version of this eternal conflict in a way with which I could live.

Eventually, I thrashed the neighborhood bully who had been preying on me for years, but I picked my moment and did it my way, realizing that a bully is really a coward working from a perception of his or her own inferiority—in this case, the presence of someone who was apparently smarter. Besides gaining a better understanding of when and when not to use violence (as a last rather than first resort), the crucible of this extended bullying experience helped me center myself. The result was a greater sense of who I am and what I'm about. It helped give me a more authentic sense of identity.

Among the things my parents did was to provide me a small weekly allowance. Beyond keeping my room tidy, which was expected, I had to take out the garbage and clean up the yard, including the dog poop that our German shepherd, Queenie, deposited. As time went on, I received a raise but had more chores. I could do whatever I wanted with the money, but it was also the only way I could get things I wanted, like model airplane kits. Other than instilling in me a strong work ethic, having chores and an allowance taught me how to be responsible to the community of my family—a good citizen in a way. It also helped me learn humility while assessing my own self-worth.

Work teaches you many things. I began to learn that during summer jobs with my dad on carpentry projects or working on farms. But more than anything, "work anoints a person with dignity," as Pope Francis phrased it for me decades later. It gives you a sense of personal value and identity in a public space. Choose your work carefully, I realized early on. Especially in America, it will define you more than ancestry or even education. Besides, you will spend more than one-third of your living hours doing it or going to or from it. "Work is love made visible," I picked up reading Khalil Gibran's *The Prophet* in college. To me, that meant if you're not happy in your work, there's a good chance you won't be happy at all or much use or value to anyone else.

Work also teaches you leadership. As I learned from John Leyen, an old, bald Dutchman who escaped with his family as the Germans invaded and later owned Orange County's last thousand-acre farm, where I worked a couple of summers while in high school, "A good boss never asks his people to do anything he isn't willing to do himself."

Having learned this from hard physical labor and Uncle Randy's example, I found it easy as a young lieutenant to get along with non-commissioned officers (NCOs) and gather numerous pearls of commonsense wisdom from them, particularly about leadership and people skills, such as how leading by example is the most powerful and enduring form of leadership because it's the sincerest way to communicate what we say about ourselves and what we value. It's also the most democratic and universal form of leadership, transcending language, culture, and other human categorizations. The resemblance or difference between what we say and what we do is the true measure of our character. If you can't walk your talk, then you're really not worth more than the material things you have, depending of course on how you got them.

Drill Sergeant Collier, who earned a Distinguished Service Cross in Vietnam, was my first exposure to that ethos in the Army. Though twice my seventeen years, he ran us into the ground on forced marches during basic training in the brutal summer heat and humidity of Fort Knox, Kentucky. Sergeant First Class Snead, my first platoon sergeant in B Troop, 158th Cavalry of the Maryland Army National Guard, who had two tanks shot from underneath him in Vietnam, taught me an important lesson after I verbally dressed down a young NCO in plain view. "L-T," he called me, "let's take a walk." As a leader, he told me, public takedowns not only make the guy you're yelling at look small; it makes you look even smaller. "You don't get respect unless you give it first." Dressing down also destroys critical unit cohesion and esprit de corps. "You need to depend on each other for your lives," he added.

"It's all about trust," I told Uncle Randy while sipping a cold beer in his downstairs man cave the day I rode into Central, reflecting back on what I had learned from NCOs like him as we waited for supper to be ready. "My article of faith has been to give people the benefit of the doubt until they prove otherwise. That's set me up for a lot of disappointment, but it's how I've expected other people to treat me. One way or another, I figure, what goes around comes around."

To illustrate, I told Uncle Randy about how, after I took battalion command, we were on our annual ten-kilometer forced march exercise, loaded with full gear and a fifty-pound rucksack. We knew we were getting ready to go to war, so we were pushing hard. Although among the oldest members, the sergeant major and I had finished ahead of two-thirds of the others. When we crossed the finish line, he was surprised to see me turn around and head back.

"Where you going, sir?" he asked.

"To police up the others. We leave no one behind, right, Sergeant Major?"

"I'm with you, sir," he said as he and other NCOs and officers joined me. Remembering what I learned from Drill Sergeant Collier, I walked all the way back to the last person and urged him forward. From that day on, my battalion knew I wouldn't ask them to do anything I wasn't willing to do myself. In that sense, I had begun to earn their trust.

"I have people like you to thank for that," I told Uncle Randy after taking another sip.

NCOs like Uncle Randy as well as some great ROTC military science instructors like Captain John Schneeberger, who was also my orienteering coach at New Mexico Military Institute, helped me learn another basic rule of military leadership: Focus on your mission and take care of your troops. It was the same guidance I gave our battalion just before going into combat. When I first returned from Iraq to Fort Bragg, North Carolina, I obtained a weekend pass, and it was Uncle Randy I first visited, talking over a beer in his den about my year at war, just as I was doing at the end of my military career. I didn't have to explain a lot because he already understood. He was the only other member of my family who had seen combat. So it made sense for him to again be the first person to see on my retirement ride, because he was also the only other member of my family who had served in the military until retirement. He knew what I was doing and why.

"Chris," he said to me in his thick backwoods drawl, "there are some things you just have to learn to leave behind."

"That's one reason why I'm taking this ride," I answered. "To think about my past so I can move into the future. You got on your tractor. I'm getting on my bike."

Whenever I ride in Rolling Thunder on Memorial Day weekend in Washington, the first person I think about is Specialist Charles Bush, a cook turned machine gunner in our battalion who was killed in action in northern Iraq. Regardless of the circumstances, every commander who has lost a soldier feels a sense of unparalleled responsibility, a sense of failure in that one goal to make sure you bring everybody home in the vertical position, regardless of how realistic doing so was. As I took the last swig of beer, I remembered how that private talk with Uncle Randy in this very same place six years prior helped me find some peace of mind about it.

Every time I visit Central, I wind up helping out on the farm, which I thoroughly enjoy. There's nothing like a good day of honest work to get you grounded again. This time, Uncle Randy, my cousin Richard, his friend Steve, and I replaced the bearings on one of the tractors and reassembled the front end. Uncle Randy's mechanical aptitude never ceases to amaze me. He can more than hold his own with those guys on the car restoration shows. After Vietnam, he brought me a lamp he had made out of ammunition casings and packing material. I still use it today.

It took me some years to appreciate the value of something else I learned first from Uncle Randy but realized much later—how civil society starts with patience. Uncle Randy speaks slowly and with an economy of words I wish I had. He never seems harried or rushed, nor have I ever seen him use expletives or lose his temper. George Washington was also noted for his outstanding sense of civility. Civility, like trust, takes patience and time. So does the loss of it.

Beyond the loss of faith in such institutions as the government, churches, or Wall Street, the General Social Survey—monitoring social change in American society since 1972—has recorded a drop of societal trust over the past forty years from one-half to one-third, with a commensurate rise in suspicion of others. Trust in others is the currency of civil society, enabling a sense of community and a better quality of life at a lower cost in social friction. "You don't have to get lawyers and accountants involved if you trust people," management guru Larry Prusak said about the importance of trust in today's knowledge-based economy. "If people trust each other, it lowers the knowledge transaction cost." After all, that's how money works. The pieces of paper we hand each other have no material value other than the trust we place in the government that prints them on our behalf. Or the trust that the figures on those electronic bank statements actually represent our personal wealth.

Distrust, on the other hand, encourages corruption. Lying, cheating, and stealing drain energy (including its coagulated form, money) away from constructive and toward distractive activities. Robert Putnam, in *Bowling Alone*, illustrates the decline of civility, trust, and other forms of "social capital" by surveying a precipitous drop in community social activities such as bowling leagues and local clubs in favor of staying home to watch TV, play video games, or engage in indirect contact from a safe distance through social media. He blames the increase in societal segmentation on rising economic inequality.

The Canadian journalist Malcolm Gladwell, who wrote such bestsellers as *The Tipping Point*, seems to agree, but also thinks it's not all that bad yet. In an interview he had with CNN's Fareed Zakaria, he pointed out how rising perceptions of inequality and unfairness could undermine the trust, confidence, and sense of legitimacy of our system of governance reflected in the high rate of tax compliance in the United States, even though, he says, individual Americans are still "the most honest taxpayers in the world."

My wife, Rosa, who hails from Spain, and others from abroad have long admired the absence of walls and fences around most American houses, itself an indicator of social trust and capital and a culture of openness and inclusion. But these days, gated communities of McMansions, like those I saw on the way to Central, are springing up around the country to segregate more of the haves from the have-nots. Reversing these trends will be quite a challenge, considering our short attentions spans, our compressed sense of time due to instant communications, and our "Look at me" culture.

Yet, the rise and fall of nations begins at the collective individual level. Having a sense of values, ethics, and morality instills a person with an identity that is personal and yet connected to the identities of tribe and nation. "Character is what defines us," Army Chief of Staff General Raymond Odierno said. "Character is about understanding the moral and ethical values that we represent as well as being able to navigate the ethical dilemmas that we face during our careers."

The Golden Rule of doing unto others as you would have them do unto you is the most universal social ethic, at the heart of any civil society, but it only works if each of us practices it on a personal level. The moral imperative of reciprocity or karma, in turn, imbues a sense of responsibility to yourself and others, in a balance between the two.

It's more than just laws that make things work. Whether over here or over there, what really makes a society resilient is a strong and widely shared sense of personal ethics grounded in common sense. Ethics are unwritten norms about what you know to say or do or not to say or do before anyone has to tell you—they're innate or intuitive as opposed to explicit, formal laws. I believe that ethical self-regulation and internally induced discipline benefit both the individual and society in far greater and more enduring ways than laws.

At my last chat at the breakfast table, with a view of the woods and chirping birds competing with the TV news, Uncle Randy and Aunt Ann shared with me a growing concern about where America seems to be going these days—a real sense of trouble beyond the usual frustration with politicians. It seems we can't get things done for the greater good because of the lack of civility and willingness to compromise.

"In more than three decades of trying to help make peace overseas," I commented, "I've learned that there are two things that tell you a country is in trouble. One is when people blame anybody else but themselves for their predicament. The other is when they talk more about the past than the future. But when people start talking more about solutions rather than problems and the future rather than the past, that's an indication that things are turning around." Whether over here or over there, a failing state is the result of a failing society.

"A lot of people here blame it on Washington and the politicians," chimed Aunt Ann, who, like my mother, has all but lost her English accent.

That raised my ire a bit. "As far as I'm concerned," I ranted between sips of tea, "I lay most of what's going on at the feet of the American people themselves. When you only get half the electorate to show up to vote in a general election, or one-third in a midterm, you're getting exactly the government you deserve. People like me and Uncle Randy have sacrificed a lot for them to have that privilege." I took another sip. "Besides, why should the politicians listen to people who don't vote? The voters obviously don't care. So why should the politicians?" Uncle Randy punctuated it more simply: "Chris, we have no one to blame but ourselves."

One of the more interesting points my aunt and uncle brought up was how people don't seem to say "please" and "thank you" as regularly as in the past. Perhaps it's generational. "It's still like pulling teeth with my nieces," I told them.

"You know, I've learned over the years to say 'please' and 'thank you' in about a dozen different languages. Those words have opened more doors for me than any other. They communicate respect, humility, and a genuine interest in other people. It's like the proverb says: 'Manners make the man.'"

Another issue my aunt and uncle mentioned is the pervasive sense of entitlement that many Americans now seem to have. "If you ask me," Aunt Ann added, "we've gotten just a little too spoiled. We're still a lot better off than most people. But we complain about the silliest things."

The baby boomers in particular, I explained to them, have weaned themselves on the strident notion that they can buy all they want on cheap credit and gain a sense of who they are through material possessions. "You see that kind of thing at Walmart and on TV commercials every day," Aunt Ann added.

"We boomers have passed our supersized self-indulgence on to our kids, coddling and overprotecting them, and telling them how special they are without making them prove it first," I replied, now on a bit of a roll. "Everyone gets a trophy, everyone graduates, and nobody's a loser. That's just not the real world. It feeds our false feelings of complacency, insularity, and superiority. We're setting ourselves up for failure, not success."

At the same time, I thought, to say that people don't use "please" and "thank you" because they lack civility strikes me as superficial. Like a lot of stereotypical comparisons between countries and cultures, it's more complex than that. Americans are likely less civil than Canadians. But as some of my Canadian friends have pointed out, they didn't have to fight for their independence, national identity, or place in the world. They can afford to be nicer.

I tend to think in the case of the United States that American exceptionalism means, foremost, remaining cognizant of one's relative good fortune. You can struggle for things and disagree on even the most essential issues, yet be civil to each other. Besides, you hardly ever value the things that were given to you as much as the things you've earned.

Saying "please" and "thank you" is not mere politeness. It's an affirmation of civil society, an expression of confidence in yourself and your identity—a confidence for which arrogance, I found out early enough through my own mistakes, is a ready but subpar substitute. Saying "please" and "thank you" is a starting point for building trust and social capital. It's how you begin to get along with people, to your benefit as well as theirs. Moreover, it conveys the greatest of human virtues—compassion.

Where else better to start to bring this all together than a place called Central?

CHAPTER 2

MISSISSIPPI: LATITUDES AND ATTITUDES

After saying good-bye to the Manleys, I took the back roads to Anderson, South Carolina, and rejoined Interstate 85, chasing 516 miles of hot, humid pavement through Georgia and Alabama into Mississippi. As I dissected Atlanta's huge suburban-to-urban-to-suburban sprawl, it reminded me that in the South, as in much of the world now, more and more people are living in or near cities, which is changing profoundly our lifestyles and outlooks.

An hour north of Mobile, Alabama, I stopped off for a slice of pecan pie (beware how you pronounce *pecan* there). Mobile (pronounced "mo-beel") is the largest Catholic city in the South. I enjoyed a short ride along its spacious avenues draped with Spanish moss. Like other southern jewels that have maintained their antebellum charm—Charleston, South Carolina, and Savannah, Georgia, among them—Mobile is a port city. I took a glance at the World War II battleship *Alabama* moored there in retirement. Then I found my way to Interstate 10. Less than an hour later, I turned off at Gautier, Mississippi, near Biloxi, along the "Redneck Riviera."

In Gautier, I spent the weekend with my friend Virginia Martin, a well-educated and traveled woman with a snowy pixie hairdo, an abundance of common sense, and the right mix of southern sweetness and northern sauciness. Ginny, whose Dixie dialect has flattened a bit, served many years overseas, as a government civilian, training troops on information technology, including in Heidelberg, Germany, where we met in 1989 while I was a civilian international relations analyst at the US Army Europe headquarters. In addition to a lot of good times then with other civil servants, we shared some history, including the fall of the Berlin Wall and the rise of the information age. After raising her two boys as a single mother and not long before Hurricane Katrina hit in 2005, she bought a retirement home at the edge of the wetlands near Gautier.

When I visited, Ginny had just moved—using private insurance, Federal Emergency Management Agency (FEMA) funds, and personal savings—into a new house tediously built after "The Storm" had destroyed the one she had originally bought. She had lived on-site in a cramped "FEMA trailer" for the nearly two years it took to build. I parked the Dyna between the massive concrete pillars holding the new house up like the arms of Atlas, well beyond regulatory requirements. I ribbed Ginny that some of that German thoroughness must have rubbed off from all those years there.

In the stretch of Gulf shore from Florida to the Texas border, you can see a cross section of how people responded to the disaster. Ginny's experience provides a good example of the social contract most Americans believe in and is akin to the most effective method of reconstruction and development assistance I've seen overseas—a hand, but not a handout, to those who should take ownership of the problem (and thus the solution). Both here and abroad, what we demand of central authorities has increased dramatically. Federal and state governments performed poorly in response to Katrina, but then we expected them to do much more than they were prepared to. They're better prepared now.

In the palatial casinos of Biloxi, however, we saw fair numbers of locals of limited means chasing the American Dream of getting rich quick. "They're betting on the house," Ginny explained as we watched. "With their money—or with the government assistance money they got," she clarified.

Like some Wall Street hedge funders, the Biloxi gamblers were looking for the big payoff. But, unlike professional money managers, they knew little about what they were doing. As we drove around, Ginny explained how government red tape and doses of lingering Huey Long–era corruption have made the recovery slow, difficult, and uneven. "It took me four years," Ginny said, "and that's because I know some things about dealing with bureaucracies."

"Looks like a lot of what I've seen overseas," I said further to her remark. "Even right here in America, recovery from natural or man-made calamities or economic development is a complex, slow, and difficult process."

"Exactly," Ginny punctuated, using one of her favorite replies as we fell back into a familiar conversational rhythm established over twenty years prior.

One of the great strengths of the United States is its ability to renew itself, having started out as a reinvention of Europe. This helped it be the greatest experiment in self-governance so far in history. Along the stretch of US 90 dividing the shoreline from beachfront properties, Ginny and I saw reminders of that positive aspect of the American character. Jutting into the air in defiance of fate are wooden sculptures of birds, fish, and other animals carved by the Florida artist Marlin Miller, who has created new landmarks from the tree stumps left by Hurricane Katrina. Miller, Ginny explained, donated his time and talent in the Magnolia State to conjure up charity support to rebuild and beautify the coast, along with a thousand volunteers for Keep America Beautiful.

A less happy story, however, was the impending impact on the seafood industry and related walks of life as a result of the most recent major disaster to hit the area: The British Petroleum (BP) oil spill, the largest in US history, had just occurred as I began my trip.

Ginny and I feasted on freshly caught shrimp in Ocean Springs between Biloxi and Gautier at the Po-Boy Express, a locally owned fast-food joint in red-and-white pop deco. Far from Bubba Gump's litany, the featured shrimp delicacy was a po-boy (essentially a grilled shrimp sandwich). We sat and speculated with others that it could be the last time for years to enjoy Gulf shrimp. After lunch, we found at the nearby marina a number of dilapidated shrimp boats awaiting some fate other than shrimping. Many crews already had contracts with BP, which has

Miller's Marlins.

since been on a multibillion-dollar, multiyear corporate social responsibility public relations binge for cleanup and recovery.

"This is historic," stated a white-haired fellow who introduced himself as George, captain of the *Desperado*, built in 1963 from hardwood
that is now nearly impossible to find. For him and his sons (it was a
family-owned business), shrimping was a matter of identity. "We survived the hike in diesel fuel prices, then The Storm. But I'm not sure
about this one," he said stoically. "People's livelihoods are gonna change

big. We've got contract work for the next year with BP, but I don't know what we're gonna do after that. We'll figure out something," he accentuated with a thin grin.

"Not exactly a Hollywood ending," I said to Ginny as I watched him amble back to the *Desperado*.

"This place isn't Hollywood," she responded dryly.

American optimism, like the Mississippi, runs long, deep, and wide, but with many twists and turns. The latitudes outlining the United States of America have shaped the attitudes of its inhabitants. By looking at its geographic history alone, you can see why the United States was destined to be the greatest power of the modern world, and how Americans came to see themselves in that world. People are who they are because of not just what they do but also where they live—and that usually involves water.

The Greater Mississippi River Basin and all the intracoastal systems of the United States have more navigable internal waterways than the rest of the world combined—and they are contiguous to some of the most prime real estate on the planet. The coastline from Maine to Florida alone contains more major ports than the rest of the Western Hemisphere. The Great Lakes, whose surrounding states and provinces comprise one-fifth of the economy of the United States and Canada, present the single largest source of freshwater in the world. Two vast oceans insulate the United States from Asian and European powers. In many ways, the formative national security of the United States is inherent in its natural seclusion and self-sufficiency.

I'm not sure what Steinbeck was talking about in *Travels with Charley*: The climate in the United States is hardly boring, especially nowadays. And yet, despite blistering summers, frigid winters, tornadoes, hurricanes, and other atmospheric vicissitudes, the North American continent is a temperate zone ideal for mass agriculture as well as mass industrial production without equal—unless, of course, it all gets destroyed by the excesses of climate change.

What's under the earth is as important as what is above it. In addition to an abundance of freshwater, the United States has some of the largest concentrations of raw material and energy anywhere—coal and iron ore, antimony, bauxite, copper, nickel, tin, salt, uranium, and of course natural gas, oil, and geothermic energy, plus vast territories receiving sun and wind as renewable energy—all in an expansive and traversable continental interior safe from foreign invasion.

Topographical factors are not the only reason why the United States is the power it is. The only thing more diverse than the landscape and the weather is the country's people, and they constitute its greatest strength. America's demography, dynamic and innovative, is sourced by a culture of immigration and assimilation—the open door and the belief in the common values of personal freedom and human dignity, regardless of heritage, summed up in E pluribus unum ("Out of many, one"). As troubled as its development has been at times, the United States has been highly successful compared to other countries. Its culture and changing demographics are at once the basis of America's great strength and social tensions. "The American solution of relying on immigration will mean a substantial change in what has been the historical sore point in American culture: race," noted strategic analyst George Friedman in *The Next 100 Years*.

In all three macroeconomic sectors, therefore—land, labor, and capital—the United States is uniquely advantaged. Its geostrategic advantages, coupled with its political, social, and economic culture, help explain its signature optimism and frontier spirit. A German friend told Ginny and me back in our days in Europe that "Americans think there's a solution to every problem; Europeans think every solution brings a new problem," to which a British fellow added, "Americans think a hundred years is a long time; Europeans think a hundred miles is a long distance."

Isolationism or interventionism for Americans is a matter of choice, not necessity. That's a luxury most other countries can neither afford nor fathom. But Americans were fortunate to have leaders who did. In *Undaunted Courage*, Stephen Ambrose's story of the journey of the Corps of Discovery, he tells how Thomas Jefferson exercised extraordinary vision in committing government funds to the controversial Louisiana Purchase and then sending Captains Meriwether Lewis and William Clark to find a passage to the Pacific through terrain I would later ride.

That early political geography required the United States to position itself in terms of Europe. For one, it has been a trading nation since the founding of the Republic. "The idea that there would be no entangling alliances was nice in theory," Friedman wrote in an online analysis. "But in reality, in order to trade, it had to align with the dominant naval power in the Atlantic—the British. Self-sufficiency was a fantasy, and avoiding entanglement impossible."

Americans like to think in terms of either/or, but geopolitical posture and commercialism prompted the United States to exercise relations with the world in a more sophisticated way than it would otherwise like to, and placed it in dilemmas between the ideal and the real—right from the time it expanded into the area where Ginny now lives. The stated ally coming out of the Revolutionary War was France, but with the failure of the French Revolution and the rise of Napoleon it was hard to side with a dictator. The main trading partner was Great Britain, but the United States had an uneasy relationship with the British until conflict erupted over freedom of the seas in the War of 1812. It was also for access to trade that the United States waged war against the "Barbary pirates" of the Ottoman Empire and sent the Marines "to the shores of Tripoli," as the hymn refers to, in the early nineteenth century. The United States has been involved in the Middle East and North Africa ever since.

Even George Washington, Friedman points out, struck a careful balance between entanglement and involvement in his oft-cited but misinterpreted Farewell Address:

Europe has a set of primary interests. . . . the causes of which are essentially foreign to our concerns. Hence, therefore, it must be unwise in us to implicate ourselves by artificial ties in the ordinary vicissitudes of her politics. . . .

Our detached and distant situation invites and enables us to pursue a different course. If we remain one people under an efficient government, the period is not far off when . . . we may take such an attitude as will cause the neutrality we may at any time resolve upon to be scrupulously respected . . . when we may choose peace or war, as our interest, guided by justice, shall counsel. . . .

Taking care always to keep ourselves by suitable establishments on a respectable defensive posture, we may safely trust to temporary alliances for extraordinary emergencies.

Understanding America's place in the world and national attitudes requires understanding the path to its rise as a world power: first, starting in the nineteenth century, by securing the interior territories; second, by ensuring that no other power would compete for domination (per the Monroe Doctrine, the war with Mexico, the Great Compromise with the British on the Canadian border, the purchase of Alaska from the Russians, and the war with Spain); third, by connecting up the continent (with the Oregon Trail and National Road, the railroads, the telegraph and telephone, the Interstate Highway System, the airplane, and the Internet); fourth, by importing labor, social intelligence, and other know-how through immigration; and fifth and finally, by dominating the continent and eventually the world economically, culturally, and militarily.

In its first century, the United States chose to be an isolationist power, concentrating on consolidating its hold on the continent. Seeking world trade beyond its shores after the Civil War, the United States became a maritime as well as a continental power, as Alfred Thayer Mahan urged, in order to control the ocean approaches to North America and then—incidentally—the world's major trade routes. Starting with World War I and climaxing with World War II, the emerging economic, financial, military, and cultural dominance of the United States made it more interventionist by default.

Both isolationism and interventionism, however, are inflections of American exceptionalism—we are a special, privileged, and even blessed land and people. If you look on the back of a dollar bill, at the left (or reverse) side of the Great Seal of the United States, you'll see a depiction of this organizing idea—the pyramid representing a new society (or, written in Latin below, "A new order of the ages," with "Annuit coeptis," loosely meaning "Divine fortune," at the top). The isolationist interpretation is that we should keep to ourselves and protect

what is ours from foreign interference or corruption, whereas inter-
ventionists believe we should share with the world our good fortune
because of our privileged position and moral obligation to do so.

Both inflections continue to compete for the upper hand in
domestic as well as foreign policies. In domestic policy, isolationism
and interventionism play out in terms of how much the government
should intervene in people's lives or how much people should be left
alone, if even to their worst excesses. This age-old Judeo-Christian and
Islamic moral dualism in the struggle of good versus evil for the soul
played out as well in the Jeffersonian versus Federalist debate about
how much faith one should have in human nature versus government,
argued equally from idealist and realist standpoints. Conservatism and
liberalism also have their roots in these interpretations.

History and geography have also shaped American identity in the
interpretation of what separates Western from Eastern culture and values. Ajit Maan, in *Counter-Terrorism: Narrative Strategies*, explained
that, in Western traditions, personal identity is based on uniqueness
and formed by separation—individuality or exceptionality. In Eastern
traditions, personal identity is understood as group identity or shared
sameness. This ongoing attempt to balance personal freedom and
sociopolitical unity in a changing society is extraordinarily difficult.
American pragmatism, which is about living in the here and now and
doing what is expedient, helps temper this tension. It has, on the one
hand, unchained Americans from the shackles of the determinism that
has plagued other cultures. It also tempers maximalist ideologies that
insist on having everything one's own way or no way at all. This intellectual freedom is a wellspring of American innovativeness, political
ingenuity in creative compromise, and sense of generosity.

When in excess, however, this same pragmatist mind-set has contributed to narrower attitudes of crass consumerism, anti-intellectualism,
and even righteous ignorance that celebrates the independence of private from public life, ranging from apathy to outright hatred of government. But there is also a thinly veiled arrogance about other countries
and cultures. If you have everything you need and can do it all yourself,
if you don't need anything from anyone else, and if no one else can
bother you, then you can afford to not care.

This insularity is the default of American populism. It is the point of orientation from which we still largely operate—except when we have to reach out beyond our immediate surroundings, which can result in close encounters of the clumsier kind. We've done what we've done abroad because we have been able to get away with it without dealing directly with the consequences. Because American grand strategy was more or less a given of geographic abundance, demographics, and an identity based on an idea of humanity transcending its categorizations, we hardly had to go about it conscientiously. Thinking and acting strategically—applying the big picture and the long term to everyday problems—doesn't come as naturally to Americans as to others, like Europeans, who are more forced to.

The conditions shaping national identity shape its narrative. "Narrative," Ajit Maan explains, "is a rendering of events, actions, and characters in a certain way for a certain purpose. The purpose is persuasion. The method is identification." Narrative is a reflection of who you are and what you are about—identity and values in the field of action. Our national narratives work for a time, but when the paradigm shifts, they don't work as well anymore, requiring a periodic update.

This larger perspective helps us understand the struggles we are going through today and how we may be coming to the end of a long era of mental insularity. After the War of 1812, we Americans did not have to care much about the rest of the world—we could afford our willful ignorance. Since 1865, we have been able to intervene in the world, win markets as well as wars, deter adversaries, and assure allies through overwhelming industrial and technological superiority and a business model predicated on an abundance of cheap resources, cheap labor, cheap energy, and cheap capital. We could afford a wasteful, surplus mentality about nearly everything, including government. Since 1945, when we went from dominating the continent to dominating the world, we've been able to hold on to a nineteenth-century view of national sovereignty while everyone else was going global. Since the country's inception, the dominant political class has been white and male. These trajectories are converging in the nation's third century, lending greatly to its latest emerging national existential crisis.

Fortunately, America is also hardwired for change by its history, geography, and demographics. Americans both fear and desire it. They like change least when it comes primarily from the top down, preferring first a groundswell of emerging consensus before moving forward. This explains how change comes about here, reflected in the elemental emotional impulses played out in conservatism and liberalism. Americans have a disdain for complexity in public, but they accept it much more readily in private. For example, Ginny is divorced, as are my parents, but we have all figured out how to maintain a satisfactory and fulfilling family life. That's because being in a real family, including a national family, is more a state of mind than an accident of birth.

Yet, we still want to understand the complexities of our world and our times in a sound bite, a 140-character Tweet, or a bumper sticker—without the entire context you just read over the past few pages, even though there's no other way to comprehend or deal with it.

Desperado George may have said more than he knew: It appears that America is, once again, in the throes of historic change—a convergence of crossroads in demographics and social values, the relationship between the state and the individual and the size and role of government, its internal balance of social and economic power, and its leadership role in the world. Because these questions are so fundamental, the arguments taking place in the halls of government, the media, and so on seem almost apocalyptic and are almost always hyperbolic. The counterweight to this inherent inner dissension is, of course, the mythology that is American nationalism.

Seen this way, the tumult and turmoil of our times is really an indicator more than an issue. Sitting with Ginny on her well-constructed wraparound porch on the second day of my visit in Gautier, overlooking the wetland waterways and the occasional alligator peering up from below the water, we concluded from our own experiences in transition and observations of historical change, at personal and public levels, that when we come to the end of one time and the beginning of another, there's always a period of pain and uncertainty, starting with denial and anger, until we accept it, process it, and learn how to move forward with it.

As do I, Ginny loves quotes. In this case, I cited Khalil Gibran: "Your pain is the breaking of the shell that encloses your understanding." Americans have been in such times before, we agreed. "Hell," she said, "we got through the Civil War." Yet, I reminded her, the words of the southern historian Shelby Foote, in Ken Burns's iconic documentary *The Civil War*, ring eerily prescient:

> *It was because we failed to do the thing we really have a genius for, which is compromise. Americans like to think of themselves as uncompromising. Our true genius is for compromise—our whole government's founded on it. And it failed.*

Understanding history at the individual and collective levels is important to contending with change and dealing with crises. I told Ginny the story about when, as a student, I rented a small basement apartment from two University of the District of Columbia history professors, Bill and Miriam Haskett. Bill, who taught American history, was born not far from where my mother's family comes from in the shipbuilding port of Jarrow in northern England—in the town of Washington. Miriam, an Israeli, taught European history. During our first chat, I told Miriam that one of my majors at George Washington University had been history.

Somewhat tongue-in-cheek, she asked, "Why on earth do you want to study history?"

My less whimsical reply was "Well, how can you know where you are and where you're going unless you know where you've been?"

Foote's observation is an appropriate admonition. Besides the weakening of civil society, trust, and national ethos, amplified by inherent self-contradictions, other factors are dumbing down the national genius he was referring to. James Madison, in *The Federalist Papers*, cautioned us "to avoid the confusion and intemperance of a multitude. In all very numerous assemblies, of whatever character composed, passion never fails to wrest the sceptre from reason." Alexis de Tocqueville called this "the tyranny of the majority."

"We need to be more reasonable, no matter where we stand on the issues," said Ginny.

I knew what she meant. Reason is a qualitative blend of thinking and feeling. Going back to the dollar bill, the reverse of the Great Seal of the United States provides a succinct explanation of how reason is supposed to work on our society. "All men are capable of reason," Joseph Campbell agrees with Jefferson in *The Power of Myth*. "This is the fundamental principle of democracy. Because everybody's mind is capable of true knowledge, you don't have to have a special authority, or a special revelation telling you that this is the way things should be."

"You know, Ginny, from a national management perspective," I said as our marathon conversation continued over a barbecue we prepared together, "the United States is a nightmare to govern. The founders set it up that way—on purpose. Our complex system of checks and balances and multiple levels of government is intended to prevent the concentration of power, political or economic, and enable reason rather than passion to prevail. So the process of change in this country is painfully slow and frustrating."

"Well, you know what Churchill said about us," she answered. "'The Americans will always do the right thing—after they've exhausted the other alternatives.'"

According to Shona Brown and Kathleen Eisenhardt, authors of *Competing on the Edge: Strategy as Structured Chaos*, people and organizations are successful because they've learned to find that edge between structure and chaos that allows them to be innovative and creative, while maintaining just enough discipline to focus on executing a plan as well as the humility to adapt it to changing realities. That ability to live on that edge, in the spaces between dualities, requires a strong sense of identity that is values based.

From its inception, the United States has been a commercial republic, and our values reflect this accordingly. Over my lifetime, however, Americans have embraced what my friends Berndt and Susie, a German-Australian couple who have likewise lived in many places, including with me in Jersey City, called "galloping consumption." It led to a standard of living that has long been the envy of a world that, in turn, has benefited enormously from the role the United States has played as a global economic locomotive. The problem with galloping consumption is that it assumes two things—one, the curve of prosperity will forever keep going upward; and two, we will never run out of resources. It also reinforces ignorance, self-indulgence, and an unjustified sense of entitlement. It reduces citizenship to residence and makes the freedom that gives it vitality a commodity.

"One thing I noticed about your new place, Ginny, is that it doesn't have a large garage to put everything in it but a car," I told her.

"I did that on purpose, Chris," she replied.

How we've become consumers more than citizens is explained in a brilliant online documentary called *The Century of the Self.* I told Ginny to look it up on the Internet. One of its main themes is that a society that lives in indulgence and is motivated mainly by emotion is vulnerable to being led around by its nose. Mass consumerism makes us more passive because consumers decide what to buy mainly on emotion. "It's no wonder we're open to manipulation by the media, the corporations, and the government," she responded. The 24/7 media and social media, tailored to our consumerism, Coke-or-Pepsi politics, and "good" or "bad" polemics have only worsened it. This limits our worldview rather than challenges and expands it.

Because Americans now have their information processed as much as their food, they think less critically or creatively, are less capable of reason, and rely less on common sense. Journalism in America today, now even more a business, is accordingly shallow and focused on the bottom line of production costs, corporate editorial agenda, quick turnaround, and advertising revenue. Balkanized to its markets, it tells their segments of society what they want to hear more than what they need to know, exacerbating the divisiveness. Members of the "Fourth Estate" (or the fourth, unofficial branch of government) no longer look to educate the public. Their most important job is to improve ratings, increase hits on the Internet, and sell their brand of soap.

Being a society that tends to champion ignorance and hate intellectuals, we're suckers for gimmicks, gadgets, and quick fixes. The TV is full of "infomercials" with get-rich-quick schemes, free-ride scams, and diet fads that let us eat, not exercise, and still lose weight. The uselessly redundant term *free gift* is now a staple in advertisements. We're saps for snake oil salesmen.

One of the most useful courses I ever took (in a public high school) was Mr. Itzkowitz's Persuasion and Propaganda, where I learned how today's ad men and spin doctors draw from techniques going back to when propaganda was earning its now-sinister reputation. In 1937, Edward Filene, Clyde Miller, and other pioneers in the advertising business established the short-lived Institute of Propaganda Analysis (IPA). The IPA's original intent was to educate the American public about the nature of enemy propaganda in the new era of mass media and how to recognize its now highly refined techniques. But it was brought down by the US government during World War II: It turned out to be as effective in analyzing our propaganda as it was in analyzing theirs.

Although the IPA no longer exists, its legacy lives on in having laid out the tricks of the trade—including "name-calling," "glittering generalities," "plain-folks," the "bandwagon," and old-fashioned fear-mongering. Although the applications vary, what they all have in common is their appeal essentially to emotion rather than reason. So that should be your first warning sign.

As a result of becoming consumers rather than citizens, what once liberated us, in excess, now enchains us instead. Living well beyond our means to feed our consumption addiction and beholden to our creditors, we look more to others than to ourselves for solutions to the larger problems affecting our lives. We worry only about what's in front of us and seek instant gratification, struggling to manage our expectations. We lurch from crisis to crisis as much as from paycheck to paycheck. We are no longer in control of our lives. We are no longer as free.

"People who are better at saving money seem to be the opposite of a lot of that," Ginny pointed out. "If you know the difference between what you need and what you want, they can't manipulate you that easily. I've always felt more in control of my life because I knew I had a personal safety net. It's helped me put this place together."

Recognizing the judgmental tendency of a fellow Scorpio, I gently countered, "Sure, Ginny, I agree that savers make better citizens. But it's become so hard for so many families to make ends meet, let alone put some money aside, that they can't get past their shortsightedness. If you ask me, I think that's a huge threat to the vitality of our country."

Citizens—versus consumers—are inherently more optimistic about the future because they can better see it. They're more confident, humble, and self-responsible. Citizens know they're important, but they don't think they're special. They understand their place in history. "Society was there before you, it is there after you're gone, and you are a member of it," said Joseph Campbell. And they can much better deal with change. Randy Bernard, when he became CEO of the Indy Racing League just before my trip, put it nicely: "It is really important in all of our lives to embrace change. When you step outside your boundaries, you grow in a different way."

There are increasing signs that galloping consumption is reaching its limits. The fact that we have been living far beyond our means at governmental, corporate, and individual levels for generations is the real reason for much of the economic and financial crisis that erupted in 2008. "We have to get rid of a lot of false notions we've held on to for too long," Ginny observed.

I asked Ginny if she remembered my friend in Germany, Andreas Nickl, the one with the pretty eyes. I told her how a couple of years ago he and I took a motorcycle trip to Memphis. It was September. The presidential election was just heating up, and the financial crisis was hitting us like Katrina. When we stopped off at a service station in Virginia, a reporter from the local paper approached us for some quick quotes on whose version of tax cuts we "felt" was better. "Don't ask me about taxes here," Andreas told him. "I'm German. Ask him."

"Tax cuts are a political gimmick," I told the reporter. "They're an inefficient form of economic stimulus. They worked better when we produced most of what we bought."

"What do you mean by that?" the reporter asked.

"Well, look at this way," I said. "Say you're a rich guy and get a tax break. What are you going to do with it? Most likely, you'll put it in an offshore account (to avoid paying more taxes, of course), invest it in a derivative or something else that doesn't really produce jobs, or buy a Mercedes that helps out people like my friend Andreas here. Or, say you're at the lower end of the social scale and got a few hundred bucks in a rebate. Are you going to put that toward your next mortgage payment? Maybe, but you'll probably go to Walmart and buy a bunch of stuff made in China. So whose economy have you just helped out? Tax cuts are just a feel-good trick. As Marx would say, it's opium for the people. Karl, of course, not Groucho." Ginny laughed.

"The reporter was stunned," I said. "He said he'd never heard anybody put it that way. I told him it was just common sense, and 'situational understanding,' as we say in the military."

"Exactly," Ginny commented.

Understanding the latitudes where we have found ourselves helps us understand where the attitudes we have acquired come from and where they both may bring us. Our geographic immensity and demographic diversity are reflected in the complexity and contentiousness of our national character. Having such a broad base of self-awareness of country and character itself gives you a well-grounded sense of confidence and reasonable faith in the future.

Things may not have worked out for *Desperado* George, like a lot of Americans, but my bet is that they somehow did. It turned out Ginny and I were both wrong about the shrimp. They came back faster than we predicted, once again proof of how much smarter and more resilient nature is than we are. My guess is he and his sons are still out there shrimping somewhere.

"It all depends on how you look at it," Ginny said to me during our conversation. It reminded me of what I had heard from older officers or NCOs as a young officer whenever I came across a problem: "Lieutenant, you don't have a problem—you have an opportunity."

Shortly before I left that Monday morning, I saw a quote on Ginny's refrigerator that she hadn't mentioned. It was from John Gardner, who was the secretary of health, education, and welfare in the 1960s, a time of great change and social upheaval in America: "We are continually faced with a series of great opportunities brilliantly disguised as insoluble problems."

CHAPTER 3

TEXAS: "IT'S LIKE A WHOLE OTHER COUNTRY"

After crossing the Mississippi in New Orleans, I encountered powerful crosswinds coming up from the southwest in the wetlands of Louisiana into Texas. At times the gusts nearly blew me and my seven-hundred-pound machine off the causeway and into the swamp, where I imagined hungry alligators lurking. Between the fatigue and the higher fuel consumption the winds caused, I had to take more breaks than planned—but still covered 435 miles that day. I felt obligated to stop off at the travel center when crossing the border into Texas on Interstate 10, which stretches from Jacksonville, Florida, to Los Angeles, California. When you see the sign at the border that says "El Paso—856 miles" and realize that's not even a third of the distance along this continental highway, you begin to get an idea of the immensity of the country, let alone Texas.

My dad's brother, George, a retired New York State police trooper who served prior to that in the Navy, called me before the trip and suggested I consider avoiding Texas. Inadvertently channeling a growing distrust among Americans when traveling, fanned by the media, he cited a documentary he saw about motorcycle gangs like the Bandidos, who apparently think nothing of killing a lone biker just to steal his ride. Some online research found very little recent reporting on them, but I stopped to ask the woman behind the counter just to make sure.

"Do you have any travel advisories for lone bikers riding through Texas about motorcycle gangs that might be some trouble?" I told her I planned to ride in the daytime, stay mostly on major roads and highways, and keep in sight of truckers, who could quickly call for help.

"Nope. But it sounds like you've got it pretty well figured out. Travel safely, and have a great time in Texas!"

"Thank you, ma'am. I look forward to doing just that."

There was a lot of urban congestion but no biker gangs as I approached the largest city in the second-most-populous state in the Union. The delays in Houston—now the fourth-largest US city—created a chain reaction of unfortunate events. I reached downtown in the middle of the afternoon commute, in time to confront the complete closure of the interstate due to an accident less than a mile from the exit to my friend Michael Goble's place.

It took me another hour to find my way back to Michael's house. First, I tried dead reckoning. Then, after passing through some barrios and more run-down neighborhoods, I began to wonder if I was totally lost. I pulled over and reached for my map in my kit bag. At that moment, a classic black-and-white police cruiser pulled up next to me.

"You look a little lost," the member of Houston's finest said through the open window.

"Yes, sir, you could say that," I answered. "How far away am I from North Street?"

"You're closer than you think," the sandy-haired patrolman said. "Just down here about a half mile, turn right at the light, then go two blocks and turn left. You'll see it," he said, pointing.

"Thanks, Officer. By the way, have you seen any Bandidos around here?" I asked a bit in jest.

"Nope," he answered. "But if I do, I'll be sure to send them your way."

We both laughed and waved at each other as he took off ahead of me.

Michael and his mother, Dolores, were waiting for me at their hacienda, as he called the tall two-story antebellum-style brick house the Gobles have called home for generations and have registered in the local historical society. Michael is a tall, lanky, and perpetually youthful fellow I worked with in the UN field mission in Eastern Slavonia. Easygoing and with a terrific sense of humor, he was home on leave from the UN mission in Haiti, having helped that unfortunate country recover from the disastrous earthquake and hurricane that had struck in January (and where a few of our international civil service friends had lost their lives).

Dolores offered me some iced tea. "It's sweet, not like you northerners prefer," she said as she handed it to me.

"No matter," I said. "I'm used to being in a lot of foreign countries."

She laughed at that and then showed me around the house. Dolores, who is very fit for her age, was always very active in the Methodist Church, having done more than thirty years overseas in missionary work and humanitarian service. She proudly showed me her scroll of honor from a community in Namibia.

"Now I know where Michael gets it from," I said to her.

Most Americans grossly overestimate how much their government spends on foreign aid, thinking it spends about a third of the federal budget on it. They would be comfortable if the expenditure were around 10 percent and are shocked to learn that it's already well below 1 percent. Most outside the United States, in turn, do not realize that for every assistance dollar the US government spends, as many as three to four more dollars come from private donors. Americans are a more charitable people than their government.

People like the Gobles also remind me of the adventurous spirit among not enough Americans. My own lifelong adventure was less motivated by a call to duty than wanderlust—the same spirit that brought many of the original European inhabitants to Texas. This is the more common, less fantastic, and more believable version of a hero— the inadvertent voyager who goes out on an adventure, thinks he's doing it for himself, and then finds out he's part of something much larger. This is how most of us are—heroic, perhaps, but less altruistic than many would like to believe.

"There are two aspects of the hero," said Joseph Campbell in *An Open Life*. "The hero is somebody who you can lean on and who is going to rescue you; he is also an ideal. To live the heroic life is to live the individual adventure, really." As in the cowboy movies, it's the unsung heroes we love the most. What makes a journey heroic is not that the hero decides one day to be a hero—that comes much later and most often not as intended. That's because the adventure the hero gets is not the one he thinks he wants but the one he's ready for. He just didn't know it. But that's why he goes on an adventure in the first place.

What makes you special or a hero is neither people telling you that you're special nor the talents or potential you have. It's what you do with your talents, in the field of action—that's where you discover your true identity. "Do you want to know who you are?" asked Jefferson. "Don't ask. Act! Action will delineate and define you." The worst thing is to say no to your call to adventure out of fear or another distraction.

All this was in my mind when considering Uncle George's advice to avoid Texas. Every adventure—from leaving home to go to school, to moving to a new job, having children, or volunteering for some kind of community or national service like the military, the Peace Corps, the police force, firefighters, or the UN—entails an element of risk. Otherwise, why bother? Only in this way, however, can we find out about our capabilities as well as our limitations. You can't do that playing video games. Or, as I like to say to myself when struggling to overcome a setback: "You can't score any points sitting on the bench."

It's the experiences in big, strange, diverse, and expansive places like Texas, the United States, or the world at large that help you realize this sort of thing—big, diverse country; big, diverse thinking. And a tolerance for alternative mind-sets? One would hope so, anyway. Texas is not the biggest state in the United States. It is, nevertheless, the biggest of the forty-eight contiguous states. Size does matter, at least in terms of shaping mind-set—but it isn't everything. In this case, it helps form the fierce sense of independence and rugged individualism of many Texans. Even the official map I picked up at the travel center noted that "it's like a whole other country."

Despite media-reported perceptions, there are liberal Democrats living among conservative Republicans and moderates in many neighborhoods—even in Texas—who actually talk to each other. Texans have almost categorically struck me as good-natured, affable, and big hearted. I joined a small group of neighbors out in front of Michael's brother's house, just a few blocks away, drinking very dry martinis, eating delicious homemade grilled fish tacos, and smoking Cuban cigars. Other members of the neighborhood sauntered by and said hello, some staying for a quick chat. On that well-to-do street were not just white Anglo-Saxon Protestants, but also Indians (the South Asian variety), Latinos, and others.

I found in Texas as in the rest of the United States that much of the talk of politics has to do with the theme of change and the role of government. Most of the argument has always been more about the nuances and inflections of democracy, not whether there should be one. I got the impression that politics were continually lying right under the surface.

Attitudes toward change among Texans seem to echo the state's surprising diversity. A shaky Republican stronghold with large pockets of liberalism scattered all around, Texas is at the forefront of a demographic conversion. Along with California, it is already among nearly a half-dozen states that are majority-minority, meaning that over 50 percent of the population is nonwhite. By the end of this decade, nearly half the fifty states will be.

After a scrumptious seafood lunch with Michael the next day, I embarked on an unscheduled 165-mile detour to Austin, a surprisingly progressive city, considering it is the state capital. Besides the huge campus and student population of over thirty thousand at just the University of Texas, the city is culturally rich, especially when it comes to music, boasting more live artist acts of all genres than any other place in the United States at a given time. To commemorate my stopover, I bought a refrigerator magnet exhorting "Keep Austin Weird."

Less than forty miles away is the town of Gruene, whose brochure chides, "Gently resisting change since 1872." Gruene, pronounced "green" by Texans, started as a German settlement in the mid-1840s and went through its own cycle of rise and fall and rise again. German dominance declined with the collapse of family-owned businesses due to the successive disasters of the boll weevil and the Great Depression and then the First World War and especially the Second World War (which did little for the German brand). With the sale of the estate of the Gruene family in the 1970s and its placement on the National Register of Historical Places, the town reemerged as a tourist attraction.

It features restored Victorian-era homes and venues such as Gruene Hall, which lays claim to staging renowned musical acts such as Rock and Roll Hall of Famers Jerry Lee Lewis and Bo Diddley and country stars Willie Nelson and Waylon Jennings.

A German car and an American pickup at the Gruene General Store.

I have had a lifelong fascination with Germany in part because it was a big part of my family heritage (on my father's mother's side), as it is for more Americans than any other nationality. More than one-fifth of this country's residents can claim German ancestry to some extent or another. Having two heritages is a great advantage for most Americans—one from the past and one from the present and future, the Old and New Worlds.

I also like to tell people that the reason for my affinity for the Germans is that I have always found myself in the middle of things. I grew up with two sisters, one older and one younger, so I knew what it was like to fight a war on two fronts at the same time (referring here to German history). Sheree, my older sister, was the bully, while Susan, my younger sister, was the spy. I was also curious to know what my paternal grandmother and great-grandmother were talking about the few times I heard them speak German. However, I did not learn it until after high school, having only French and Spanish as my foreign language choices before then. The stories about "The War" I heard as a kid from English and German relatives prompted me to read about it, including a 128-volume magazine series called *History of the Second World War*, which my father bought me week by week. In college, I took courses in German and European history and was amazed at how such a talented and industrious people could produce Goethe, Mozart, and Immanuel Kant and, yet, could also be responsible for Buchenwald and Auschwitz.

The question vexed me until I talked with my friend Miriam Haskett, who also spoke fluent German and was a European history professor in Washington, DC. She helped me put it in perspective. Just like Miriam, I do not believe that any one country or culture is inherently more good or evil than another. Germany was the right country, at the right time, and under the right conditions for the rise of Nazism and the fate it conjured. To its credit (and with the help of people like General Eisenhower), it faced the horrors done in its name during the war and took responsibility for it through years of introspection, especially through the media—although German history in school curricula ended at World War I until recently.

More than from books, however, I really learned the language, history, and culture during eleven years of service in Germany. In the 1980s, I saw how the United States descended from its German pedestal, beginning with Vietnam and Watergate. The understandable process of disillusionment continued with the Iraq War, followed by the National Security Agency (NSA) and Google data-collection scandals. But I also reminded Germans that it was they who put us on a pedestal in the first place in the wake of World War II and the realization of what their country had done in Europe. On a couple of occasions, I encountered their early, awkward moments of assertiveness. During the Gulf War, when I was a civilian international relations analyst for the US Army at Europe headquarters in the iconic and idyllic city of Heidelberg, German leftists were leading the protests outside the *Kaserne* under the mantra that there could be no just war.

My retort: "And what about the war against Hitler? Was that also unjust? Where would you be now if that had been the prevailing mentality in my country then?" They were not amused.

The second US military incursion in Southwest Asia was rather different. The German Social Democratic government committee I spoke with at an Atlantic Bridge meeting in New York in 2004, criticizing our less defensible casus belli, pointed out that "real friends tell friends when they're wrong," to which one member added, "We are no longer beholden to the politics of gratitude."

"Fair enough," I said. "It shouldn't be about gratitude, anyway. It should be about pragmatic, long-term interests. So, let me ask you: Which country has had the best track record of being supportive of your interests, from the Marshall Plan to reunification, the expansion of NATO and the EU, and the eurozone?"

The discussion went on, but it was now clear that the relationship between the United States and Germany had matured from senior–junior partners to peers. In fact, we now have to deal with many other powers as partners rather than as clients, as we did during the Cold War, while our partners must now assume greater responsibility for many of the things we have managed alone.

The Germans deserve credit for taking some international responsibility, and not just recently with the Syria refugees. When a congressional delegation in Heidelberg couldn't understand why the Germans weren't eager to join us in the Gulf War, let alone were protesting it, I explained: "We just spent the last forty-five years beating into their heads that they should be nice people and not invade their neighbors. Now we want them to go off to the front." Just a few years later I ran into colleagues from the *Bundeswehr* in Kosovo. The idea of German troops returning to Yugoslavia for the first time since World War II was unsettling to them, to say the least. It was just as hotly debated in Germany as was the US discussion of putting boots on the ground then.

Much larger than a unified Germany, Texas compares in temperament with the Free State of Bavaria, the Federal Republic's largest and southernmost province, where I had spent nine of my eleven years in Germany. The Texans are the Bavarians of America—or the Bavarians are the Texans of Germany, with all the stereotypes that find truth and contradiction. Bavaria has yodeling forest dwellers in lederhosen; Texas has tobacco-dipping cowboys. Bavaria has BMW; Texas has Texas Instruments.

Yet, like Bavaria, Texas is anything but monolithic and belies predictability. Like other big states with diverse populations, such as California and New York, Texas is an analogue of multicultural America, with its own twists and surprises. The Gobles' neighborhood has broad boulevards canopied by huge dogwood trees and Spanish moss, as I just saw in Mobile, Alabama. It reminded me that Texas is still part of the South, despite its fierce independence. As in Bavaria, separatism stirs from time to time in Texas, although its founder, Sam Houston, did not favor secession in 1861.

Near Austin, I visited the home of Monica Kovacs-Barnes, a friend of my cousin Richard in South Carolina, who helped arrange the impromptu visit. Like Richard, Monica is among hundreds of thousands of "military brats" born overseas—in her case on the huge air base in Ramstein. I stayed with the Barnes family in their home just outside of town, a newly developed suburban community of prefab houses representative of how most Americans still live. The neighborhood is not altogether inspiring, and Monica and Kevin struggle mightily to earn a living and raise their kids to give them a chance to get a good education and a respectable job with a decent income—the stereotypical middle-class American Dream. They are everyday heroes who do little things in little ways that add up, but their stories are of little to no interest to Hollywood or the news media—and, increasingly it seems, to most of our political and economic elites.

In Houston and Austin, as well as San Antonio, I was constantly reminded that there seem to be two states of Texas as there are two Americas—one smaller but increasingly rich and the other larger but increasingly poor, with fewer in between. Economic inequality and a shrinking middle class create a predicament throughout the United States, but the boom and bust is hardly as stark and substantial as in Texas, with consequences felt well beyond the Lone Star State.

Wealth disparity has grown to endemic levels worldwide. The Generalized Inequality Index (or "Gini coefficient") that roughly measures national income distribution since the *Titanic* went down has been steadily rising since the 1980s, with indicators (ranging from 1 to 100, with 100 being the highest disparity) averaging in the 50s and 60s in Africa, the Middle East, Central Asia, and Latin America. There is a strong correlation between inequality and instability. Even in the United States, the Gini index has steadily grown from the mid-30s to the upper 40s, intersecting China's rising economic disparity as a result of its state capitalism as well as Mexico's falling inequality as a result of economic reforms. Meanwhile, the United States is falling relative to other countries in many measures of the stability of states, such as in the Fragile States Index, and the peacefulness of civil society in the Global Peace Index.

Something much larger is afoot. As Mark Twain said, "History doesn't repeat itself, but it does rhyme." Last time we saw such wealth disparity and political fecklessness was in the days of the robber barons, those imbalances leading to the social turbulence and middle-class deconstruction starting with World War I, through the Russian Revolution and Hitler, and culminating with World War II.

In the United States and Great Britain, at least, with the dismantling of many Depression-era and postwar socioeconomic reforms, the cyclical result of the enduring debate about the pie and its pieces, the forces of freewheeling capitalism have once again been at play, creating new economies and destroying old ones. What many capitalists cite as Joseph Schumpeter's "creative destruction" does impel significant transformation, innovation, and growth, but it is destabilizing and incurs tremendous social cost. There are ups and downs in all of this. The trick is how to meet and manage them.

Although a certain degree of wealth disparity has been more accepted in the United States than in Europe, given America's strong sense of national identity, the country has also been built on the belief that a rising tide lifts all ships. Despite its rough-and-tumble reputation as a country of winners and losers, the American social contract presupposes that all are owed a chance to get a larger slice of a bigger pie. As in Europe, however, prosperity is no longer a given, especially for youth, and a growing number also no longer feel represented by mainstream political parties and other traditional institutions. Larger numbers of both Americans and Europeans are looking for the simple answers to complex problems that fringe movements offer, and debates about national identity are framed by rising anti-immigration and Islamophobia—a determination of identity not by who one is but by who one is not. Meanwhile, the idea of what Churchill called a "United States of Europe" looks more and more remote. With all these parallels, it would seem we have as much to discuss across the Atlantic as during the Cold War.

During the time I spent in Europe, I got to see a different sociopolitical management model based on what the Germans call the *Mittelstand*. They learned from their own history, more than from us, the centrality to sustainable democracy of a robust and vibrant middle class. Theirs was wiped out in successive generations, leading to the catastrophes of the twentieth century. Today, Germany has a nationally supervised pension and health-care system that features a mix of public and private mechanisms. Germany's public education system benefits from a society that looks upon schoolteachers—in social as well as professional status—as something more than sanitation workers, resulting in schoolkids who score way above ours in math and science and are fluent and literate in their own as well as at least one foreign language. Public unemployment assistance there emphasizes retraining for a changing job market.

Then there are labor–management relations that are more collaborative and include "codetermination" (*Mitbestimmung*), where labor and management sit on the same board and make decisions about what's good for the company and the industry as much as what's in it for the shareholders. Many Americans call this socialism, but it doesn't stop them from buying products from Germany's "social market economy" by the boatload. In addition, laws there prioritize the protection of personal data and privacy versus nearly unfettered government or corporate access, something less seriously addressed here. In Germany, you can refuse to receive junk mail; in the United States you cannot.

The result of all these policies is a proportionally larger and more resilient middle class with a social mobility that has overtaken what was once the trademark of America. The system is so compelling that hundreds of former GIs have joined it. Although they still love their home country, they've found it difficult to live there. James Albright Jr., who hails from Dallas, was the civilian public affairs specialist when I was his military chief in the 2nd Armored Cavalry Regiment in Nürnberg. Even as the regiment left in the early 1990s, Jim had already decided to remain there with his German wife, Gabi, and their two sons. Two of my colleagues from Heidelberg, Ron Rasch and David Lange, also stayed on for decades, returning to the United States for a few months at a time.

To be fair, I also have quite a few German friends who found it equally compelling to retire in places like Florida or California. Josef Joffe, editor of *Die Zeit* and author of *The Myth of America's Decline*, whom I've known since my days as a research assistant at the Woodrow Wilson Center in the early 1980s, is at home *hüben wie drüben*—here as there. Still, many Americans view people like Jim as ex-patriots rather than expatriates, forgetting America's largely European heritage and the nearly twenty million Americans who have lived in Europe temporarily during their military service. Of the top thirty countries in the Organization for Economic Cooperation and Development, the United States ranks about last in the number of persons working overseas. It's embarrassing how much others know about the United States versus the other way around.

Our ignorance feeds an attitude that Americans have little to learn from other cultures—but we do, as much as our distant cousins across the big pond have to learn from us. Among these is the most important of American traits—a sense of national identity that is more inclusive. Europeans may poke fun at our campy patriotism, but secessionist movements in Texas and other states are a joke compared to the more than one dozen separatist movements in Europe that have already partitioned countries such as Czechoslovakia, torn apart the Balkans, and threatened to tear asunder countries such as Spain and Ukraine.

Unlike in Europe, Muslims in the United States see themselves, by and large, as first and foremost Americans. They are more integrated in America because Europe does not have America's longstanding immigration-assimilation culture. With respect to national identity, the significance of America is that its citizens identify themselves based mainly on an idea rather than human categorizations such as race, religion, ethnicity, or language, although these are significant second-tier determinants of identity. The United States is a true nation of nations. Unlike identity in most countries, American identity in its diversity is a strength and not a vulnerability. E pluribus unum.

I spent most of my years in Germany between the ages of twenty-three and thirty-two—some rather formative times in a person's life. Although I lived in German neighborhoods, in time had more German than American friends, and spoke fluent German, I never felt that I could, nor did I want to, fully integrate into that society. By contrast, because being an American is mostly a matter of mind-set, anybody may become an American within a generation.

Despite all that, and despite the fact that much of my work in Germany was about fostering German–American relations, I also never felt that I really understood Germany and Germans with the same kind of *Fingerspitzengefühl* (the feeling at the end of your fingertips, or intuitive sensibility) as native Germans. One thing I was fortunate enough to do was to visit, every few months, towns in eastern Germany such as Erfurt, Weimar, Dresden, and Berlin, starting from six months after the Berlin Wall came down to just before I left Germany three years later. I stayed in people's homes in bed-and-breakfast arrangements so I could talk with them and see how they lived. It gave me a great chance to watch the start of the psychological as well as physical transformation of that society and to gain appreciation of the complexity and difficulty of such a transition. Yet I still understood that I was little more than a visitor.

Before I left Germany, I told German friends and colleagues that the most significant issue in Europe's most significant country would be to find a durable and workable answer to the question, "What is a German?" This is true in any country, but particularly in Germany since then because Germany's demographics have been changing to a more diverse society than any other time in its history. Since the fall of the Berlin Wall, Germans have had more asylum seekers apply to their country than to the United States, and Germany has the same proportion of foreign-born people living there as in the United States— around 13 percent.

They're still at it. As in the United States, Germans are having an enduring discussion about who they are and what they're about. The future is uncertain, but the past is not an option. The Germans cannot return to the nineteenth-century nationalism that a half century of American military presence helped put to an end. (The witticism for years during the Cold War was that NATO existed to "keep the Russians out, the Americans in, and the Germans down.")

The only way forward is for the Germans—and much of Europe with them—to come up with a narrative of multiculturalism and inclusiveness that works in a European context, north and south. That can best occur in an enduring and multifaceted dialogue between the two most powerful countries on either side of the Atlantic, from which both sides could benefit. Nation building is generational and homemade. Looking at younger Germans, who are staunch democrats and multiculturalists practically from birth, I'm confident their generation is even more committed to that process than *Oma* and *Opa* were. We have always known that the fate of Germany is the fate of Europe, but what the Germans seem to have bought into is that the fate of Europe is also the fate of Germany. This is good news for both Europe and the United States.

National and international integration is a common theme for Europeans and Americans, in different ways. In addition to interrupting the cycle of wars of runaway nationalism in Europe—making what happened in the twentieth century nearly unimaginable today—the United States introduced a global system that has, paradoxically, encumbered a dominant power. What seems to be missing for many Europeans is a unifying concept with which individuals can identify, which is where America may come in. Joseph Campbell may have been onto something when he suggested in *The Power of Myth* that the organizing idea for a truly global multicultural world is indeed the concept of the United States itself.

The transatlantic nexus is more relevant than ever to global peace, security, and prosperity, if only to shape a future world less controlled under it. The practicalities go well beyond security. The Transatlantic Trade and Investment Partnership, a long-negotiated free-trade agreement, will cement a financial and economic bloc composing over half the world's gross national product and nearly two-thirds of its financial power, and one that still leads the world in advanced manufacturing, higher education, and scientific and social innovation. It

would be poised to gain further energy independence from less stable and reliable sources, such as the Middle East and Russia. All of
this portends the strengthening of the most stable and secure quarter
of the world for decades to come, with its possible extension south-
ward into Latin America and Africa as well as toward Asia from both
sides. NATO remains the principle agent of this zone of stability. The
United States remains the guarantor of the security and stability of
the European Peninsula, which in turn is still more vital to American
interests and international peace and prosperity than any other region
of the world except perhaps the Asia-Pacific. That's why all the news
about European economic and financial stability registers not only in
the media but also on Wall Street.

Besides, Western norms and values still dominate institutions in
international cooperation, peacebuilding, and security. The dignity of
the individual is still a most attractive sociopolitical value. The proof of
that is twofold: Democracies in general have been growing in number
and robustness, and the lines outside US and European embassies are
longer than at those from anywhere else.

America has much to teach the world, but the world has much to
teach America. That requires humility, engagement, and leadership by
example—living your values and walking your talk. It made a great deal
of sense to me to think about all this while riding through Texas.

After Austin, my next stop was San Antonio, whose own transformation in diversity can be seen in the River Walk. Still, you don't go to
San Antonio without seeing the Alamo, a shrine today that is central
to American as well as Texan identity. "Remember the Alamo" is, of
course, among a long train of rallying cries including "Remember the
Maine," "Remember Pearl Harbor," and "Remember 9/11." This particular slogan mobilized commitment to what was described as national
liberation by Daniel Cloud two months before the battle in February
1836: "If we succeed, the Country is ours. It is immense in extent, and
fertile in its soil and will amply reward all our toil. If we fail, death in
the cause of liberty and humanity is not cause for shuddering."

"When you consider who was here and what happened afterward,
you have to figure that it was more than just about defending their
property," noted one of the curators at the Alamo. "We still want to

believe that we don't go to war unless we have a real good cause," he added.

Nonetheless, the Alamo was as much a story of diversity as about disaster. Most of the nearly two hundred who died there were not Texans by birth, including men straight from Denmark, England, Germany, Ireland, and Scotland. In fact, nearly half spoke no English at all—the majority of them German.

Just thirty miles outside of San Antonio, the gusty winds diminished, leading me to think I might have left them behind for a while. Within a stretch of only about twenty miles, I saw the change in foliage from the familiar thick deciduous trees and surrounding greenery to the scrub brush and brown dirt countryside that characterized a different topography altogether. I had left the Eastern United States and was proceeding into the West on my own, like a pioneer, with no more friends or family to visit until I reached California.

Like many times before throughout my life, it was as if I were in a whole other country.

CHAPTER 4

NEW MEXICO: OLD POST AND NEW POSTS

Making my way through West Texas, about eighty miles east of Fort Stockton, where I was to turn north on US 285 to head toward Roswell, New Mexico, I took advantage of my good pace and enjoyed a break at a rest stop in the cool midmorning air. Having at last come out from under the blanket of clouds following me since San Antonio, I absorbed the warm sun and wide open spaces of the desert landscape. Besides the changing topography, you can tell you're in the West when you see signs at roadside stops warning "Poisonous Snakes and Insects Inhabit This Area."

Just as I resumed my ride, a gaggle of nine Harley-Davidsons roared past. They were mostly touring bikes—Electra Glides, Street Glides, and one or two Softails. I caught up with them and exchanged the biker wave to join them. More than security, they offered companionship on a long and lonely stretch of two-lane highway. When you buy a motorcycle in general and a Harley in particular, you've joined a subculture of adventurers. Handing you the keys to your first Harley, the dealer usually shakes your hand and says, "Welcome to the family."

Like cowboys on a cattle drive, we meandered along on the smooth asphalt of our twenty-first-century trail. One member of the group was bringing up the rear in a black Chevy Suburban pulling a matching trailer. I later identified him as the chuckwagon driver at our lunch stop at a great Tex-Mex restaurant in Pecos, Texas, sharing my cowboy analogy. It set off quite a bit of laughter.

From our impromptu highway hookup, we rode sixty miles before pausing at a truck stop at Fort Stockton and filling our near-empty tanks. Then we made introductions. Like a lot of Harley riders, they were mostly middle-aged professionals. We went by first names—Terry, Bob, Jim, Dave, and so on. All were from the Corpus Christi area and out for a long weekend at the mountain resorts in Ruidoso, New Mexico, about thirty miles short of my day's destination.

Once we got to Pecos, I told them about my trip, and they were intrigued when I explained that I would be closing a circle that I had started thirty years ago in Roswell. They had some difficulty grasping how I could float back and forth between two connected, parallel careers, one civil and the other military, as a Reserve officer. So I told them what I've told many: "Just think of me as both Bruce Wayne and Batman. Same guy, same cause, but sometimes I wear the costume and sometimes I'm the other guy—at least until I get to New Mexico Military Institute and retire tomorrow. Then I'll be just Bruce Wayne. Only not rich."

They chortled and then said, "Thank you for your service, Chris." They were obviously sincere, but I'd heard it so many times, especially over the past few years, that it had begun to sound pro forma. For the first half of my military career, few Americans made a big deal of being in the military. After 9/11, whenever in uniform, I saw surging esteem from fellow citizens. Besides the free dinners, discounts, flight upgrades, and other bennies, what struck me was how people would say the same thing: To "Thank you for your service" many would add "to our country." It seems many see the military as the ultimate public servants. That's a good thing.

Nowadays the military is the most esteemed institution in America. That wasn't always true. Such reverence for the military—or those in the military—was not always a given. Prior to World War II, the regular military was kept small in peacetime due to distrust of a large standing army going back to the country's inception. Yet, inasmuch as Vietnam may have been a low point in our civil–military relationship, it appears we have swung to another, equally unhealthy extreme. It's time for us to move on again toward a new normal near the middle. The veneration and outright hero worship of the military is an unhealthy distortion of the time-honored yet taken-for-granted civil–military clause in our social contract.

Our culture has militarized considerably since Eisenhower warned us about the military–industrial complex just before I was born—and civilians are much at fault. For one, the shift has led to overpoliticization. An important principle in what I call military civics, other than the primacy of civil authority, is that the military should remain apolitical. Yet, political pandering that's soft on the troops and hard on national security has become today's version of kissing babies and a quick and easy way to justify defense spending. In TV programs, movies, and video games, as well as military displays at sports events, Americans are subjected to a daily diet of folklore valorizing the military and celebrating a culture of violence—war and killing being antiseptic and abstract to a society that has hardly seen it. Football, the most martial of our sports, has unseated baseball as the national pastime. Our political, economic, and media elites are unabashedly opportunistic in pursuit of their own agendas. Businesses of all kinds have also been cashing in on the good PR it all engenders.

These and the catechistic utterances of "Thank you for your service" are, however, as West Point professor Elizabeth Samet put in an op-ed, a "mantra of atonement" reflecting the chasm between what many civilians admire about the military and what they themselves will not do. The bumper-sticker patriotism that came from "a nation at war" that was basically told to be consumers more than citizens inspired a picture of a Marine barracks whiteboard that went viral: AMERICA IS NOT AT WAR; THE MARINE CORPS IS AT WAR; AMERICA IS AT THE MALL." Another one that summed up how the role of the Reserves had changed is a picture of a sign a GI in Iraq made from a box of rations and put in the windshield of his truck: "ONE WEEKEND A MONTH, MY ASS!"

Meanwhile, the Army, with the brunt of combat casualties, had the most difficulty meeting recruiting goals during what after 9/11 the Pentagon called the Decade of War, targeting parents more than kids in their advertisements and raising the recruitment age to forty-two, even in a slow economy. Businesses have habitually hired fewer veterans than civilians, revealing their ignorance about war and the profession of arms and their distorted assumptions about military life and post-traumatic stress disorder (PTSD). As I've scolded some business leaders, "These guys have taken chances on your behalf—the least you can do is take a chance on theirs."

"Freedom isn't free," one rider in our group contributed, reciting the slogan.

The launch of initiatives like the Wounded Warrior Project is less because the greatest casualty is being forgotten than because the US Department of Veterans Affairs has been underresourced and mismanaged for decades. "If you can't afford to take care of your veterans, then don't go to war," Vermont Senator Bernie Sanders reminded us. The widening civil–military gap has prompted private or public–private initiatives to help veterans find their way back into civil society, such as The Mission Continues, The Code of Support Foundation (for military families), One Mind, and Joining Forces, the latter headed by Michelle Obama and Jill Biden. Riders for Resilience looks to improve the resilience of the military community (and its connectivity to the larger civil society) through "the healing and therapeutic power of riding a motorcycle." Carry the Load looks to better connect civilians with the sacrifices made by military and first-responder personnel by honoring them equally on Memorial Day.

Yet, as Samet has also said, "the successful reincorporation of veterans into civil society entails a complex, evolving process." Indeed, soldiers would rather be socialized than idolized. The psychology of civil–military apartheid and anonymous adoration of the military is intrinsically undemocratic and elitist—exclusive and not inclusive. Our decision in 1972 to pay the economic rather than social costs of the historic anomaly of a large standing peacetime army has resulted in an increasingly professional but correspondingly disconnected warrior class. And the more disconnected they are from us, the more we have been willing to use them in an era of perpetual warfare against terrorism or for reasons such as "humanitarian intervention."

Perhaps most disturbing is how a national decision that once took a declaration of war or an act of Congress now seems far too easy and painless. American power abroad is now seen largely in terms of its military. The use of force is too often the only real solution applied to settling conflicts or providing humanitarian and disaster relief. It has contributed to the militarization of our foreign policy. Then there is the overlay of a military–industrial complex contributing a lion's share to our fiscal insolvency.

"What I do worry about," retired Admiral and former Chairman of the Joint Chiefs of Staff Mike Mullen said on *The Colbert Report*, "is that we have become some version of the French Foreign Legion. 'Please go off and fight our dirty little wars and let us get on with our lives.' And I think that's a disaster for America. We need to be connected to the American people, and we need to do that through the system that's here, those that are elected, and I certainly agree that those who are elected ought to vote on what we do. And we ought to have a fulsome, raging debate about that in this country."

"I find all this very interesting, Chris," said Bob while we were munching on Mexican food. "There's no doubt we're asking the troops to do the kind of things we should have other parts of the government do. But who else is gonna do it?"

"It's complicated, I admit," I said. "But one of the reasons we get deployed to take care of this stuff is because our government under-resources the agencies that can either help get at the causes of a lot of these conflicts—and thus prevent the use of force—or be the right responders to humanitarian crises. You wouldn't send a fire truck if what you really needed was an ambulance, right? A lot of this is because many of us think we spend too much on foreign aid. We don't realize the connection between one and the other—foreign aid and national security." They were astounded to learn that their country spent less than one penny of their tax dollar on foreign assistance.

Another topic we got onto was social change in the military, despite its conservative overtones. "Take ending 'Don't ask, don't tell,'" I offered. Sure, the military resisted it, but its integration has gone smoothly since due to an ethic that says while we may or may not at first like what we're being told, once we get our orders, we salute the flag and give it our best.

"Wasn't quite the same after we desegregated the Army," piped up Terry, an older African American gentleman, referring to the integration of African Americans in the late 1940s.

"You're right, Terry," I said. "Look at the experience of Vietnam. But we've come quite a long way. Think about this: A black female officer receives exactly the same pay and allowances as her white male counterpart with the same pay determinants. You can't come close to that in most of the private sector. The problem's not so much that there's segregation within the military; the problem is the segregation of the military itself."

An unintended consequence of the professionalization of the military since Vietnam, I told them, has been an institution that has learned to talk less about citizen-soldiers and more about warriors. Even now, the Pentagon is hardly taking seriously the obviously huge potential benefits of relying more on the most operationally experienced citizen-soldiers in our history, the Reserves. Many have forgotten that what Jefferson called the "unnecessary soldier" has been at the heart of the paradox of the national strength and character of the United States. It has not been just the professional warrior that has won our wars or made America much the envy of the world. It has really been the citizen who becomes one, whenever and wherever the need arises. Stephen Biddle, a scholar at the Army War College, concluded in a study that armies from democratic societies have tended to outperform those from autocratic societies.

It's clear to me, as a former citizen-soldier, that a whole-of-society ethos of national service would make all of us better citizens of a better nation, prepared to meet the largely whole-of-society challenges we now face in an interconnected world. The national mythology that summons our psychic as well as physical energies to face them should likewise champion role models from all walks of life and every corner of our country, tapping the essential strengths and comparative advantages of this nation-of-nations. The heroes we revere reflect the values that brand us as a people. We have to come to a similarly expanded understanding of national service. There are many ways to serve your country other than wearing a uniform.

My nephew Brian, who chases down drug dealers and gangsters with the New York City Police Department in the Bronx and Harlem, yet finds time to call me every November 11 to thank me for my service, has been serving his country. The work of a police officer in a democratic society, like that of a soldier, is not primarily that of killing, but of keeping others from killing.

My cousin Richard, who was a firefighter for nearly twenty years before retiring as a result of injury, has served his country, as have a multitude of government civilians, like Ginny Martin. So have people like Michael Goble. And so have the journalists and charity workers beheaded by Islamic militants, and aid professionals helping countries find an alternative to conflict or dealing with Ebola and other crises. And then, of course, there are military spouses.

Professional public and private educators like my high school teachers—Kevin McIntyre, Joan Cashon, and others, now retired from helping hundreds of young people over decades find their own paths as self-actualized individuals contributing to their communities—have served their country. In fact, they still do—Kevin remains a scoutmaster and Joan, a multiple cancer survivor, continues to write and lecture to inspire others going through their own trials.

The increasingly vast number of private volunteers—people like Dolores Goble performing countless other acts of compassion at home as well as abroad, working in kitchens, providing meals, building houses, and cleaning up slums, and the Salvation Army volunteers ringing bells in front of the stores every holiday season—are also serving their country.

Americans celebrate individualism, but the country has a tradition of those same individuals opting out of hierarchical systems run mainly by government and pursuing personal goals in a local volunteer society. Volunteerism is the way Americans reconcile individualism and community. It defines much of our national character and identity as well as brands our sense of citizenship. "American volunteerism," wrote author of *Made in America* Claude S. Fischer in the *Saturday Evening Post*, "is the merging of our individual and communal strains—the worldview that individuals forge their distinct fates with like-minded people in groups that they have individually, freely chosen to join and are individually free to leave. People attain their personal ends through community, but through voluntary community. And thus they are both sovereign individuals and community citizens."

The keys to American community are in the acts of opting in and out. That is why collective action through the state is anathema to so many Americans. It's also why Americans say "Love it or leave it." Being an American is more mind than matter. Go watch a naturalization ceremony and you'll see what I mean.

Service to others is woven into the American moral and social fabric. "Successful life in America," said President George H. W. Bush, "must include service to others."

Whenever you serve others in society, you are serving your country, to one degree or another. Our long-standing sense of charity and volunteerism in the private sector is one of the things that has made the United States a great country. And like charity, citizenship begins on the block. In an interconnected world, when you serve your community, you serve your country.

"We need some kind of national service bill," said Dave, with other voices muttering approval.

A movement of some kind no doubt has been afoot for some time. In August 2007, *Time* magazine's edition on "The Case for National Service" kindled a wider discussion perpetuated in part by ServiceNation, a coalition of over five hundred organizations inspired to work "towards the day when a year in a national service program like AmeriCorps is a common expectation for Americans, and when national service is universally accepted as a strategy for putting people to work, tackling pressing social challenges and uniting Americans in common purpose." It is gathering many champions, such as retired general Stanley McChrystal. Barack and Michelle Obama, the First Couple, have in turn supported United We Serve, led by the Corporation for National and Community Service. Linking service at home and abroad and encouraging Americans to serve in organizations other than the military and the foreign and civil services, United We Serve includes AmeriCorps, Citizen Corps, and Learn and Serve America as well as the Peace Corps, Senior Corps, and Volunteers for Prosperity.

"I don't mean a military draft," Dave went on. "We don't want to go back to that."

"Right you are, Dave," I responded. "Any concept of national service starts with common values and their connective effect. Civil society, after all, comes from a personal sense of responsibility to others in all ways, at all levels." In terms of the civil–military relationship, it means understanding the military as part of our national identity and civil society rather than an aberration.

One of the reasons for the near deification of the uniformed services, besides the threat of terrorism, is because of the vital unifying mechanism that patriotism has in the United States. As in many countries with diverse populations and a contentious political culture, such as Great Britain, China, and Pakistan, hardly any national institution plays a more unifying role in national identity than the military. This was certainly true to a great extent for Iraq—which is why our deliberate dismemberment of the Iraqi army after our invasion was such an odd decision.

Another reason we exalt military service is that the military lifestyle is the most outstanding model of a service ethic in a nation hungry for role models. Soldiers voluntarily place themselves in harm's way, in relative discomfort, and endure long separation from loved ones—but then so do many police, firefighters, and aid professionals. It's also worth noting that well over half in the military never deploy to danger areas, and a minority of them actually see combat. When put in harm's way, however, the reason a soldier fights is well known; it is first for his comrades, then his country. Since the 1980s, the Army has institutionalized its values: "Loyalty, Duty, Respect, Selfless Service, Honor, Integrity, and Personal Courage" reads the little "LDRSHIP" dog tag I've had since then. Value-basing is enormously compelling in a society awash in complexity and moral relativism, and for which such sacrifice for the greater good has been made by a tiny minority. But what is enjoyed by many cannot be long upheld by a few.

No doubt the celebrity status of the military will eventually abate, hopefully not in another overcorrection. This is the greatest danger of the disconnection: The higher the pedestal you put people on, the farther they tend to fall. Before the inevitable demystification comes

and we fire and forget the military, it would seem prudent to capi-
talize on both the military role model as well as a resurging service
ethic in America. We have an opportunity to transition the meaning of
national service to one that is more inclusive and democratic. Besides,
in the long run, the best way we can support, take care of, and honor
the troops is to make sure they are among us and not apart from us—
socialized, not idolized.

Shared values also come from shared cost. We have to clearly link
sacrifice with service because it's the sacrifice that qualifies the service. Each year we lose many more police and firefighters at home than
troops abroad. We have lost as many Peace Corps volunteers proportionally in the line of duty as soldiers on behalf of our national values.
We've also lost thousands of contractors, scores of journalists, and
many others in the UN and NGOs. Too few Americans are aware of
these sacrifices.

Multiple times I have ridden the day before Memorial Day in
Rolling Thunder, the world's largest single-day motorcycle event, as
well as with about twelve hundred or so other bikers in the annual
LawRide honoring fallen law enforcement officers, which takes place
two Sundays prior in Washington, DC. I've wondered why Rolling
Thunder, three hundred times larger than the LawRide, shouldn't
join in remembrance of all those who have died for their country
in uniformed service. And why isn't the National Fallen Firefighters
Memorial on the National Mall instead of in the middle of the woods
in northern Maryland?

"A national service bill of some kind makes a lot of sense," Dave
concluded as we asked for the check. "But I doubt it will happen any
time soon—hell, we can't even get a budget passed."

While waiting for consensus on that, I suggested, one thing
Congress could do to shape a whole-of-society sense of national service is to update Veterans Day (which used to be Armistice Day to
commemorate the end of World War I) by calling it National Service
Day to honor all those in public service. In turn, they could revise
Memorial Day to honor those fallen in the service of community as
well as country. Memorial Day in particular evolved along a path of
greater inclusiveness. It was first called Decoration Day, to honor those

who died preserving the Union in the Civil War, but in 1926 Congress directed the secretary of war to designate Memorial Day as a national holiday and changed it from honoring Union soldiers to honoring all Americans who died fighting in all wars. We should continue to march along that long road of inclusiveness.

Besides revitalizing the meaning of citizenship, a more universal sense of service and sacrifice will do more than regenerate the civil–military relationship in America. It will help put the *unum* back into *E pluribus unum*. Although we still may not respect each other's opinions, at least we should respect each other's commitment to community and country—real common ground for much-needed civil dialogue on the issues of our day.

It could also start restoring public faith in government. A comprehensive ethos of national service and sacrifice also makes us better citizens of a better nation among nations, tempering our narcissistic tendencies. Although it makes us a better example to others in the world and helps restore our all-important moral credibility, it most importantly makes us better examples to ourselves. There is no reason why we cannot honor all who serve neighbor and nation on National Service Day and stand up for all the fallen on Memorial Day. Lincoln was right: "Any nation that does not honor its heroes will not long endure." That's true for all of the people all of the time and not just some of the people some of the time.

"Your bill would be a good idea," Dave said. "But I'm not sure most of your fellow veterans will want to share a holiday that honors them with civilians. And they're a powerful lobby last time I checked."

"You've got a great point, Dave," I answered. "But that may be just the problem: We can't lose sight that all soldiers are citizens, first and foremost." We all shook hands and wished each other luck, knowing we would probably never see each other again. We rode together on US 285 and crossed into the mountain time zone in New Mexico, until they peeled off to the left, toward the Ruidoso Downs resort in Artesia. They threw me the biker wave; I threw them a salute.

As I headed into Roswell, I thought it was good to be alone while returning there for the first time in thirty years. I also thought about how lucky I was to have had a career since then that steered me to an intrinsic and not just superficial understanding of the civil–military relationship and the issues I had just discussed with Dave and the others. Had I not gone to New Mexico Military Institute (NMMI) first and then to a civilian university, I would not have had that understanding. It inadvertently gave me the best possible exposure to the civil–military dynamic I was talking about. It also explains why I eventually gravitated to Civil Affairs during my military career. None of this was premeditated; it just worked out that way. Serendipity, in many ways, is indeed a wonderful thing.

Back in high school, I decided for a number of reasons to go to NMMI, some two thousand miles and two time zones away, instead of West Point, near where I grew up. I had applied to the United States Military Academy, met the requirements, and received a nomination from Congressman Benjamin Gilman, who surprised me at graduation with a Congressional Medal of Merit (for outstanding community service and leadership while maintaining a high academic record). By then, however, I had told my family I had changed my mind. Instead, I was going to a military junior college "out West" where I could obtain my Army commission in two rather than four years and then finish college at a civilian school. And I could learn to ride a horse.

LEFT: Graduations and other gateways: Receiving the Congressional Medal of Merit from Congressman Benjamin Gilman. RIGHT: Graduation from the New Mexico Military Institute on May 16, 1980.

"Know thyself" the ancient aphorism goes—I knew that I was not structured at the time for success at the United States Military Academy. The required degree for all students was a bachelor of science in civil engineering—and that would have been impossible given the way the left side of my brain functions. So I wound up going to NMMI, got my commission as an armored cavalry officer in the Army, completed an associate's degree in liberal arts and military science, and joined the Maryland Army National Guard while finishing my undergraduate work in international relations and German at George Washington University.

Private military schools abound in America. College preparatory schools, junior colleges, and four-year colleges and universities all parallel the structure and practices of the armed forces. These institutions aim to educate the whole person with rigorous academics, physical training, and character development—a classical education, if you will. The structured atmosphere fosters discipline and self-regulation, good time management and interpersonal skills, teamwork, and critical and creative thinking. Military junior colleges feature a liberal arts education, but like military academies, they strive to teach a young person how to put foundational values into practice through hands-on leadership training—personal integrity, respect, community service, and selfless sacrifice to imbue a sense that everything's not about you but, rather, something larger than you.

Not all graduates of military schools go into the military. As many as half go on to successful careers in business, science, the arts, education, and public service. In fact, most military officers are not service academy graduates. For the past century, four-fifths or more have received their military training right along with their civil education in hundreds of colleges and universities through the Reserve Officer Training Corps (ROTC). Junior ROTC is also found at thousands of high schools.

New Mexico Military Institute is just one of scores of such civil–military academies in the United States. Founded in 1891, it has been called the "West Point of the Southwest," consistently ranking among the top five junior military colleges in the country. Although about half the students come from the Southwest, NMMI goes out of its way to recruit cadets from at least forty states and nearly two dozen countries around the world.

Among the things I realized there was that a uniform was either something to hide behind, a persona given to you, or a platform from which to project yourself. No doubt when you join the Army and put on the uniform you become something else—less an individual and more a functionary. But if you lose yourself too much to that given group identity, instead of developing your own, you risk becoming a cog in a machine and not a person.

I also learned a lot about problem solving—mostly about not being afraid to meet problems head-on, and to be relentless in pursuing personal goals: Don't quit just because it's hard to do—if it's not hard, it's probably not worth doing. When I later went to George Washington University (GW), I wound up obtaining two bachelor's degrees in successive years. It was a workaround against what I dubbed *bureaucrapia*. You could not obtain an interdisciplinary double major there: I was enrolled in the School of Public and International Affairs and wanted to add to my three-year language study requirement and round out my fourth year of German to get the most from my tuition dollar; however, the German Language and Literature Department was in GW's Columbian College of Arts and Sciences. Dean Lindon, who took the time to meet me and answer my letter of petition, was sympathetic but powerless, as it required a decision by the Board of Regents. (My case was later instrumental in having the rule changed; it just didn't benefit me.)

So I researched the rules, met the minimum residency requirement, and graduated the following year, much at my own cost, with the coveted German major and, for good measure, a major in history. These turned out to be fateful decisions, not just because the process introduced me to thinking both inside and outside the box, but also because it led me to a career in, among many others, civil–military matters. Your life experiences really do evoke your character.

Thirty years later, rather than a retirement ceremony with my last unit of assignment—the 304th Civil Affairs Brigade in Philadelphia, with which I had served long but done little as of late—I decided to retire on my own terms. What better idea than to return to where it all began, watch the latest generation of cadets obtain their commissions and degrees, share a few words of wisdom with them, salute the flag one last time, take off the uniform, climb back on the Harley, and ride off into the sunset? Storybook ending to this movie, right? Well, not exactly.

Despite what I thought was ample planning and coordination, little of what I envisioned happened. First, the school had made no arrangements for me to publicly mark my retirement due to some confusion between the Alumni Association, of which I'm a member, and the offices of the superintendent and the commandant that were in charge of the events. When I got to NMMI, it was apparent that everyone was focused on the ceremonies and had little idea how to deal with some old alumnus riding in on his Harley. Roswell was clearly not ready for this alien visitor.

As the SNAFU unfolded, I was at first rather disappointed. But I soldiered on, watched the cadets take the oath of office on Friday morning, May 14, and attended the Celebration of Diversity at the chapel later that day. As I strolled across the quiet, starlit campus after the final ball, I recalled two pearls of wisdom gathered during my quarter century in civil–military affairs. First and foremost, manage your expectations. Second, it's not about us; it's about them.

I was not there to participate; I was there to observe and, once again, learn. At the graduation ceremony, I sat with the noncommissioned officers to pay tribute to them as the soldiers from whom I had learned the most, and we sang "Old Post" together. As we chatted after the graduation, I told the superintendent and the commandant what I thought I had gleaned from all this.

I also told them that during my last tour of duty overseas, as Senior US Military Observer and Chief of Civil–Military Coordination at the UN Mission in Liberia, I oversaw the rotation of three groups of young officers from all service branches. They had suddenly found themselves in a place where practically no members of our military go—in a true multinational operation in which the United States was not in charge, a highly visible post where our deeds would be watched and scrutinized closely and would have considerable impact on the image of our country, for good and for bad. To help guide them, I gave them three watchwords—*professionalism, discipline*, and *humility*.

Professionalism, I explained, is really being yourself in what you do best and falling back on what you've learned and know as an officer—especially the principles and ethics of doing the right things the right way—when dealing with strange, complex, uncertain, or stressful situations. It's doing your duty.

Discipline is doing the right thing even when no one else is looking—but you can bet someone is. Even when you're off duty, you're never off-line. It's upholding your own as well as your group's honor—be that group a team, a branch of service, or your country.

Humility is the ultimate self-confidence. "Everybody knows," I told them, "that we're the biggest, baddest mothers in the valley. Don't beat your chests. Besides, you have as much to learn from them as they do from you. So be as respectful to a colonel in the smallest army there as you are to me. Come in low—you'll gratify some and astonish the rest," I said, channeling Mark Twain. "And you'll end up on a high. You'll get a lot more done and enjoy it even more."

Just about every one of those young officers told me how much that guidance helped them. And it showed. They performed brilliantly in their multinational liaison-and-support mission, punching way above their weight in raising the level of play among the UN military staff and generating tons of goodwill. They achieved a lot for their country and had a great time doing something very few do, even making friends along the way.

I told the generals how it had dawned on me that each of those three watchwords could be traced back to the motto of NMMI—"Duty, Honor, Achievement." I had not made that connection until returning to where I first learned about values-based leadership and principled operations. It was then I realized how much I had drawn from my education there.

The lesson of my return was to remind me of the value of enduring principles and their situational adaptation. The moral imperatives and ethics taught at schools like West Point and NMMI were not just theory. They *worked*. I told them that this is even more relevant in the complex and uncertain world of the twenty-first century, when young leaders will have to provide more sophisticated leadership much earlier in their careers.

At that moment I realized that my return to NMMI was anything but a disappointment. Just as it was for me back when I was an undergraduate, and for the cadets I was with that day, the function of any ritual—such as a graduation, a wedding, a divorce, or even a funeral—is to introduce you to the next stage of life, not to bring you back. They are gateways. Irrespective of my return to NMMI, I had much to offer beyond the last salute I performed alone and in silence on my last day in uniform. Things had worked out, just not as I had foreseen. Somehow or other, my old post had given me a new one.

Riding northward in the crisp morning air and rejoining US 285, I recalled another bit of refrigerator magnet wisdom I had seen at Michael's house in Houston a few days prior: "No one can go back and make a brand new start, my friend, but anyone can start from here and make a brand new end."

CHAPTER 5

THE SOUTHWEST: HUMANS AND HARDWARE

After a pleasant ride up US 285 from Roswell, I spent two days in Santa Fe—the oldest capital in North America. It's tempting to see the original thirteen colonies as the oldest European-developed sections of the continent. But the Spanish empire preceded the British here—Spanish was first more widely spoken than English in much of what is now the southwestern United States. Santa Fe boasts that "The Oldest House," a squat adobe structure on De Vargas Street, is allegedly the oldest standing dwelling in the United States still in use. Two streets away, where I had parked the Dyna, the Chapel of San Miguel is considered among the oldest churches in North America. The nearby Cathedral of St. Francis of Assisi contains the country's oldest Madonna, of the Cofradía de la Conquistadora, dating back to 1625. Kateri Tekakwitha, the first Native American saint, is commemorated in front of it.

I spent the summer of 1980, right after graduation from NMMI, at New Mexico University's *Deutsche Sommerschule*, north of Santa Fe near the artistic town of Taos. In an alpinelike ski village, I let my beard and hair grow, spoke only German, and was totally civilian for the last time until now. I meandered through the same aspen valleys thirty springs later, sensing a timelessness that only great works of nature can convey. I was glad to see the school still going strong. Dr. Richard Rundell, whose beard was now as white as the snow on the mountains and who introduced me to German poetry then, was still teaching there.

Things were not so idyllic when I got going again. Heading down to Albuquerque and losing about three thousand feet in altitude, I turned west on Interstate 40 not too far from a place called Truth or Consequences. For three hundred miles or so, with nothing in front of me except the handlebars, I wrestled with headwinds of up to fifty miles per hour caused by seasonal atmospherics, as the ranger at the Petrified Forest National Park explained when I took a much-needed coffee break. Only two days before, the winds had forced temporary closure of most of the interstate system in Arizona.

After more wind wrestling, I turned south again near Flagstaff, Arizona, and rolled through the stunning scenery of the red rock country along US 89A, negotiating countless switchbacks along steep mountainsides. With my physical reserves as low as the fuel left in the tank, I wasn't sure which would run out first—man or machine—as I coasted into Sedona. A route of 430 miles that should have taken just over six hours took nearly ten.

It was the scenery that kept me going—reviving and pacifying in its honest grandiosity, the splashes of evergreen on the warm sandstone. I spent what was left of the evening in the hot tub at a resort on the edge of town, ordering Italian delivery and going to bed much too early. The benefit of waking up at four thirty the next morning, however, was to witness a spectacular sunrise while strolling along the peaceful Verde Valley and catching a couple of balloons floating silently above it. Soon, I was off and running again. I had a schedule to keep, and it meant I had no time to meet with some of the locals and have a chat or two.

Fortunately, I had seen Sedona before (and have returned numerous times since). A small town of about ten thousand when I rolled through, it was named over a century ago after the wife of its first postmaster. For the previous eleven millennia, North American natives inhabited the area, the latest from the Yavapai and Apache tribes. The home of significant spiritual portals—vortexes—coming down into and up from the earth (male and female, respectively), people consider it among the most sacred and spiritual of places. Whatever you believe,

Sedona has an energy that somehow improves a sense of inner tranquility and equilibrium. Despite the short stay, I felt rather revived.

The headwinds obviated my original plan to ride a hundred additional miles along the South Rim of the Grand Canyon before going on to Las Vegas. Luckily, I had seen the Grand Canyon before—first in 1980 during spring furlough from NMMI when I hopped on a bus and backpacked down to the canyon floor alone. Instead, I continued south the next morning and picked up US 89 North after breakfast in Prescott (pronounced "press-kit"), a former Wild West town. It turned out to be fortuitous in that I got to see parts of Arizona that were new to me, including the town's Palace Restaurant and Saloon, whose patrons included Wyatt Earp and his team of vigilantes. I also got a reprieve from the winds along a very scenic roadway before rejoining Interstate 40 for about ninety miles, then turning north on US 93 toward Las Vegas. My travails with machine and nature in Arizona brought me back to how I first saw this ongoing dichotomy as a young armored cavalry officer.

It's no coincidence that so many of our lives lack real action—despite an insatiable appetite for facsimiles in "reality" TV, action/adventure films, and video games like *Call of Duty*. True adventure entails risk, but we have become a risk-averse society. This is the downside of encroaching creature comfort in consumerism, materialism, and technology: We get lazy, physically and intellectually. "The lust for comfort," Khalil Gibran called it, "that stealthy thing that enters the house a guest, then becomes a host, and then a master."

Technology is the great accelerator of human history, but as former Navy SEAL J. Robert DuBois wrote in *Powerful Peace*: "If unprecedented technological advances are allowed to run ahead of rational, compassionate, and moral human guidance, the consequences will be devastating."

It's tempting to be antitechnological, but Robert Pirsig's *Zen and the Art of Motorcycle Maintenance* advises that the "condemnation of technology is ingratitude" and itself a road to nowhere. Still, from health care to national security, technology—like the money that affords it—is not a panacea. What's really needed is a new, conscientious approach that transcends the dilemma.

Another way of looking at it is seeing that we live in a world of metaphors. Understanding technology as metaphorical for nature—both internal and external—expands our perception of it. The roads we ride on are a metaphor, too. Interstate 40 in Arizona generally runs along the same path as US Route 66, connecting Chicago to Los Angeles. When the highway opened in 1926, the United States was already the world's first motorized society, with far-reaching cultural and socio-economic implications.

Machines like airplanes, spaceships, automobiles, and even motorcycles have become the mythological metaphors of our time, much like birds were for the Greeks' Icarus and Daedalus, a story I have often found relevant. The moral for Icarus, of course, was moderation and understanding what you're getting yourself into with a new invention. (In the story, Icarus, the high-spirited youth, flies too close to the sun, melting the wax on his homemade wings and sending him plunging into the sea.) Along similar lines, one thing I eventually came to realize in the Army is that it's not material shortfalls that get you into trouble most but, rather, a lack of situational awareness and understanding coupled with a failure to understand the future implications of decisions and actions made today.

Among all the machine metaphors of mobility, motorcycles offer an ideal and reasonable balance between passion and prudence—manageable risk. They best embody the bond between man and machine, between our inner and outer natures. Motorcycling is an active rather than passive use of technology. You have to be fully into what you're doing, mentally as well as physically. Motorcycling has consequently made me a better car driver—more aware of my surroundings on the road. For example, not looking over your shoulder into the blind spot to change lanes in a car can result in trading some paint—on a motorcycle, it can be fatal.

Weapons are also metaphors—of the power of destruction, control, and coercion well beyond our physiology. Passing the saguaro cactus as I left Prescott, I recalled how the Colt revolver and the Winchester repeating rifle enabled the winning of the West. Guns are one thing, but Santa Fe had reminded me of the most extreme example of our enthrallment with weapons. Less than an hour away from this charming artisan city is Los Alamos, where Robert Oppenheimer's team set off the most revolutionary weapon in history in the desert near Alamogordo in July 1945. As the first atomic bomb exploded, Oppenheimer recited from the Bhagavad Gita, among the oldest of India's sacred texts—"I am become Death, the Destroyer of Worlds"— wondering what Faustian bargain this creation had just struck.

Challenged by geography and steeped in a Puritan ethic of material fortune as a sign of providential approval, Americans have leaned heavily on technology to breach frontiers, overcome obstacles, and parse time and space. Our progressively technological approach to warfare goes back to the Civil War, when the industrial North outlasted the agricultural South. It shaped what Russell Weigley, in his classic *The American Way of War*, called the "strategy of annihilation" (or attrition warfare) through technology and firepower. The pinnacle of this was World War II.

A country's approach to warfare is an extension of its social and cultural norms and values as much as it is policy by other means. In 1944, most of Germany's ultraprofessional *Wehrmacht* was still supplied by horse-drawn wagons. The US Army, an ocean away from its industrial base, supplied its front line troops almost entirely by trucks. The military–industrial feats were astounding: In addition to providing for its own forces, the United States supplied nearly half the tanks, trucks, and aircraft used by its allies, including the Russians. The Americans and their allies beat their enemies mainly because they had more of everything. Even today, the United States remains the only military power able to move massive amounts of personnel and materiel from one side of the globe to the other, or strike at its enemies from a safe distance with everything from killer drones to nuclear missiles. That is unprecedented, but it also conceals our overreliance on material solutions and a dearth of historical or cultural understanding that has played out in America's most recent wars.

It has also belied a still underappreciated truth best conveyed by a quote attributed to Napoleon, which I came across shortly before leaving for Germany and have come to appreciate more over time: "In war, the moral is to the physical as three is to one." Or, as Anthony Cordesman of the Center for Strategic and International Studies and a foremost strategic thinker observed, "Technology has not triumphed over the human dimension of warfare. . . . Tactical victories become meaningless without civil victory, and military forces alone cannot defeat the enemy." War, in other words, is more about people than platforms. The wars we have fought—more so now than then—have essentially been wars of identity. Those who have a more firmly and widely rooted sense of it are usually the winners.

The wars we have clearly won were also those in which our cause was clear. This moral factor is the great strength of armies from democratic societies. As Stephen Ambrose noted in *Citizen Soldiers*, "At the core, the American citizen-soldier knew the difference between right and wrong, and he didn't want to live in a world in which wrong prevailed."

The backbone of the American army is its noncommissioned officers (NCOs). Whenever an officer is taken out of action, NCOs step up and get the job done with commonsense leadership and initiative. The NCO corps of the Army in particular is unequaled—it is the main reason for the success and resilience of the US forces and their adaptability in the field.

Yet, for most of the time I served, technology drove military development. The first real indications of the limitations of Weigley's "strategy of annihilation" have already come in Southeast Asia. Denial, however, was the response of many of the military elite then. When I became an officer in 1980, Vietnam was already in the rearview mirror of a big-war Army with institutional amnesia on small wars (*guerilla* is Spanish for "small warrior"). The lesson-learning process concentrated on industrial-era rather than information-based warfare, much as our corporations clung to hierarchical business and industrial models belonging to an older era.

During my time at NMMI, and later as a research assistant at the Woodrow Wilson Center in Washington while attending George Washington University and drilling with B Troop, 158th Cavalry in the Maryland Army National Guard, I worked for top strategic thinkers like Cordesman. At that time, a debate intensified among strategic and military thinkers regarding the champions of art and of science in warfare, between maneuver and firepower, between the roles of men and machines—a debate that's been going on for a very long time.

This argument was peaking as I postponed pursuit of my master's degree, due to academic fatigue, and worked for a year at the *Armed Forces Journal International*. Thanks to Benjamin Schemmer, the editor in chief and my boss, I got to meet key actors in defense and military–industrial policy as well as national security politics. Among them was Colonel Charlie Beckwith, who had formed and headed up the elite Delta Force commando group.

Meeting Beckwith convinced me that I had had enough of Washington's contrived world of policy and politics. It was high time for this young armored cavalry lieutenant to get away from think tanks and get into armored tanks, knowing you really can't understand the world merely through books, the media, or weeklong fact-finding trips. I realized that one has to get out in the field and experience even what one might know intellectually to be true, because that's how you validate and internalize that truth. To better understand the issues I was witness to, I had to see how they played out in the field of action, and not just on weekends.

So after Ben made a few phone calls to the Pentagon, I reported in the spring of 1984 to the 2nd Armored Cavalry Regiment (ACR), once the vanguard of Patton's 3rd Army and now keeping vigil at the border of West Germany in Bavaria as the covering force of the 7th Corps. At that time, the Army was developing the AirLand Battle combined arms theory of operational art along with battle systems that it still has today, like the M1 Abrams tank, the Bradley fighting vehicle, and the Apache helicopter. It was the beginning of the warrior ethos to professionalize the still new all-volunteer force. The term *warfighter* was entering the vocabulary.

This new concept and the tools of the trade would eventually not find use where originally intended—on the North European Plain against the Soviets, who deprived us of that opportunity by going out of business. Instead, it played out in Desert Storm, scene of the largest tank battles since the Russian front, then in the coercion of the Serbs to abandon Kosovo entirely through airpower in the late 1990s without a single loss of an American serviceperson, and then again in the short-lived success of the shock-and-awe military doctrine in the first months of Operation Iraqi Freedom—and now, it seems, with the use of armed drones and air campaigns to destroy terrorist networks. After the Gulf War, the concept was recast as the "Revolution in Military Affairs"—modern warfare predicated on information, communication, and space technologies. The invincibility of our technology became synonymous with the invincibility of our military and thus our nation because we had come to see our power abroad as largely a function of military power.

Over the course of my military career, I witnessed some challenges to this catechism. But we didn't think of overhauling our way of war after our first clear loss in Vietnam—in essence a small war fought like a big war as Max Boot explained in *The Savage Wars of Peace*. This approach to war necessitates a surplus mentality, so it was no coincidence that grunts (infantry soldiers) in Vietnam described one of their own killed in action as having been "wasted." Mogadishu and the peace operations of the 1990s should have prompted further insight that, as Cordesman explained, "the civil dimension in creating greater political stability, more effective governance, and adequate employment and economic development is at least as critical as the military dimension, and at times the political effort in fact supersedes the military fighting." The 9/11 attacks, the threat to the cyber infrastructure of our twenty-first-century economy, and improvised explosive devices (IEDs) are further evidence of how technology we invented can be adapted against us, with egregiously disproportionate costs.

"Asymmetric warfare"—a term adapted after 9/11 but in essence something much older—must be seen as an economic and strategic as well as a ground concept. Economically, warfare is asymmetric when a couple hundred people spend a few million dollars on actions to make us lose or spend billions or trillions of dollars in direct and indirect costs. Strategically, warfare is asymmetric when you're fighting a war of limited ways and means while your opponent sees it as total war, with all moral as well as material ways and means in the state of play—something we had seen in Vietnam (or the British saw when fighting us in the War of Independence). The latest batch of bad guys we see in the news today went asymmetric, not just because they couldn't go toe-to-toe with the world's most professional fighting force. They had identified the Achilles' heel of our industrial-era strategy of annihilation in attrition warfare. They understood better than we do that war is and always has been more a psychological than a physical struggle.

Asymmetric warfare as such is really maneuver warfare. It is humanism in the field of human conflict, the psychological over the physical. In a long war of attrition, we cannot outlast this kind of adversary by just trying, as Mitt Romney put it in his debate with President Obama, to "kill our way out of this mess." Besides, it's not really about the guys with the guns—it's about the conditions that allow them to use them. So why haven't we learned this—if not as a country, then at least institutionally?

For one, Great Power militaries rarely reform themselves unless defeated in detail on the field. The US military has only had what George W. Bush later called "catastrophic success" in Iraq (we won the battle but lost the war). Going back to the civil–military relationship, it's also because the American public has been less critical of its military since Vietnam. The military is less compelled, as Tom Ricks mentioned in *The Generals*, "to conduct the kind of self-examination" critical in contemporary warfare. John Nagl, in *Learning to Eat Soup with a Knife*, called this being a "learning organization."

Because no one yet has been able to beat us at our own game, our military has gotten away with its force-on-force, technology-centric brand of battle. So it plans and prepares for the wars it prefers but not the ones in which it often finds itself. This has been its modus operandi throughout most of the late twentieth century, as Max Boot's books explain. That incongruence eventually got exposed in Iraq and Afghanistan, as our adversaries inconvenienced us again, choosing not to appear as we wished—sort of like the Huns and Visigoths inconvenienced the Romans, or the Minutemen did the Redcoats. It's the human factor that is the ultimate determinant in war, as military intellectuals like Arthur Cebrowski, Robert Scales, H. R. McMaster, and many of their kind have long argued.

Even as I joined the Army, I was already struggling with the concept of attrition warfare. My ability to comprehend what was going on over my last decade in the Army was because of what I was fortunate enough to understand in my first decade. In addition to the Napoleonic dictum, I discovered this while conducting research in the National Archives (my translation):

> *War is an art, a free-flowing and creative endeavor rested on scientific foundations that place the highest of demands on the human personality.*

It is the opening statement of the *Truppenführung*, or the operations manual of the *Wehrmacht* of 1936, a half century before the US Army AirLand Battle concept. What I found remarkable was how this quote suggested a more comprehensive understanding of warfare than anything I was reading in the new doctrine. Even the technological one-up-manship with the Soviets at the time reflected Carl von Clausewitz's "contest of wills." In his "remarkable trinity" of popular emotions, military skills, and political calculations, this early nineteenth-century Prussian philosopher of war, long the guru for Army officers, set the terms for the overarching primacy of politics, of which war is a continuation. Or, in the first of the "Special Operations Truths" I later learned as a Civil Affairs officer: "Humans are more important than hardware."

It was both my upbringing and civil–military education that helped me understand my trade in this way. It was also because of the unique attributes of "the Cav," which operated based on a combination of holistically applied maneuver and firepower. This more integrative understanding helped me whether I was on border duty at Camp Hof in Bavaria, at the corner between the two Germanys and Czechoslovakia, or leading armored columns around the countryside in exercises like REFORGER (Return of Forces to Germany). While doing something unimaginable in the United States at any time and in Germany now, it struck me then how the US Army had more exposure to the German people than to Americans, especially as we got closer to the Inner-German Border and the enemy.

The cavalry is the elite of armored units. Its mission is mainly operational reconnaissance (the eyes and ears). Back then, the 2nd ACR was the covering force (facing the enemy first) of a large, lumbering mechanized corps of seventy to eighty thousand soldiers. Armored cavalry relied more on the tactics of maneuver and economy of force (doing more with less) than the big divisions. Even though they were one-third the size, with about four thousand troopers, they had about half the firepower and a far smaller logistical train. The real mission of the cavalry was to force the Soviets to commit their main forces so the firepower of the Army's big mechanized divisions and the Air Force could "attrit" them before getting too far. An ACR had a tactical "signature" similar to that of a division—to deceive the enemy and develop the situation favorably. The paradox was to exercise restraint and avoid decisive engagement. Explaining it to my troopers, I channeled the boxer Muhammad Ali: "Float like a butterfly; sting like a bee." This use of hit-and-run tactics to goad the enemy into the desired response was, in a sense, like being mechanized insurgents. It was brains over brawn.

Being leaner and meaner inculcated a cowboy mentality going back before Custer. The Cav was steeped in tradition and élan. The 2nd ACR, whose 150th anniversary jubilee I planned and directed as a young captain, is the oldest continuously serving unit of regimental size or greater in the US Army. Its motto was "*Toujours Prêt*" (Always Ready). Regimental commanders, as colonels, were then among the most powerful in the Army—nearly 90 percent of them went on to become general officers, far more than colonels from other branches.

Maneuver versus firepower, however, was not the only enduring dichotomy in the Army, as I saw when I first arrived in the picturesque Upper Franconian city of Bamberg. As far back as the American Revolution, Army regulars have looked down on the militia. Yet, beyond the citizen-soldier ethos, Reserve forces maintain many other advantages. Back then, I noticed how cohesive my Guard unit was, able to hone its skills because of team stability. Reserve soldiers were in their positions two to three times longer. In graded tactical exercises, B Troop got high marks from its 82nd Airborne Division graders because of the high percentage of combat veterans that trained together so long. Many aspects of unit management and maintenance were tidier, due to not having the time for what we called unnecessary or foolish work. The contrast led me to adapt something I had heard many say about Vietnam—"The US Army has not been in Germany for forty years; it has been in Germany for one year forty times."

A few months after first reporting to the 2nd ACR's 2nd Squadron in Bamberg, I had an amusing encounter with some of the troop commanders who sat with me one day at the mess hall and harassed me a bit, much as veteran players rib a rookie. One of them, a tall and affable captain named Tom Burnett, really got into it.

"Well now, Lieutenant Holshek, now that you've been in the *real* Army for a while instead of the *National Guard*, how are you finding it?" he asked in his nasal midwestern drawl.

"Well, sir, now I do in a whole month what I used to do in a weekend."

They all laughed but stopped haranguing me. I had passed some kind of initiation rite.

After a year of rumbling around the German countryside, I climbed off the tank for the last time and moved from Bamberg to my adopted German home of Nürnberg. Germany's largest medieval city, "Lebkuchen" City (as I nicknamed it after its trademark gingerbread) was the New York of the sixteenth century in trade, finance, economics, and the arts—and later the spiritual capital of Nazi Germany and the scene of the Nuremberg trials. It was also the location of the 2nd ACR's Regimental Headquarters, situated in the former "SS Kaserne," renamed Merrell Barracks.

When I reported in the spring of 1985, one thing I noticed was how the power structure of the 2nd ACR ran a bit, ironically, like the Soviet Politburo—with concentric circles around the innermost circle usually consisting of the regimental commander, executive officer (XO), intelligence officer (RS-2), and operations officer (RS-3). The only other officers with direct access to the commander, guarded carefully by the XO, were the squadron commanders and sometimes the chaplain—and, of course, the regimental sergeant major.

I nonetheless decided to take on one of the least understood and glamorous of staff positions—the Regimental S-5, who was responsible for civil–military operations and public affairs—by essentially snookering the new commander, Colonel John H. Tilelli Jr., into giving me the post as a junior staff officer. Even openly wanting to be the

RS-5 in the 2nd ACR was a bit like coming out of the closet. What self-respecting cavalry officer would be interested in people, culture, and other touchy-feely stuff? But competent cavalry officers who could also speak fluent German were not easy to find. So when Tilelli found out I was interviewing for a similar job in a nearby command, he told me, "You're not going anywhere. You're going to be my S-5."

I took to the job like a fish to water, having already performed numerous civil–military missions in Bamberg as the unofficial protocol and liaison officer of the 2nd Squadron, dealing with mayors and German Army commanders. I had also earned the reputation and endearment of many troopers by finding comfortable places to sleep and—most important—places to take a shower in the field, usually at an Olympic-size indoor swimming pool (or *Schwimmbad*). My handle on the Squadron radio was "*Schwimmbad* 6" (6 is the part of a call sign of someone in command or in charge; so it meant, ironically, that I was in charge of swimming pool procurement).

My routine was simple: Look on a map, find the nearest *Schwimmbad*, then go to the lord mayor's office. After charming his secretary with my *akzentfrei* (accent-free) German, I gained an audience with the OB (*Oberbürgermeister*). The OB was inevitably a war veteran who, conveniently, had never fought Americans. After some chitchat, listening to the OB's war stories, providing a briefing that gave him the skinny on our doings, and presenting him with a small token from the regiment, the OB would ask the inevitable question: "So, what can I do for you, Lieutenant?"

Which prompted my spiel: "Well, sir, as an old soldier yourself, you know after a few days in the field it's good to find a place to clean up. We were wondering if we could make use of the *Schwimmbad* after normal hours. Of course, we'll reimburse the town, say, one deutsche mark per soldier, and have a crew clean up after we're done." The OB would then call the *Schwimmeister* and arrange for us to pick up the keys. *Einwandfrei*, in German slang, indicates how easy something is (or, in my penchant for literal translations of German directly into English: "one wall free"). Or, as New Yorkers say: "Badda boom, badda bing."

Once at the Regimental Headquarters in Nürnberg, I was first assigned as the Regimental Protocol Officer, finding myself at times teamed up with my good buddy Captain Bill Plumlee, an artillery officer I met in Bamberg who was even more fluent in German. Our job was to help entertain entourages of German and American politicians at the border, including then vice president Bush and Bavarian Minister President Franz Josef Strauss (who loved to hang out with us after the "dog and pony show," drink copious amounts of beer and schnapps, and tell us raunchy jokes).

So I already had a liking for this civil–military stuff because I was good at it, enjoyed it immensely, and figured it was all the same after you got off the tank. One time I briefed Chancellor Helmut Kohl at a tank range, along with Strauss, US Defense Secretary Caspar Weinberger, and the top brass from both countries. We also showed Kohl how to eat our new field rations—MREs, or "Meals, Ready to Eat." He picked the frankfurters.

Another interesting duty was as the liaison and coordinator of the regiment's participation in the anniversary celebration in Lunéville, a small town just on the other side of the French border, which the Regiment had liberated in September 1944. My French counterpart from the local cavalry unit spoke no English, whereas I spoke just enough French to get my face slapped. So we discovered a lingua franca. It was quite a scene for passersby in Lunéville to see two young captains—one French, the other American—sitting in an outdoor café casually discussing the parade plan in German. They must have wondered who had really won the war after all.

As the RS-5, I learned how civil–military operations were not simply a form of public relations. They were a form of maneuver and economy of force, more in the psychological than physical sense. They should be integral to the operation rather than nice to do. If war was primarily a human endeavor, then civil–military operations could hardly be a sideshow—they were part of the main act. As part of war planning, for example, they included protected target lists and refugee movements to protect civilians and limit what was starting to be called "collateral damage" (or civilian casualties). They also included cultural dos and don'ts as well as "Wartime Host Nation Support," or supplies and services obtained from the local economy. In all the planning sessions and exercises, however, we never talked about how to help Germans recover from the obvious devastation. We gave no thought to what would later be called Phase Four post-conflict stability operations.

Connecting this to my experience in the Iraq War as I maneuvered the Wide Glide back on to Interstate 40, heading west once again directly into the wind, I realized that our Phase Four failure in Iraq was not that much out of character, because we weren't thinking of it in Cold War West Germany either. Then I remembered how I had learned from my father, as a carpenter's understudy, that it wasn't the framing and shaping work of posts, beams, and rafters that was most difficult or time-consuming. It was the finishing work—joinery, windows, doors, walls, and trim—that ultimately decided how good a job you had done. Civil–military operations and Phase Four stability and reconstruction operations are, in a way, the finishing work of war.

Your mind can really wander and make all kinds of connections when riding on a motorcycle through the vast and varying landscapes of America.

Being responsible for the finishing work of civil–military operations and public relations in an area the size of Connecticut was a challenge for anyone, let alone a junior captain in a senior major's position and the counterpart of both a lieutenant colonel and a senior major at a division headquarters. I got the job, as I said, because no one else really wanted it, but also because no one else could really do it—at least as I understood it. As a small fish in a small pond of bigger fish, I drew on three methods to hold my own—sheer competence, a sharp wit, and chutzpah.

At the time, the regiment did not exactly have a great rapport with the Germans—creating lots of damage on field maneuvers and behaving, well, like cowboys. But I stressed to the leadership that good relations had pragmatic payoffs. As I told Colonel Tilelli, "Sir, the mayor is always going to shake your hand and be polite, but it's your troopers who will get nasty treatment from the neighbors. So this stuff is also about taking care of our people." In any war, I reminded him, based on his own tours in Vietnam, you can win battles but never a war without the support of the population.

Being interviewed by Jim Clancy of CNN while on a tour of the Inner-German Border.

We had a small shop that punched way above its weight, thanks to an excellent German/American lineup including Sergeant First Class Kenneth Morris, Jim Albright, Manfred Barthel, Winfried Blümel, Helmut Juegl, Christa Lachner, and a rotation of fine young military photographers. My leadership approach was simple: Challenge them to excel, provide good guidance and top cover, listen to them, keep them informed, and then stay out of their way.

Within a few months, the regiment, hardly mentioned in the German papers and the *Stars and Stripes*, was getting regular coverage, most of it positive or neutral. This included left-leaning newspapers such as the *Abendzeitung*, after inviting reporters like Susanne Koelbl (long since a security policy analyst with *Der Spiegel*) to spend eighteen hours with a soldier and his family to get an understanding of what their everyday lives were like. When, at a 7th Corps public affairs conference, the corps public affairs officer asked, "Chris, how the hell are you guys getting all this great press?" I replied, "Sir, we're just telling them our story—glasnost and perestroika," referring to Soviet leader Mikhail Gorbachev's new policy of openness and transparency. They all laughed, but "telling the story" became a moniker for Army public affairs in Europe.

As I learned from others, humor is the best way to maintain perspective in a high-stress environment. One of my close friends on the staff was Father Gregory Jude D'Emma from Roselle Park, New Jersey, who was the regimental chaplain. After weeks of an inclement early spring, I marched over to Major D'Emma's palatial office in the old SS headquarters, complete with a huge oak desk and swastikas still inlaid in the parquet flooring. He swung around in his sumptuous leather chair, looking a bit like Al Pacino in *The Godfather: Part III*, puffing on his pipe.

"Yes," he said. "What can I do for you?"

"I'm here to file a complaint."

"What are you talking about?"

"This weather sucks!" I bitched. "What are you guys doing over here? We haven't seen the sun for weeks. Do you think you could say a few extra novenas, you know, pull some strings, and get this fixed?"

He took another puff on his pipe. "Hey," he shrugged and said in his North Jersey accent, "I'm in sales, not in management."

As much as Father Gregory was my friend, the Regimental S-3 (essentially the chief of plans and operations), Major Robert Young, was my nemesis. Rather full of himself, he was a real empire builder who eyed my little shop of wonders like Hitler licking his chops over Austria. No one wanted to work for him, as he had a reputation for driving his people into the ground. His nickname was Darth Vader. Being type A+ and übercompetitive, the regimental staff worked many hours even if not all of them were essential. After a few months in my new job, I realized I had to work smarter, not harder. Most things had to be done when my contacts were available, from nine to five. So I rewarded myself one evening by going home around seven o'clock. As a friend and I were walking out of the headquarters, Darth came swooping down the stairs.

"Where are you going, Captain Holshek?"

"Home, Major Young."

"Well now, you know you're a regimental staff chief now. We burn the midnight oil around here at Regimental Headquarters."

"Well, Major Young, it appears some of us are efficient enough to get our work done by seven. You have a great evening." And with that we were off.

More than my impertinence, Young was perturbed that my office was only three doors down from the commander's, and that Colonel

Tilelli and I had developed good rapport. Tilelli would at times come down, sit in my office, and just chat. I was one of the lowest-ranking officers in the regiment to have direct access to him. Beyond the access and my insolence bordering on insubordination, I knew Darth more than minded that I never addressed him as "sir."

So Young made his final power play, after already annoying me by intensifying his habit of directly ordering my people around without checking with me first, as he tended to do with most of the other staff sections—purely to flex his positional muscle. One evening after he received a promotion, he barged into my office. As when any officer of higher rank enters the room, I stood up and said, "Yes, Colonel Young"—I figured dropping the *Lieutenant* in his new rank, not an uncommon practice, was enough unearned deference—"how may I help you?"

"Yes, *sir!*" he growled. "I've had enough of you. You might be a staff chief here, but you're still a junior captain and I'm a senior field-grade officer, and you will afford me the appropriate recognition," he breathed, edging closer to me, his face growing red like that of a baseball manager arguing a call with an umpire. Respect, in my mind, was something you earned and not simply an entitlement. I stood my ground.

"Tell you what, Colonel Young," I said. "You are indeed a senior officer and among the most important staff chiefs in this regiment. I'll always acknowledge that, in public as well as private. But I don't run my shop the way you do. Let's make a deal. I'll address you as 'sir' if you don't treat me and my people like your action officers. If you want one of my people to do something, kindly let me know and I'll tell them. How's that?"

"I'm the Regimental S-3. I can task anyone I damn well need to. That's how it works around here. Get it? And I don't make deals with you!"

"Well, then, Colonel Young—no deal, no 'sir!'"

We stared at each other like a couple of bulls for a minute (though it felt like an eternity). "I need to have a talk with the XO," he snorted and stormed out. The executive officer came to me after Young saw him and let me lay out my case. As a result, I had to display more deference, but he could no longer directly task my staff without first seeing me—which was the deal I was offering in the first place. After that, we actually got along a bit better.

By that time, the XO and I had already come to a very good work-ing relationship, based on trust and mutual respect. When I had first become the RS-5, I had inherited my predecessor's campaign to fire Winfried Blümel, our German public affairs officer, apparently due to a clash of personalities. The only thing that stood in the way was the German union (the Works Council). After my predecessor had failed, it was up to yours truly. In fairness, I recommended to the XO that he should give me two or three months to evaluate Blümel on my own, in order for the whole thing to be as objective as possible. But he reminded me that the regiment had already made up its mind. As far as he was concerned, we were going through the motions.

After three months, I provided a special evaluation and did not give Blümel as low marks as my predecessor. True, he needed to improve his English-language writing and event-planning skills, but highly valuable was his long-established (and underutilized) network among German journalists and community leaders. I concluded that, with some coaching and assistance from me and his peers, Blümel's contributions would far outweigh his shortcomings. We were already showing that in improved press coverage. I also had gathered copious written testimony, including that of a squadron commander whose relations with the German community in his area specifically bene-fitted from Blümel's intervention. I provided a copy of the evalua-tion packet to both the Command Group and the Works Council, as required.

The XO was less than pleased. He cross-examined me and pres-sured me to change my findings, threatening to write his own report to override mine and even hinting that "this may reflect" on my own evaluation. To that I replied, "Sir, you do what you think you have to do, but I just hope you can document your case as well as I've docu-mented mine."

It was a very tense moment. The XO was obviously irritated and uncomfortable. It wasn't the regiment's reputation that was on the line as much as it was his. He had bought into my predecessor's narrative, made it his own, and briefed the commander about what was going to happen. After a moment, I suggested, "Sir, I recommend I brief the commander myself and explain that you did not have the benefit of the information that my investigation revealed. More important, the evidence also shows that both the investigation and evaluation reflect extreme prejudice on the part of my predecessor, as the affidavits show."

The XO thought it over and eventually said he was fine with that. It's one thing to stand up for what you think is right, but if you can give somebody a decent way out, so much the better. It's never too early to use diplomacy when you have the chance. No sense in tilting at every windmill.

By May 1987, I had fulfilled my initial active-duty obligation. The regiment offered to have me go "Regular Army," but I turned it down and returned to the Reserves. The decision was not based on how well I was doing then—I had simply realized that the active component was not something 100 percent for me. As Blümel, among others, observed, "Captain Holshek, *Sie denken zu viel*" (you think too much). Besides, I had chosen to go into Civil Affairs, which was then 95 percent in the Reserves. I probably never would have heard of it had I not joined the 2nd ACR. Working there had prepared me well for it.

In the sense of tradecraft, the cavalry helped me develop the right understanding of civil–military operations as a form of maneuver. I learned to appreciate the importance and value of situational aware-ness and understanding the operational environment, anticipating actions as well as adapting, achieving results with fewer resources, and looking constantly for the win–win. It also taught me a lot about how to play within the system without being eaten up by it, and how to deal with people with all kinds of backgrounds in a range of situations. I also came to see that my chosen profession was more about humans than hardware. In all these senses, it helped me find my professional military identity.

Despite my decision to leave active service, my final performance evaluation could not have been better, which gave me a sense of affir-mation. The regimental commander placed me in the top block of his part of my evaluation, reserved for a handful of the thirty or so captains he senior-rated in the regiment. A few days before he changed command and a few weeks before I left, he dropped by my office.

"Did you get your evaluation, Chris?"

"Yes, sir, I did. Thank you very much. But if I may, I think you shouldn't have wasted a top block on me and should have given it to someone who's staying Regular Army and can really benefit from it."

"That doesn't matter," Tilelli came back. "You earned it. I learned a lot from you, and I wish you the very best of success wherever you go." Then he shook my hand firmly and walked out.

I never had the honor and privilege of working for him again. Years later, while walking down the halls of the Pentagon in uniform after coming back from Kosovo, an entourage of high-ranking officers—among them General Shalikashvili, then chairman of the Joint Chiefs of Staff; General Tilelli, then Army vice chief of staff; and a couple of other four-star generals—approached from the opposite direction. As soon as Tilelli spotted me, he came over to me and shook my hand.

"Chris, how are you?" Then he introduced me to the chairman. "General Shali, you remember Chris? He was my S-5 when you were at the 1st Armored Division."

"Yes, of course I do—I wanted to steal him from you," Shali chuckled.

If I had ever become a general officer, General Tilelli would have been an ideal role model. He never saw himself as so far above a person that he couldn't learn from them, and he remembered those who did well by him. He knew how people and things came together.

It wasn't about men or machines—it was about both—about understanding that technology, as metaphors of the interplay between inner and outer nature, should work to enhance rather than be a substitute for moral conscience. War, like any collective human endeavor, is ultimately an exercise of the moral *in* the physical, not just *over* it. As such, therefore, the role of art and science in our lives cannot be understood any more separately than can humans apart from their hardware. This more expansive understanding of who I was and what I was about helped prepare me well for later challenges that I could not have foreseen during those days in Central Europe.

As I rumbled into western Arizona, I turned off the still blustery highway and took a short twenty-mile detour to look at the Meteor Crater—a nearly mile-wide hole in the ground created by a hundred-fifty-foot piece of composite metal that crashed into Earth from outer space some fifty thousand years ago—an eternity to humans but a mere blink of a geological eye. After seeing the crater and the ten-minute film *Collisions and Impacts*, I recognized a vulnerability in our existence wholly different from war's threat of annihilation. A meteor pummeling Earth and sending up a cloud of ash and dust could shut down more than air travel, as the volcano in Iceland would do later that summer. It could shut us all down—and our technology could do nothing about it.

Places like Meteor Crater help us see a far more expansive paradigm, where the same nature we have striven to conquer occasionally forces us to expand our minds and not just our possessions. Technology has made the planet smaller, helping us see it from a different perspective—from outer space. It behooves us humans to think more on that scale.

The natural disasters we are witnessing today in both greater frequency and intensity should remind us that we belong to a natural world much greater than we are. Global climate change—whether natural or human-made—should be reminding us that humans are part of nature and not separate from it. We are, after all, renters on this big round piece of real estate. We are not the landlords. That being true, all that we bring into the world is a product of our own nature, in concert with the nature around us. How well we bring together our human nature and the natural world, through the fruits of our labor, is the measure of our tenancy.

CHAPTER 6

SIMI VALLEY: GUNS N' IDEAS

Thankfully, US 93 North into Nevada was smooth riding, with long stretches of straight roadway through desert less colorful and without the dramatic rock formations typifying western Arizona. Even in the spring, southern Nevada is more brown than green, with rocky formations that look almost like those on Mars.

That day, I saw three more examples of our attempt to conquer nature. The first was Hoover Dam, in the Black Canyon of the Colorado River between Arizona and Nevada. This public infrastructure project required eight years to pass through Congress during the Roaring Twenties, before the government was cash-strapped. Work continued through the Great Depression, with 112 associated deaths. As I paused to look at the structure, I wondered how the media would have handled that today. Thinking of the builders' sacrifice, I rode the overpass across the dam.

Then came Las Vegas, where I caught a late-night comedy show. The town's gambling industry, connections to organized crime, and hosting of various forms of adult entertainment earned it the title of "Sin City." But it also has the highest number of churches per capita of any major US city. Contrary to the urban legend about mobsters building it, Las Vegas started as a stopover on the pioneer trails to California and became a popular railroad town in the early 1900s. Nevertheless, it is situated in one of the most desolate areas of the United States, in thriving defiance of the natural world that Americans say they value but still strive to subdue.

The Mojave Desert air was dry and fresh, as long as I kept moving. It was equally surprising to see how Southern California is essentially an extension of that russet desert, all the way into the Los Angeles area—truly amazing, when you think of the millions of people who inhabit the area. When entering it from the east, California looks like little more than a gigantic wasteland leading to the Pacific Ocean. Most people wonder what's so great about it and don't realize until they've seen a lot more of it—not unlike many places I've seen.

An even greater man-made wonder than the Hoover Dam is the sprawl of cities and towns in Southern California, which would hardly exist without the Governor Edmund G. Brown California Aqueduct, a system of canals, tunnels, and pipelines that conveys water collected from the Sierra Nevada Mountains hundreds of miles to the north. Construction began in 1963, and the system was operating fully by 1997. During that time, California overtook New York as the most populous and productive state, then surpassed France as the world's fifth-largest economy (if it were its own country). All this marked a tipping point in America's socioeconomic and cultural center of gravity in a shift from east to west, now looking more toward Asia than Europe. At the same time, the Cold War peaked and unexpectedly ended. Today California is facing its greatest threat in the worst spate of droughts, forest fires, and floods it has seen so far.

Like a mid-nineteenth-century prospector from the East, I felt I had navigated an unknown expanse to a strange yet familiar place. When the Dyna pulled up to the home of my grandmother's cousin in Simi Valley, the trip odometer read 3,594 miles. I was now retired from a career of military service that began in the Cold War and accelerated into a world that had become much flatter.

For the first time since Texas, I was no longer among total strangers, and for the first time since South Carolina, I was in the company of family—but this was family I hardly knew. Hilda Nighswander is one among a number of my grandmother's extended maternal bloodline who immigrated to the United States from the village of Bindersbach, near the French border, after World War II. This was the last of five great movements of Germans to America—from the colonial era, giving us the Amish and the Pennsylvania Dutch (*Deutsch*, or "German," has been confused with *Dutch*), to farmers before and industrial workers after the Civil War, to the aftermath of two world wars.

Many in Hilda's clan stayed with my father's family in the Bronx for a few months in the late 1940s before taking a three-day train ride across the country to join the others in Simi Valley from the Seyfried and Kuntz families who had managed to leave before the war. Now, at least two more generations have grown up there, obviously far more American than German (many of my distant cousins don't speak more than a word or two of German).

Hilda and her husband, Dick, first met in the United States shortly after he was drafted into the Army in 1948. He spent most of his enlistment in postwar Germany. Originally from Warsaw, Indiana, Dick was the classic Cold War American soldier. He hated the Army (or so he said) and was scheming to get out "A-S-A-P" (or so he said). Judging by his yarns over iced tea in the kitchen of their ranch-style house, he was technically gifted and had liked his job as a tank mechanic. He looked back on his time in the Army as "character building," talking far more about those four years than the forty that followed in technology jobs in Southern California.

I first met Dick and Hilda a few weeks before leaving the 2nd Cavalry, when they were touring Germany. I showed them around Nürnberg, but Dick most liked the Regimental Museum. This stop in Simi Valley was the first time we'd seen each other since Germany, and the last time I saw Dick. He passed away a year later. Along with my father, Uncle Randy, Uncle George, and others, I count Dick among the many upon whose shoulders my generation has stood. National service was second nature to them in a way it isn't to many of us.

The debt we owe to those who came before us is to try to become better stewards of our times than they were. I've always felt the successive generation is going to do things as a matter of course that the previous generation saw as extraordinary. That's a good thing, but it doesn't make the current generation greater than any other. What it does is put into perspective their challenges. The only way to measure any generation is to see how it meets its own challenges rather than compare it to how others met theirs. At the same time, it's up to the current generation to help the next one be ready to meet its challenges as best as it can. That's our obligation to the members of the next generation. Their obligation to us is to do the best they can with it and pass it on to the next generation. And so it goes.

The day after I arrived, Hilda took me as a matter of first order to the Ronald Reagan Presidential Library, Simi Valley's most famous attraction since the early 1990s. It became even more popular after the death of the fortieth president prompted a national discussion of his legacy and of the Cold War. I was interested because my military career began just before the Reagan era and because I wanted to gain an impression of how his legacy was portrayed there.

It didn't take long. I wandered through the displays that carefully cast "the Gipper" as the towering hero who brought down what he called "the Evil Empire." Through moral and material superiority, an economy with a military–industrial complex (the United States) won over a military–industrial complex with an economy (the USSR). Beyond the simplistic moralism reminiscent of his B-grade movies, the Reagan era was touted as a time of "peace through strength."

Americans especially love their interpretations of history and the outside world rather summarized, as in CliffsNotes. Besides how it rhymes, Mark Twain also warned us that "those who have no sense of history have no eyes and ears." It's little wonder how mythologies such as Reagan's feed nostalgia that still shapes current debates on how America engages the world. Indeed, the bipolar world that emerged from the worst calamities in history, ushering in an age that made the suicide of our species entirely possible, was easier to decipher than the one today. But even that world was more complex than we saw it.

There are many other legacies the Reagan Presidential Library left out. Among them is how the threat of thermonuclear war was made frighteningly real in *The Day After*, a 1983 TV movie watched by more Americans at one time than any before or since. It incited an unprecedented culture of conspicuous consumption by yuppies (young upwardly mobile professionals) and Gordon Gekko's *Wall Street*–type financial speculation, which arguably linger today, a materialistic rejection of the 1960s counterculture. Another is the deficit spending that rose dramatically then. In an edition of the *Stars and Stripes* in 1984, I had read how the United States had suddenly transformed into the world's largest debtor country from the world's largest creditor nation—a position held since entering World War I. I saved the clipping, thinking it was a game changer.

Because Americans have little appreciation of history's bigger picture and longer-term view of events, it's no coincidence that they have difficulty grasping the totality and complexity of strategy in the here and now. Just before Reagan assumed the presidency, a political science instructor at New Mexico Military Institute told our class that "true power is when you don't have to care what anybody else thinks, says, or does." He was right, but things have long since changed. Now Americans can less afford that worldview because of the greater connectedness between over there and over here, resource restraints, and issues like climate change. Strategy is fundamentally about making choices regarding the future, and a strategic mind-set is driven mostly by limitations in those choices. If you can do everything, you don't have to make choices.

World War II seems to be the reference point in American collective memory for a lot of reasons. For one, we've tended to think it is what all wars are supposed to look like. But the halcyon days of the Greatest Generation and the forty-four years that followed were an anomaly in world history. In many ways, however, the "new world order" that Reagan's successor, George H. W. Bush, identified began to look like the older world order of messy and indefinable coalition conflicts that preceded Reagan's lifetime. Many countries in the Middle East and Africa were not nation-states to begin with and are still sorting out their identities. Then came globalization, the rise of nonstate or transnational actors, and the increasing role of international organizations. Coupled with the forces fragmenting societies, these are all tearing at the fabric of nation-states and the international law notion of Westphalian sovereignty to which we still cling.

My visit to the Reagan Presidential Library helped me better understand how we got to where we are now. The museum did mention Reagan's diplomatic engagement, particularly his support of the pope and the Solidarity movement in Poland that was instrumental in ushering in the collapse of communism. It also cited Reagan's other famous role as "the Great Communicator." Regardless of how one felt about his policies, Reagan was able to effectively connect with most Americans and convey his evolving vision—from shutting down the Evil Empire to engagement with Gorbachev.

Talk is one thing, but what really brought down the Berlin Wall was neither that nor the half-million troops in Europe, the missiles in silos in the Dakotas, or the arms race and Star Wars that helped bankrupt the Soviets. What brought it down were the rising expectations of the people living behind the Iron Curtain. When I visited those East German households for months after 1989, East Germans told me how they all watched West German television. Rather than *Dallas*, *Dynasty*, and *Miami Vice*, what intrigued them were the ads. Their Western cousins could choose among Mercedes, Audi, and BMW while they waited a dozen years for a plastic twenty-six-horsepower car called the Trabant. The narrative they had been fed was that they were in the "workers' paradise." By the late 1980s, the lie of communism was too obvious. It was not Gorbachev who tore down the wall, despite Reagan's exhortations. It was *das Volk* (the people).

"Soft power" was at work, a term coined in the early 1990s by Harvard professor Joseph Nye. An inflection of personal or national power, it is more about persuasion than coercion, inspiration over intimidation, incentive over deterrence. This is in recognition of both the limits, risks, and costs of "hard power," resident mostly in the military and economic sanction, as well as the fact that soft power has been proving more efficacious, less costly, and sustainable. Its disadvantages are that it's harder to measure its effects, being more about art than science, and that it takes longer for those effects to take hold, as it had taken over four decades in the Cold War. Another is that it doesn't always work by itself. Although, as Max Boot later put it, "The Tweet is mightier than the sword," you still need both.

The alignment of the soft power of persuasion and the hard power of coercion framing US Cold War strategy is laid out in National Security Council Report 68 (NSC-68), now declassified and well worth reading because it is one of the rare examples in history of an articulated grand strategy in a single document. In NSC-68, diplomacy—not defense—was in the lead, and military or hard power was a holding action until moral or soft power, the offensive long game, could help the Soviet system collapse under the weight of its own self-contradictions through the "corrosive power of freedom." This is how the Cold War strategy of containment really worked. Even Reagan was talking as much about what the United States was for as what it was against. American identity has always been based on enduring national values, embodied most of all in the Declaration of Independence.

Americans couldn't understand how the Cold War could come to an end because of how hard power was—and still is—more visible and understandable to them than soft power, not really seeing what is behind the mask of our power. It has been a handicap in responding to foreign and security policy challenges since. I got a real understanding of this when I was on border duty with the 2nd ACR. One of the more interesting little towns in our sector of the border with the German Democratic Republic was Mödlareuth, which we called "Little Berlin" because it was also divided in two by a wall. We got news of Soviet officers appearing not far from there one day, a rare occurrence. East German *Grenzaufklärer*, or border guards, normally patrolled in front of the minefields and wire-mesh fences (based on a design patented in Georgia, USA, in the early 1950s).

Just a few meters away from the stones marking the actual border, we stood equidistant from the Russian officers. We stared at each other for a while, neither allowed to say anything or make any gestures for fear of causing an international incident. I somehow sensed, although they were standing at the edge of a geopolitical tectonic plate defined by their ideology and I was standing on mine, that we both knew that what was there was forced and artificial, yet we could not imagine how it could end. Only a few years later, I crossed the border at that spot for the first time into the new eastern states, wondering whatever became of those men.

After leaving active duty and the 2nd Cavalry, I took on a civilian job as the civil–military plans officer of the 1st Armored Division. I decided to pursue my master's degree in international relations in Boston University's overseas program. My first course was on political and military strategy and taught by an Army colonel who worked at the Supreme Headquarters Allied Powers Europe. My class paper, on (West) German grand strategy, argued that reunification was the raison d'être of the *Bundesrepublik* based on its *Grundgesetz* (Basic Law) and reinforced by the policies of every chancellor from Konrad Adenauer to Helmut Kohl. Colonel Heinlein, my professor, thought it should go to a major foreign policy journal. It appeared in *Global Affairs* magazine's summer 1989 edition, earning me an invitation to Washington to take part in a conference early that November on the future of NATO. With all expenses paid and a nice honorarium to boot, I was put up in the luxurious St. Regis Hotel, two blocks from the White House. When I showed up, the participants, mainly former NATO secretaries general, supreme allied commanders, and senior policy pundits from both sides of the Atlantic, were surprised to see the youngster who had written the article.

On the second day—November 9—we were in hot debate. The older, more cautious majority argued that NATO was strictly a military alliance and should remain as such against the opposing Warsaw Pact that would linger. A tiny minority countered that NATO was essentially a political alliance that could only maintain relevance in post-communist Europe by expanding eastward as a vehicle of European and transatlantic unity. While we were summing this up to our unreceptive colleagues impatient to get to lunch, an intern barged in, exclaiming, "It's on CNN! The Berlin Wall is coming down!" Our little insurgency treated ourselves to champagne and caviar that evening, knowing that, while we might have been good, we were certainly lucky.

The NATO alliance is more than just a political or even military instrument—its efficacy and strength are found in that it represents a community of basic values about governance—a common collective identity, which is the real reason for its durability. A decade after that peak moment, I republished a paper on the "Legacies of the US Military Presence in Germany for Peace Operations" for the American Council on Germany in New York. It noted, "In the more than half century since 1945, at least fifteen million American military personnel, civilian employees, and family members spent part of their lives working and living in the Federal Republic of Germany. In this regard, the stationing of American troops in Central Europe, though not its first intended purpose, was one of the most successful peacebuilding operations, of a sort, in history."

Even the Great Communicator had learned to place more faith in soft power than we seem to recall. And despite his reputation for not being gun-shy, he also knew when to exercise restraint. After Hezbollah blew up the barracks in Beirut in 1983, killing hundreds of Marines, he realized how much it would take to even try to stabilize Lebanon, so he withdrew the rest of the troops. Lebanon was not a vital US interest, Cold War notwithstanding.

Of all the quotes in the library, the most revealing is from Joseph Stalin: "Ideas are more powerful than guns. We would not let our enemies have guns, why should we let them have ideas?" Soft power is what autocrats like Russia's Vladimir Putin most fear. Their slavish control of the media is the biggest proof of that. Later, at the National Steinbeck Center in Salinas, I came upon a remark Steinbeck made at the time the Berlin Wall was erected in August of 1961: "I'm amazed that anybody would confess so completely that he failed. That's what this amounts to. A failure in competition, a failure in everything. It's like a little kid who takes his football home when he can't play very well. I don't understand that ability to confess failure. I can't see that this wall has any other purpose."

Fast-forward from 11/9 to 9/11. As I read Steinbeck's quote, I thought: Weren't the attacks on September 11, like all acts of politically charged terrorism, a resort to violence in a similar admission of failure? Their medieval ideology cannot compete with the inherent strengths and values of a society and political culture more compelling than their own, let alone go toe-to-toe with its economic and military might. Violence of this kind is a sign of weakness—a sign of an inferior narrative. If our success in defeating communism was based on playing our strengths to correspondingly attack their weaknesses, then shouldn't we be leveraging the same power in response to violent extremism? The communists feared our moral power more than anything. So do jihadists, because they have no real counter to it other than to distract us from it with acts of terror.

The Arab Spring that began a few months after my visit to Simi Valley may have signified the start of the long and very messy demise of minority and authoritarian rule in much of the Arab world, redrawing the map lined out following World War I, as the fall of the Berlin Wall signaled the collapse of communism, redrawing the map of Europe that armies drew at the end of World War II. But that, too, will be a generational, people-powered process. Our soft or moral power is more relevant in this century than in Reagan's. The good news is that America has a great résumé for this leadership position—as long as it keeps up its qualifications. As we have seen, freedom is better promoted through SharePoint than at gunpoint, and the relationships between peoples are as important as between governments, as sovereignty shifts downward from states to communities. George W. Bush may have broken the eggs in the Middle East, but it will be the people there who will make the omelet.

As we're beginning to understand, democracy cannot come about through sheer rhetoric, let alone by force. There as here, it's much easier to get rid of a bad government than it is to institute a good government—it's easier to campaign than it is to govern. Still, if we learn to understand moments like the fall of the wall, 9/11, the Arab Spring, Ukraine, and others as opportunities as much as problems, we could be better able to seize upon them.

Despite all the jubilation in 1989, I sensed some unease. We weren't fully grasping the meaning of the moment, as we didn't again a dozen years later. We weren't "watching the world wake up from history" as one popular song then celebrated and Francis Fukuyama proclaimed in *The End of History and the Last Man.* We were watching the world wake up *to* history, given the nasty, noisier little wars that followed the end of the bigger, quieter one. Another thing that troubled me was our triumphalism. Somehow we interpreted the fall of communism as complete vindication and even infallibility of laissez-faire capitalism. It was obviously not that simple, and it has blinded us from honest self-examination at times like the Great Recession.

My own rather naïve hopes were dashed that the collapse of (Soviet) communism would lead to more of an end to ideology than the end of history. Ideology is useful as a means of helping us reconcile philosophical views with reality, but it is more often a shortcut or even a substitute for critical or creative thinking. Because ideology leads easily to groupthink and discourages dissension, it encumbers rather than enhances individuality and freedom of personal thought and expression. Pope Francis is right: "We must not let ideology trump morality."

However, something more disturbing than that was going on. In the waning days of the Warsaw Pact, the head of the Soviet Institute turned to US journalist Daniel Schorr and relayed a warning from Mikhail Gorbachev: "We will deprive you of an enemy and then what will you do?" Although the United States had won the Cold War, the loss of an existential enemy capturing our otherwise ephemeral attention spans, as well as damping our divisiveness, turned out to be another form of "catastrophic success"—as President Bush's son later described the invasion of Iraq.

That's because Americans suffer from a permanent enemy complex. "Since the end of the Cold War," David Rothkopf of *Foreign Policy* noted, "America has been on a relentless search for enemies," adding that we seem to have "a visceral need for them." In a sense, September 11 rescued us from that predicament, when new monsters to destroy— Islamic terrorist networks like Al Qaeda and other violent extremist groups—were served up just in time.

So why do we have this chronic fixation on "bad guys"?

Our enemy complex goes back as far as Puritanism's fire-and-brimstone brand of Christianity. It frames our moral dualism manifest in Hollywood good-guy/bad-guy movie plots, Coke-or-Pepsi politics, or the idea that "If you're not with us, then you're against us." Evoking Tip O'Neill's observation that "All politics is local," America's foreign-enemy complex is merely an extension of—and an excursion from—our own feuding family, stoked by the 24/7 media. It's no coincidence that our failure to find a new existential enemy after the fall of the Berlin Wall has contributed to and enhanced readiness to look for them at home.

This enemy addiction, coupled with our ignorance-based politics, helps explain our lack of mental aperture to find new and coherent ways to see ourselves and the world since the Cold War. Nothing helps make things look simpler and mobilize the physical and psychic energies of the base for party and policy than making those who don't agree with you the personification of evil—it's no wonder we evoke Hitler or the Nazis when painting those pictures.

Based on the negative motivator of fear and threats, our power paradigm inflates enemies to the point of conflating them with the drivers of conflict and instability—the poverty and wealth disparity, civil disorder, and political dysfunction that characterize the spawning grounds of violent extremism—much as symptoms are confused with the disease. It's self-disarming, taking all the other tools out of the foreign policy toolbox, among them diplomacy and development and the opportunities they present—like fighting with one hand, powerful as that is.

It also makes us think the bad guys are bigger than they really are. As I traveled through East Germany and Poland in 1990 and saw the dilapidated barracks and run-down equipment of the Red Army, remembering all the "intelligence" and propaganda, including the Pentagon's glossy public diplomacy publication, *Soviet Military Power*, which helped the Reagan administration justify its defense spending surge, I thought to myself: And we thought these people were ten feet tall? We do the same today, scaring ourselves with stories of jihadists, rapists, and other bad people crossing the Mexican border.

This neurosis, bordering on psychosis, is now at the point of being a conspicuous strategic liability. It blinds us from seeing many solutions within our grasp, as hard power masks soft power. The sheer weight of our power and dominance covered this for a long time, but that's becoming less true, practically by the month.

The good news—if you want to call it that—is that our greatest threats are not from overseas, and thus are more within our span of control. "They don't come from terrorists," Rothkopf further explained. "They come from political obstructionists and know-nothings who are blocking needed economic and political reforms, whether fixing a health-care system that poses a debt threat many times greater than the immense US budget deficit or tackling the growing inequality in American society or overhauling the United States' money-corrupted, dysfunctional political process." As Pogo said: "We have met the enemy and he is us."

Whether beyond or within our shores, our love of enemies begins and ends with us. Or, as Abraham Lincoln eloquently stated some twenty-three years before becoming president:

Shall we expect some transatlantic military giant, to step over the ocean, and crush us at a blow? Never! All the armies of Europe, Asia and Africa combined . . . could not by force, take a drink from the Ohio, or make a track on the Blue Ridge, in a trial of a thousand years. . . . If destruction be our lot, we must ourselves be its author and finisher. As a nation of free men, we must live through all time, or die by suicide.

Our enemy dependency and threat obsession are not necessarily un-American, but they are anti-American because they are the antithesis of reason and civil society. They also erode another critical capacity that Alexis de Tocqueville observed: "The greatness of America lies not in being more enlightened than any other nation, but rather in her ability to repair her faults." Let's hope he's still right.

Keeping things in historical perspective is part of thinking and acting strategically. It improves insight into both problem and solution, and it helps remind us that America abroad is about much more than its military power. Besides, being an extension of policy by other means, military power supports and sets up political and civil progress, not the other way around. That is a lesson from the Cold War that we have yet to learn.

If we are witnessing what Fareed Zakaria has called "the democratization of violence" and war—as combatants can include women and children as suicide bombers—then the necessary antidote is the democratization of governance and peace. That means applying the plethora of our power in communities as much as capitals through our aid and development programs more than we've been used to—something good Civil Affairs operators have long understood.

What gives us greater advantage in this new age of engagement is the inherent strength of a national identity predicated on American values. Our approaches to the world must reflect more of what we're about than what we're afraid of—right more than might.

With my newfound extended family in California. Hilda is
on the upper left and Dick on the upper right.

Shortly before I left, Hilda and Dick threw me a backyard barbecue party—for one, to celebrate my retirement from the Army, but also, more important, to reacquaint me with once-seen relatives and some I had never seen and to learn even more about my past. We spent hours sharing lifetimes of photos and stories that I heard for the first time but somehow felt were familiar. It was like finding another home I never knew I had.

Knowing more about where I've been and the things that have shaped the circumstances of my life will certainly help me understand better where I am now and where I may be going. It was a wonderful retirement gift, and it helped me greatly on my way forward.

CHAPTER 7

LIBERIA: LEARNING FROM THE OUTSIDE IN

Leaving the Dyna in Simi Valley for some well-needed scheduled maintenance, I took a flight from Burbank, California, via Dallas to Ronald Reagan Washington National Airport. Two days later, I joined thirteen graduate students and my good friend Professor (and retired Army lieutenant colonel) David Davis. Dave founded the George Mason University Peace Operations Policy Program in 1994, a unique graduate program that takes the commonsense approach of co-learning peace operations—for practitioners by practitioners.

From DC, we went on a field trip to look at and learn about the United Nations Mission in Liberia, or UNMIL, where I had been and served the two years prior as the senior US military observer and chief of Civil–Military Coordination (CIMIC). UNMIL was my first time in a UN uniform but my third time in a UN field mission. Hardly many more Americans have been in UN peacekeeping operations in both civil and military capacities than you have fingers and toes.

The purpose of the trip was for the students to get a firsthand look at a country struggling to emerge from one of the longest and most vicious civil wars in African history. The students met with representatives of UNMIL, the US team, the Liberian ministries, NGOs and other civil society organizations, and of course ordinary Liberians. All are players in the complex, difficult, and patient work of building peace in a place that's hardly known it—an entire generation had gone by without any education to speak of, among other things.

It wasn't my original intention to take this international diversion from my national tour of discovery. However, while finalizing my plan, Dave called me that March to ask if I could accompany the students to Liberia mainly because of my experience there. For the past few years, he had been taking them to Haiti, which was much closer. That was no longer an option. The disastrous earthquake had struck there that January.

The field course showed how the UN really works—in the field and not in New York. It also showed how the United States can have great international impact at low investment and risk. Our support of and participation in the UN generates tons of lasting goodwill. Before the end of the Cold War, the UN was peripheral to our foreign policy and national security interests. Over the past two decades, however, it has moved closer to the center of them.

That's because our engagements abroad (beyond requiring greater balance and synergy between soft and hard power for both preventing and responding to conflicts) are going to occur more and more in truly multinational environments where the United States is not calling the shots, nor should be. Still, these sorts of programs enable us to go places and do things we might not be able to otherwise. In any case, if we want to concentrate more on getting our own house in order over the next few years, then we need to work more with partners abroad and through multilateral institutions so they can do more of the heavy lifting.

In this emerging new world, the military has to be a force of cooperation as much as confrontation. Professional soldiers of the twenty-first century must be as adept in the use of restraint as in the use of force. Most pathways to peace don't call for boots on the ground. Partners like the UN, NGOs, and other civil society organizations are better at performing humanitarian and reconstruction tasks once left to the military. The military's role is now more indirect, and a supporting rather than leading role—it's also really more a matter of winning the peace rather than wars alone. This is more apparent in Africa than it was in Iraq or Afghanistan, and the UN plays the central role in international and even regional security in Africa. Well over half of the UN's peacekeepers are serving in field missions in Africa; nearly half of those peacekeepers are African.

How I got to Liberia the first time is a story in itself. While working with DynCorp International as a civilian in the late summer of 2007, I was sitting in the office of retired general and former CENTCOM commander Anthony Zinni, who was a DynCorp executive board member then. In his plush office, viewing the lush summer woods of Falls Church, Virginia, we were discussing a concept I was toying with in order to propose to the Defense Department that it should provide client countries with education and training in civil–military operations. Beyond improving effectiveness at peacekeeping, counterinsurgency, and counterterrorism, the idea was to sensitize them operationally to the civil–military principle of the primacy of civil authority and perhaps help them democratize incrementally through generational improvements in civil–military relations. It would also make them less unstable.

"Chris," Zinni asked me, "why *aren't* we teaching Iraqis and Afghans Civil Affairs?"

"Great question, sir. Should I send General Petraeus a message and ask him?"

I first met General David Petraeus at the Holiday Inn in Washington in early 2004. We were among the first commanders to come back from Iraq. Petraeus, who had commanded the 101st Airborne Division, was the keynote speaker. We had a chance to talk off-line. In addition to pointing out that we were both born in Cornwall, New York, I complimented him on his remark that "every one of my soldiers had a Civil Affairs mission." We then traded e-mails once every blue moon, as he and General James Mattis, the 1st Marine Division commander under whom I had served in the first few months of the war in Iraq, were overseeing development of the new counterinsurgency doctrine. Then Petraeus went out to take charge of the surge in Iraq. But when I relayed Zinni's question after he took command in Iraq, he replied that they were "rather busy." Zinni was disappointed, thinking Petraeus didn't quite get it.

My personal concern, however, was with the rest of Petraeus's response. In his reply, he also queried my interest in being a Provincial Reconstruction Team leader there. I was about as interested in going back to Iraq, or deploying to Afghanistan, as I was in getting on a sinking ship. So my question to Zinni and another retired Marine and fellow UN veteran, Buddy Tillett, was—paraphrasing the famous definition of diplomacy—"How do you say no to a four-star general and make him happy to be on his way?"

"What's the problem?" Zinni asked, sipping on his coffee.

"Sir, Iraq and Afghanistan are emerging legacy operations," I said, using national security wonk-speak to convey the idea that we were, in many ways, already fighting yesterday's wars. "We're just trying to figure out how to get the hell out of there."

I told them that the US Military Observer Group at the Pentagon was interested in having me take the senior US military assignment and top civil–military post in a UN field mission in Liberia. Not only was Africa the place for much of our future foreign and security engagements, I told them, "but I have the opportunity to do something very few people can—go and help the UN learn civil–military operations and thus help a hell of a lot of partner militaries. It's a great strategic opportunity that I think could pay huge dividends in the years ahead."

"Then why don't you tell him that—the last part?" Zinni asked.

Petraeus got that. It was, in fact, a great strategic opportunity.

In Liberia, I learned about a way our military can engage the world in a very different but much more productive way than it did in the wars in Iraq and Afghanistan. Having a few of us placed in these UN field missions as strategic scouts and strategic enablers, as I later tagged them, helps Uncle Sam in many ways.

First and more than anything else, strategic scouts directly represent the commitment of the United States to these missions, fostering their legitimacy and encouraging the participation of other nations. Whether with one or a hundred thousand, America makes no more powerful a statement of its national interest than when it places its men and women in uniform in a troubled area. As such, the military is the multiplier to civilian-led diplomacy and development.

As I had already seen in Germany, soldiers serving as unofficial national ambassadors can enhance (or ruin) America's international standing and image with great efficiency through personal behavior and engagement with people from many nationalities in UN agencies, NGOs, and of course with the locals themselves. A typical UN field mission can have civilian, police, and military personnel from as many as forty countries. In addition to media coverage and US policies, the direct interaction of these officers affords a valuable and unique way to shape local perceptions of Americans as well as act as on-ground sensors of how the locals perceive the United States.

Leadership being a form of learning, our men and women in UN blue berets obtain much-needed and rare exposure to real-world multinational operations (versus US-led coalition operations). These officers join a few dozen Americans with working knowledge of the UN. The institutional understanding and international engagement skills they gain are a precious resource for our diplomacy abroad. Educating officers on how to work with foreign partners also helps them learn more about us—much like student exchanges are intended to work.

As such, US military in UN field missions can help balance Uncle Sam's understanding of the situation, the effectiveness of the international intervention there, and the circumstances in many African countries, without a large military footprint. US military observers can also act as strategic and operational enablers. An example is the assistance I saw our team give to the building of a Bailey bridge (a portable, prefabricated truss bridge) by Armed Forces of Liberia engineers along a strategic supply route in the volatile Southeast, involving a number of players from the US team, the Liberian government, UNMIL, and NGOs—scoring an inimitable contribution to building capacity and confidence in governance there.

Less episodically, US military observer teams help raise the UN's peacekeeping prowess just by being in key military staff jobs. Their professional example and their unique expertise in intelligence, planning operations, logistics, and civil–military operations significantly enable and sustain a higher level of play, sometimes beyond the mission area. This included my own efforts to help the UN develop a civil–military coordination framework based to a great extent on what we had done at UNMIL. If these small teams can help UN operations work better, it may mean not having to send a lot more US troops at much greater cost and risk to play globo-cop.

Finally, the presence of even a handful of colonels and captains publicly monitoring things sends a clear message to everyone out there that Washington is watching. "Glad you lot are out here," one British colonel at UNMIL quietly admitted to me. "It's one thing to outflank and embarrass standard UN infantry, but quite another to play games in front of your people."

This actually got played out about a half year into my tour of duty in Liberia. One of our US observers, living and working up-country in Bong County, had witnessed some bad behavior Nigerian peacekeepers exhibited toward Liberian civilians. He sent the pictures to me, which I discreetly shared with the UN mission leadership, including the senior Nigerian officer, a mild-mannered brigadier general named Paul Boroh, who also happened to be my UN boss as force chief of staff. The Nigerians already had a reputation of harshness toward the locals, due to their regional hegemonic self-image. But they were slow in corralling the problem.

"Sir, I wanted to make sure you saw these pictures before anyone else. I know full well this does not reflect on the professional standards you demand of your troops, or the many who work hard to perform their duties in an excellent manner."

He thanked me profusely. For the remainder of my time there, negative reports of troop behavior in the Nigerian sectors went to zero from two or three each month. In fact, General Boroh had me provide for the Nigerian officers a special session of the civil–military coordination course we had developed for the mission at large. Then he had a tall Nigerian Air Force wing commander named Samuel Babalola assigned as my deputy. "Learn from him," Boroh instructed Babalola, who did an outstanding job as my right hand. When I left the mission, he took the brunt of managing the UNMIL CIMIC operation (having already been doing it under my advice and counsel) and took over as chief instructor of the UNMIL CIMIC course, which he helped refine.

I had tutored other officers in my shop, including an Ethiopian medical officer and a Jordanian major named Amjad Al Majali, who like many on our team went back to their countries among the most knowledgeable in civil–military operations in their armed forces. A couple of years later, Amjad helped me find a gold dealer in Jordan to purchase wedding rings for me and Rosa, whom I met in Liberia only a few months before we both left on the same day. A dark-haired Castilian beauty who shares (or should I say, puts up with) all my silliness, but with far greater humanitarian instincts, Rosa was then and still remains in the service of peace with the UN Refugee Agency (UNHCR), going to places such as Bukavu in Congo, Irbil in Iraq, Kabul in Afghanistan, Beirut, and now in Baghdad. We see each other only a couple months at a time these days—proof that true love transcends both time and place.

Liberia helped me appreciate the value of multinational engagement in many ways, you could say. Despite its complexities and the frustrations the United States sometimes has with it, the UN is a cost-effective way for Americans to engage the world. Instead of paying 100 percent of the costs for a unilateral deployment, with all the bad karma that tends to generate, the United States pays a little more than one-fourth of the costs for UN peacekeepers, with other UN donors like Britain, France, Japan, and Germany collectively sharing the burden. No UN mission starts up without American say-so. In addition, UN peacekeeping forces work at operational costs far below those of US and many NATO forces. The reimbursement rate set by the Department of Peacekeeping Operations for them is around $1,300 per soldier per month. That's about one-fourth of the salary and benefits of their US counterparts.

The kind of mission I was on at UNMIL increasingly represents our emerging international security engagements, in this case with only thirty to forty US military officers from all services in UN peace operations worldwide. We could easily double or triple this contribution to these relationship-building programs and with it our visible commitment to the UN and partner nations, further generating international goodwill. It's a no-brainer.

I was fortunate to be the most senior US officer in a UN field mission and to head up the largest contingent. I was also fortunate to do it for eighteen months rather than the six months called for by the

Pentagon. In a business requiring extensive networking and relation-ship building, you just can't parachute into these places and expect to make a difference in a short time, although that has often been the expectation. When I joined a Defense Department ministerial capacity-building program as the project manager for Liberia a couple of years later, I critiqued this belief at a conference in Washington: "You know, we Americans think we can fly in on a Monday, make paradigm shifts and behavioral changes, and then be home in time for the Friday night happy hour." Those kinds of insights can only come from having been there and doing it over time.

UNMIL was my last duty overseas—collectively, I spent twenty years in Europe, the Middle East, and Africa—learning many things about those places and, perhaps most important, others' views of America. No doubt we are going to have to become more of a team player in the interdependent, globalized world we have largely created. Americans are not well known for getting into other people's sand-boxes and playing by their rules. "We're the foreigners here," I would remind my younger officers. Yet, I've often said to international col-leagues, "The world's challenges are so many, so huge, and so import-ant that even if we had perfect cooperation we couldn't solve them all, given our limited resources. Even then, we would have to prioritize. That alone requires even more collaboration."

Another thing I've learned from being there and doing it is that no one human category—race, ethnicity, religion, nationality, gender, and so on—has a disproportionate share of either genius or idiocy. Americans are no better than anyone else. They're just luckier. For that reason, and due to the collaborative nature of their work, I used to tell my Civil Affairs soldiers, "Check your ego at the door."

It was with that hard-earned appreciation that I thought helping this group of young George Mason students learn more about the world, as someone who had been there and done that, would give value to those experiences and insights. So when Dave nonchalantly sug-gested GMU fly me from California back to Washington to pick up the students, go to Liberia with them, fly back when I was done, and then jump back on the bike and continue my ride, it made all the sense in the world. For one, having an overseas portion of the trip made sense since I had spent so much time abroad during the part of my life I was now reflecting on. For another, it fit the paradigm of a different world than the one in which Steinbeck lived.

The excursion to Africa was integral to this trip, not an interruption. If the purpose of my road trip was to look back to see my personal and collective future, then I had to extend this journey beyond America to see it from the outside in as well as the inside out. In a sense, it was also a first for me—I had never returned to any of the places I served overseas and looked back at it. The experience turned out to be more than gratifying.

The students noticed right away that the only thing warmer than the persistently humid climate in Liberia was how I was greeted by so many people, almost every minute, as we walked through the UNMIL headquarters and traveled around Monrovia and up-country. It was a validation of the work I previously had done there. It became comical pretty quickly, so they dubbed me "the Don of Liberia." After a couple of days of their lightheartedness, I turned the tables at our daily after-action meeting. "Okay, I've got a teaching point," I told them.

"Whatever you want to call this foreign engagement stuff—diplomacy, development, security cooperation, peacekeeping, peacebuilding, stability operations, conflict management, conflict prevention, counterinsurgency, counterterrorism, whatever—it's all about building and maintaining relationships. Why? Because that's how you get things done in most places. It's how you build trust—the social capital you need to move things forward. When you think about it, we do it at home, too, just in a different way." The product is in the process, as the destination is in the journey. My good friend Sam Burnette, who was with the Liberian Ministry of Youth and Sports then, taught the students an oft-used proverb from there: "When you walk alone, you go faster; when you walk together, you go farther."

Liaison and exchange programs like those I was involved in throughout my career and student exchanges and field trips like this are a rare opportunity for upcoming generations both in the United States and elsewhere to connect on a personal level. I was as amused by the naïveté and insularity of some students as much as I was impressed by the knowledge and maturity of others, but they were all sincere

With the George Mason University Peace Operations Policy Program
students at UNMIL HQ. Ellen Margrethe Loej (center), the special
representative of the UN secretary general, surprised us by finding
time to chat with us. David Davis is on the far right.

learners. Although most had never been outside the United States and almost none had been in Africa, they were engaged, interested, well-read on relevant subjects, tough questioners, and amazed by most of the people they met. In the seven days we were there, they learned a lot, as did I.

Beyond all the learning, the students brilliantly performed their other, implied mission as informal ambassadors of their country and culture. One deputy minister took the appearance of such a group of American students who felt it safe enough to come to Liberia as a very good sign that his country was at last returning to a state of normalcy unimaginable for half his lifetime. As the much younger Liberian UNMIL Radio jock who live-interviewed some of them the night before we left said, "You guys really repped" (represented). Their characteristic openness and optimism, without pretense or forcefulness, helped them make friends with just about everyone they met. I was as proud of them as of the soldiers I led who had done likewise.

And to think that we accomplished all of this for the cost of a tricked-out Cadillac Escalade. I later mused on Facebook: "Imagine, if we were to take a couple of billion out of the Pentagon (which would hardly miss it) to finance more of these kinds of personal-level engagements of our young people, what that would do for our national security and the quality of our foreign relations, especially in the long term." This isn't some kind of utopian fantasy.

With social media, more and more enduring contacts between people and not just governments are possible. Yet, personal interactions multiply—and are multiplied by—networking technologies inconceivable when the Liberian Civil War started in the waning days of the Cold War. Beyond globalizing and humanizing peace and security, such contacts help empower people and democratize their countries, creating and connecting communities without borders. It's a very powerful and meaningful way to use this technological platform—and people used to think it was just for entertainment. It could be a game changer for all of us.

In the year of our trip, the State Department–sponsored student-exchange budget was $635 million, involving about fifty thousand exchange participants, helping eight thousand US students learn strategically critical languages, and promoting two thousand partnerships between US and sister cities abroad. Every year, twice as many students visit the United States as there were US military and civilian personnel in Afghanistan, which has cost $50 billion to $100 billion in each year of the "Decade of War." According to the Association of International Educators and others, international students generated nearly $20 billion and almost three hundred thousand jobs for the US economy in 2009–10. Beyond the intangibles, programs like these pay for themselves many times over. In numerous ways, they are an investment, not a cost.

Shifting priorities and rebalancing our commitment of resources to meet new realities is not idealism—it's good strategy. Rather than cutting programs like student exchanges, we should be investing more because of their high long-term return-on-investment ratio, in good part because the learning goes both ways, doubling the results. A transfer of less than 1 percent of what we would spend on weapons of mass destruction to weapons of mass instruction would probably do more for the safety, security, and quality of life for Americans and others than the other 99 percent.

Many in Congress with whom I now speak on behalf of the US Global Leadership Coalition's Veterans for Smart Power acknowledge the goodwill and payback these initiatives create, yet too many see them as a nicety rather than a necessity to our national security—which makes you wonder whether they really understand what national security is in this day and age. They should have heard what one of the Liberians told us: "The best way to create lasting peace is to help people put bread on the table. Improving daily lives is the best way to security."

As far back as my time in Germany, I saw that formal, high-visibility, top-directed events do less than informal, low-profile activities at the community level. That's because they create more enduring bonds and impressions from substantive person-to-person contacts, promoting this increasingly vital aspect of international relations. Building relationships and trust is nothing more than getting people together and kicking off the conversation. Simply juxtaposing people along common lines of interest like education, business, sports, cultural and social groupings (e.g., women, religion), and of course the military and allowing them to interact freely has been the most effective formula. As I saw over my years in service, the behavior of especially our younger

A rare sight, indeed—an American Army colonel with blue UN headgear, receiving an on-site briefing at a vocational training farm run with the help of NGOs and Bangladeshi peacekeepers.

informal ambassadors, for good and for bad, transcending language and culture, have more impact on the success or failure of our foreign relations than anything else.

In March 2005, the Army (which never makes a mistake) promoted me to colonel. My brother-in-law, Bill Smith, gave me a clock as a promotion gift with the inscription "Leaders are like eagles. They don't flock. You find them one at a time." By then and especially during my tour of duty in Liberia, thanks to people like Paul Boroh, I also realized that I was at a point in my career where a lot of what I was doing was mentoring and coaching younger officers to do a better job of learning the kind of things I had been learning. Leadership is both learning and teaching. After all, the Latin term *educare* means "to lead." Up until that time, my job was primarily learning by doing; now it was more doing by teaching. I also discovered that every good teacher must first be a good learner, and if every good leader must be a good learner, then the prerequisite to all of that must be humility.

When I went to Liberia the first time, I had the opportunity to apply the sum of many hard-earned lessons, even though I hadn't yet figured out what they all were. When I went with the students for the second time, I had the opportunity to sum up those lessons and pass them on by sharing them right in the field.

Besides the fact that this business is essentially building relationships and trust, I conveyed to the students what I have come to appreciate as the two important rules of the road. I had also used them in my course to help UNMIL CIMIC officers understand civil–military operations. The first is about managing expectations. The second is "It's not about us; it's about them."

Managing expectations—yours and those of the people you work for, the people you work with, and the people you're trying to help— is the most supreme of the two. Besides an understanding that the environments of engagement we find ourselves in are predominantly psychological, we Westerners have a habit of setting the bar too high, whether in personal relationships or what we expect of government and think can be accomplished. Although it pushes us to achieve more, if we find ourselves consistently falling far too short, we need to adjust our aims. I have suffered from this, being a bit type A—expecting a lot of myself but then, unfairly, transferring those expectations to others. As I grew older and more aware of psychological as well as physical limitations, I cut myself—and others—a little more slack and learned to be more compassionate. Accepting your own limits teaches you patience, and thinking like a man of action and acting like a man of thought, as the philosopher Henri Bergson suggested, demands it.

This maturation process applies at both collective and personal levels. Because of the insular mentality of the country and continent we come from, along with the success we've enjoyed for so long, we Americans in particular tend to wonder why others shouldn't be more like us. We tend to overlook how many global issues we have deemed to be peripheral because they don't affect us personally. Until now, our children didn't have to live with the consequences at home if we failed at our attempts to do well abroad. That's changing, however, in a flatter, more interconnected world—not just because of terrorism, but also because of everything from the spread of diseases, financial melt-downs, and global climate change. We could get away from Vietnam, but we can't get away from the Middle East and Africa. Nonetheless, that doesn't mean we have to keep doing everything the same way. Quick fixes don't do it anymore—we're in it for the longer game it increasingly is.

As did the young officers I mentored in Liberia, the students gained an appreciation of the enormous difficulty of multinational peace oper-ations but also the common sense of commitment to peace among so many different walks of life, which is very powerful. The advancements we've seen at home, such as the rights of women and minorities, have taken generations. Involving a complex and difficult process, they are still a work in progress—and that's without the hundreds or even thou-sands of years of sociocultural inertia many of these countries have experienced.

This speaks to the issue of what peacebuilders call "absorptive capacity." A person can learn only so much at a time before reaching the TMI (too much information) threshold. That's why you have to understand others' capabilities and limitations as well as your own. In Kosovo, I saw a well-meaning woman from the Italian government who wanted to start recycling in a place where people were just trying to figure out how to get the trash picked up. It was a miserable failure, and it reinforced how much I appreciate Maslow's hierarchy of needs, which orders the factors that most motivate human behavior, as a model for figuring out what needs to be addressed first and foremost. In Iraq, I saw so many people coming in to assess the same things over and over again, yet delivering nothing, so I reported how local leaders were suffering from "assessment fatigue" and "low delivery disorder," as we dubbed the situation then.

In this business, you need to keep the big picture and the long run constantly in mind, and apply common sense—think globally, act locally (or, in military-speak, think strategically and act tactically). Besides understanding, as Dorothy realized in Oz, that "we're not in Kansas anymore," it's taking into account what T. E. Lawrence would tell us—this is not your country, and your time here is short. I often referred to Joseph Campbell's sobering sense of hope:

> *The warrior's approach is to say "yes" to life: say "yea" to it all. Participate joyfully in the sorrows of the world. We cannot cure the world of sorrows, but we can choose to live in joy. When we talk about settling the world's problems, we're barking up the wrong tree. The world is perfect. It's a mess. It has always been a mess. We are not going to change it. Our job is to straighten out our own lives.*

"Spoiler alert," I said to the students during one of my informal chats over a beer back at our hotel in Monrovia. "You can't save the world, but maybe a little corner of it. I've learned to tell myself that if I could make a real difference in at least one person's life before I went to sleep, then I've had a real good day. If you've done the best you could, that's all you can reasonably expect. This work is a marathon, not a sprint," I said, relaying an aphorism I had often heard.

Another thing is to work from positives rather than negatives. There is an interesting parallel phenomenon in motorcycle riding. To avoid potholes and other hazards, you have to first see and then look away from them, because where you look is where the bike goes automatically. So if you focus your attention and energy on negatives, that's where you wind up steering yourself. More times than not, what you look for is what you get.

Focusing more on the negative of threats than seeing the conflict as an opportunity for positive change is no doubt one reason we've not done so well in some places, such as Iraq and Afghanistan. We've poured immense resources into provinces and areas where we've had more trouble than traction—reinforcing failure and then wondering at the results. Although it's important to contain threats, it's more important to invest your time, energy, and other resources where you have the greatest chance of success—in opportunities. As Jesus taught us, it's the fertile soil where the seeds fall that produce the greatest fruit. Then the power of attraction takes over and, by that example, encourages others to follow suit—making it *their* decision to change, not your change to induce. "Success begets more success," I said to the students. "So it's better to do a few things really well rather than everything half-assed." The idea is to grow from your successes rather than attack the problem on a broad front. Counterinsurgents call this the oil spot theory.

In helping people, you have to resist the impulse—per the Chinese proverb—to give someone a fish, which is relatively quick and easy, versus making the commitment to teach them how to fish, which is much more painstaking. "Giving people a fish makes you feel good about yourself. But it also makes them dependent on you. Teaching them how to fish gives them independence and is ultimately a more sincere gesture of respect," I told them.

I also told them how, especially in Liberia—one of the most aid-dependent cultures I've seen—I'd come to appreciate a tough-love approach. "I'm not here to win your hearts and minds," I often told my Liberian colleagues. "When I'm done here, I get to go home and ride my Harley-Davidson. You get to stay here. So you can take advantage of people like me to learn to take better care of yourselves after we leave, or you can hope they'll keep coming back. But one day a lot of these people will be gone, and you'll still be here. So use us before you lose us."

"It sounds harsh," I ended the talk with the students that day, "but if you really care about these people, you'll do what's best for them as they see it and not what's best for you as you see it. That takes patience, compassion, and—most of all—humility. It's not a job for everybody, which is one reason why peace—and not just war—is for professionals. It's a protracted process of helping others manage change that begins with managing expectations."

That leads to the second rule of the road for building peace: "It's not about us; it's about them." If it's their problem, then it has to be their solution—otherwise they'll never take ownership of either one. That's why it's up to you to see it from their perspective— empathetically rather than sympathetically. As far back as my days in Germany, I had learned that most people (forgoing Maslow's hierarchy) operate from two prime motivators: "What's in it for me?" and "So what?" One involves persuasion, the other coercion. If you're there to help, you have to understand how the people with the problem see those things, not just how the people with the solution think they do.

Understanding the country, especially its history as well as its culture—without assuming that you'll really understand it, as locals do—is the key. As I explained to my troops in Iraq, "There's the cultural space you're coming from and the cultural space you're entering. You have to know both, because you're really working in the space between and not within cultures. And what you're doing in that space is mostly looking, listening, and learning. Think of yourself as a management consultant: You're here to help others develop the tools and capacities they need to improve their own lives, not to do it for them."

The best example I could give the students then was how we worked to build governance from the bottom up in southern Iraq. My Civil Affairs operators didn't choose who would be the mayors or in the governorate councils. Nor did we extoll Thomas Jefferson or constitutionalism. It being their future, not ours, our main themes were accountability and responsibility—not to the Big Man in Baghdad but to the people right there in their communities. The governorate council meetings were at first chaotic and unproductive. The grandstanding these people put on made Congress look tame—even less talk and no action, if you can imagine. In the meantime, little was getting done to restore essential public services and improve the lives in neighborhoods.

At the same time, people were lining up outside our civil–military operations center, waiting to see me about their problems and expecting me to solve them, which was indicative of the "big daddy complex," as I told the students. "In autocratic or hierarchical societies," I explained to them at another evening beer session, "big daddy is the personification of not only who makes the decisions but also who is to blame—like Charles Taylor or Saddam Hussein. In either case, it puts people off the blame line. Whether you're an occupying army, as we were in Iraq, or a UN peacekeeping mission, you become the new big daddy, whether you like it or not."

After a while, there were so many Iraqis lining up that I couldn't possibly sit and listen to all of them. So I had the word put out, to avoid crowds standing for hours under the hot sun, that I would have limited *mushkele* hours (*mushkele* is Arabic for "problem") and then only some days each week. Equally important, I explained to the students, is that, after spending time with each petitioner and employing active listening techniques to better understand their problem and communicate care, I would end by asking them, "So, what do you think the solution is?" This would surprise them, as they expected me to have the solution. Instead, I worked with them through the problem-solving process to empower them. "I'm not here to solve your problems for you," I would tell them. "I'm here to help you find a way to take them on yourself." I would employ the same methods in conversations with local Liberian leaders.

After a while, I got the mayor of An Nāṣirīyah to join me. In a matter of weeks, he was not only taking over the talks but also telling people to see him in the city hall we helped restore. I had worked myself out of at least that job.

We employed a similar transition process with the NGOs, all of which (except for the Iraqi Red Crescent) came to the meetings we hosted. We wanted to provide a secure place for them to meet, get the benefit of our information, and coordinate among themselves as much as with the military. "I'm not interested in co-opting you—I'm interested in supporting you," I told NGO leaders. We initially organized the meetings, set the agendas, provided reports on the situation and security advisories, and coordinated logistical support. Over the next few weeks, I told the students, the NGOs took control of the meetings and set the agenda. Then they simply no longer showed up. They were now hosting their own coordination meetings on the other side of town. It was exactly the result we sought.

In the same period of time, after the Marines got the local television station up and running, I reported at the governorate council meeting that, beginning with the next such meeting, we would have the TV station present to record the meetings and air them later those same evenings. "That way," I told them, "the people can see who is working for them and who is not." It was C-SPAN in the sand. Again, over the next two months, the local governorate council began to run the meetings and set the agenda.

When someone brought up an issue, like a nearby mayor who said that the trash was piling up or the water supply was low, the governor turned to his director of public works and asked him to explain how he intended to help out. They started to get a grip on the many *mushkeles* they had to face, and that they had to be responsible and accountable to those who saw them on TV that night. Without ever mentioning democracy, we were helping the Iraqis to learn grassroots governance. We even got them to debate and adopt a budget for the upcoming year with the money we had captured there from the regime when we invaded, instead of just issuing it to them every time they told us they had a problem to fix. There was still a very long way to go by the time we left, but we had given them a start in the right direction, because we realized this was not our country and our time there was short, and that it was about them and not about us.

Whether in Bosnia, Iraq, or Liberia, civil–military operations and peacebuilding are ultimately about transition management—from conflict to peace and military to civilian lead. Building peace is about maximizing stakeholders and minimizing spoilers by empowering the former, marginalizing the latter, and converting the uncommitted through the example of success.

US identity around the world is forged in our actions, which reflect our character. I had the honor to serve in Liberia with Major General Muhammad Tahir, an outstanding multinational leader from Pakistan (where anti-American conspiracy theories run rife). He taught me a lot about Liberia, demonstrating tremendous cultural understanding, which he used to promote good relations among diverse and often contentious groups. When he left—and subsequently retired—he got a huge send-off from the UN and the Liberians, including a parade and many honors.

Later on, he sent me an e-mail marveling at pictures of thousands of military aircraft in the "boneyards" of Arizona. "That was nothing," I wrote back. "In 1945, the US possessed 50,000 combat aircraft, 5,000 naval ships, 96 divisions, 10 million men under arms, 45 percent of the world's gross national product, and of course a monopoly on nuclear weapons. If America were to have taken over the world," I went on, "that would have been the moment. Instead, it did the Marshall Plan," referring to the US aid program to reconstruct Europe after the war.

Balance in and between thought and action seems to be even more crucial than ever. It's how you emphasize and align idealism or realism, coercion or persuasion, hard or soft power, wisely applying Theodore Roosevelt's advice that if you "speak softly and carry a big stick, you will go far." Balance is found in those three watchwords I gave the officers I led in Liberia and recalled in Roswell—*professionalism*, *discipline*, and *humility*. No idea or value has validity if it isn't lived. And no one who doesn't live them can be respected for his or her values.

Sure, Americans are privileged to be exceptional, but if they are humble and confident in their exceptionalism, they don't need to go out of their way to advertise it. It speaks for itself. Actions always speak louder and longer than words. Pope Francis noted that the word *authority* in English comes from the Latin "to grow." "Authority," he said, "implies creating a space where a person can grow. When you have to assert you're in charge, then you've already lost your authority to lead. Having the upper hand means to serve, not impose."

I've seen many young American men and women in uniform who have served overseas, and they are most effective when they are just themselves. There is, after all, something quite good about the American character. These civilian kids from George Mason demonstrated that just as well as the many young soldiers I have seen, I thought as our plane winged its way back over the Atlantic.

As for me, I have found my own confident humility in the gratitude of having been in places, done things, and met people most Americans can only imagine meeting, knowing it has made me both a better American and a better person. I left Liberia, for the second time, a bit more hopeful than the last. But I also felt a bit better about my own country, because I had the vantage point of once again learning to see it from the outside in.

CHAPTER 8

THE PACIFIC COAST: BUILDERS AND ARTISTS

On Monday, June 7, I was road bound again. It felt good to be back on the freshly serviced Wide Glide after a two-week hiatus. In contrast to hot and steamy Liberia, Southern California was anything but warm and sunny, as I thought it would be, as I made my way to the Pacific Coast Highway (PCH). The weather improved as I slipped out of the June gloom that produces little rain in California. After lunch at Pismo Beach, I found lodging at San Simeon, just a few miles from Hearst Castle, today a National and California Historical Landmark.

William Randolph Hearst, the great entrepreneur and media magnate, wanted to be known as a builder. Of his many estates in the United States and Europe, this one is the site of his boyhood campground: La Cuesta Encantada (Enchanted Hill) was returned to the state of California after his death in 1951 and has been a moneymaker since. When I saw its opulent Mediterranean Revival mansion and guesthouses, and its prodigious collection of art and artifacts from Europe and the Middle East, the estate struck me as the ultimate self-indulgence of a nouveau riche American who would spare no expense in materialistic acrobatics. But as I learned more about how Hearst and his chief architect, Julia Morgan, blended its carefully chosen and placed collection with the surrounding landscape, I had to agree with the architectural historian Lord John Julius Norwich that "Hearst

Castle is a palace in every sense of the word." But it is a truly American palace—where else could something so new come from things so old?

Along with many other families, such as the Fords, Carnegies, and Rockefellers, Hearst collected artwork from European aristocrats who were broke or under pressure to abandon their belongings for political reasons in the 1920s and 1930s. In this way, many treasures were preserved that might have been looted or destroyed during the Spanish Civil War or World War II. During and after World War II, the "Monuments Men" prevented the loss of millions of priceless pieces of art. This was the first time on such a scale that a conquering army deliberately saved, salvaged, and returned cultural artifacts, including from the enemy country. In my own time, Civil Affairs officers like Major Cori Wegener did the same kind of thing in Baghdad. I decorated a Marine officer with an Army Achievement Medal for saving hundreds of artifacts in our sector. Increasingly, civilians are trying to protect and preserve cultural artifacts in Egypt, Mali, Burma, Tibet, and especially Iraq and Syria due to the deliberate actions of the Islamic State.

It is common knowledge that wealthy families in America, in recognition of their own good fortune and what is now called corporate social responsibility, organize and support numerous charities. The middle class, however, has been proportionally more charitable than the rich—a testament that "generosity is giving more than you can, and pride is taking less than you need," to quote Khalil Gibran.

My thoughts as I departed San Simeon were distracted as I saw my first zebras in the wild—in California, not Africa. On the advice of a fellow traveler, I enjoyed a short interlude at Point Piedras Blancas to see the elephant seals coming to breed and shed their skins for the next winter. As they basked in the sun, I met up with Uwe, a young German from Hamburg riding from Florida to San Francisco, and we shared the ride up the PCH as far as Monterey. The scenery was so spectacular that we risked, especially on motorbikes, becoming part of it. Fortunately, Uwe's eighteen-year-old Dyna made us stop every hour or so to readjust the shift lever.

The stopover in Monterey had two purposes. The first and most important was to enjoy a long lunch with a friend and colleague who was then at the Naval Postgraduate School, Dr. Karen Guttieri, one

of the rare serious historians on Civil Affairs and civil–military operations and the author of *Masters of Peace*. A stately woman with an
encyclopedic mind, she explained during lunch at a Mexican café that
Monterey had its own chapter in the history of civil–military operations. Military government began with Texas before it became a state,
followed by Reconstruction after the Civil War and the "winning" of
the West. In the wake of the Spanish-American War at the turn of
the last century, a military government was in place for short times
in Cuba, Puerto Rico, and other places, then in the Philippines until
independence in 1946. The largest and most successful examples were
in the occupation of Germany and Japan right after World War II.

After the Treaty of Guadalupe Hidalgo in 1848 to end the war
with Mexico, California was under military governance until General
Bennett Riley grew impatient with the inability of an increasingly dysfunctional Congress (obsessed with the balance of slave and nonslave
states) to form a civilian government, so he convened a constitutional
convention in Monterey, serving as California's first capital, to write
the state constitution in English and Spanish. The "fecundity of the
Californians" described by Navy Chaplain Walter Colton (for whom
Monterey's constitutional hall is named) also resulted in proposition
voting, since a hallmark of California politics. In 1850, California
joined the Union as the thirty-first and a nonslave state.

For me, Karen's story was just another example dispelling the "We
don't do windows" myth that many in the military perpetuated in
the early 1990s, especially after Desert Storm. At the Armor School's
Officers Advanced Course at Fort Knox, Kentucky, we had animated
discussions about these lessons. The minority I was in asked, "So what?
When are we going to do this again?" Like sports teams, you can't learn
from lopsided wins like this. "Against no other opponent in history
has the US military enjoyed so swift and unqualified a success," Jeffrey
Record wrote in an op-ed in May 1981. "The Plains Indians put up a
better fight against the US Cavalry."

The groupthink was stifling. The instructors cited the "Powell
Doctrine," a journalistic term from the Reagan era. Also called
Invincible Force, it was a checklist of preconditions for the use of force,
in the form of questions:

1. Is a vital national security interest threatened?
2. Do we have a clear attainable objective?
3. Have the risks and costs been fully and frankly analyzed?
4. Have all other nonviolent policy means been fully exhausted?
5. Is there a plausible exit strategy to avoid endless entanglement?
6. Have the consequences of our action been fully considered?
7. Is the action supported by the American people?
8. Do we have genuine broad international support?

Powell would later elaborate on the canon named after him. An application of the American strategy of annihilation, it framed our involvement in Desert Storm. More (in)famously, it was the rationale to avoid involvement in multinational peace operations as a result of the mission creep in Somalia that led to the disaster depicted in the book and film *Black Hawk Down*. It reinforced the notion that we should not "do windows" of small, unconventional wars. This military attitude also stoked public and political reluctance toward US military involvement in the growing UN peace operations in the 1990s and in nation building.

The polemic, in fact, drove the virtual disappearance of the word *peace* from the doctrine that underpinned Army training. *Stability operations* became the less offensive substitute in the growing warrior ethos of the military. But even stability operations have been seen as a supporting activity of warfighting. No doubt the Powell Doctrine makes a great deal of sense in restraining the military option to one of last resort. (Too bad it wasn't as stringently used for deciding on the second war in Iraq.) But when there's no war in the classic national-army-versus-national-army sense, it's hard to identify the enemy.

Among the most significant things I later heard someone in the UN explain to me was "In peacekeeping, the enemy is not a party to the conflict—the enemy is the conflict itself." That's really the paradigm we're in now. The Powell Doctrine has had limited application for the unconventional or what are now called irregular-warfare situations between peace and war that have become the new normal.

After the Cold War ended in the early 1990s, I sensed it was the end of an era for me as well. A lot of times the thing about change is recognizing when it's time to move on. So much of what I had done those nine years in Germany was to represent my country there. Because I hadn't lived in my own country for so long, I sensed I had lost touch and needed to reconnect, so I made a life decision to repatriate in 1993. Before I left, I received a gift from a lifetime friend, Wolfgang Zahn. In Thorwald Dethlefsen's book *The Challenge of Fate* I came across a simple symmetrical principle: "As above, so below." It helped me see the parallels between public and personal history. I was now in my thirties—when first confronted with personal limitations, physical and psychological—and realizing you can't do everything you want to do when you want to do it.

Analogous to the times and, to some extent, anticipatory to further changes, life became more complex and unpredictable as I went in and out of uniform—so much, in fact, that some people were convinced I was in the CIA, because no person in their right mind would live this way. Between 1993 and 1995, I served on numerous short tours of duty in support of both the Army's 21st Theater Support Command and the vaunted 173rd Airborne Brigade that comprise the Southern European Task Force. The 21st was based in Kaiserslautern (or K-Town) in Germany, providing logistical support to the US forces in Europe and Africa, while the 173rd was based in Vicenza, Italy, as the quick-reaction force in the same theater command area. The Powell Doctrine aside, the Army found itself in many contingencies, such as emergency assistance in the form of water purification units in response to the mass atrocity in Rwanda in 1994 and planning for US involvement in the Balkans the next summer. One thing I learned in those days was that if you really want to know what's going on, hang out with the logisticians, because they seem to know where everyone is and what they're doing. Because the "loggies" need to supply or support everyone in some way, they are often the first in and the last out.

My deployments were on behalf of the 304th Civil Affairs Brigade in Philadelphia, which I joined in early 1994, quickly becoming one of their go-to guys in operations and planning support to both of those Army commands. The 304th was near Wilmington, Delaware, where I spent the first year after returning from Germany living with my father, who worked at DuPont after a series of accidents some years prior forced him to make his own transition from blue-collar work as a carpenter to white-collar work as an electron microscope technician. He received his training at Orange County Community College in New York at the same time as my older sister, Sheree, was studying to be a nurse. Their friends were amused to see them meeting between classes. Change and transition were all around.

Beginning with the Gulf War, the old world order was also breaking down for the Reserves, which had been intended only for a mass call-up during a big war—when "the balloon went up," as we referred to a Soviet invasion of West Germany. There was a reason we would call up the Reserves only in extremis. As the draft ended in 1972, ushering in an era that professionalized the armed forces over the span of my career, the military instituted another key reform that transformed our ability to wage war, at least on a large scale. Still smarting from the body politic's failure to do what was done in every major war prior to Vietnam—call up the militia—a group of Army generals, among them Creighton Abrams, introduced the Total Force Policy.

More than just a way to manage another postwar demobilization, the Abrams Doctrine transformed the Army Reserve and the National Guard from being shelters to avoid service into integral parts of the nation's war machine. The policy made it impracticable to engage in serious conflict without calling up America's part-time troops. By placing the majority of the Army's combat support in the Reserves, it ensured congressional involvement in deciding matters of war and peace, making it harder to get in a major war without the support of the American people. Also, by weaving citizen-soldiers back into the fabric of the military, the military was woven back into the fabric of the country to sustain a healthy, democratic civil–military relationship.

Over time since then, the role of the Reserves in maintaining vital civil–military linkages has become even more important. This is especially because of the long-term effects of making the decision a long time ago to pay the financial versus the social costs of the anomaly of maintaining a large standing peacetime army. As I pointed out in a May 1995 *Stars and Stripes* op-ed, for the first time since World War II the majority of our political, economic, and cultural elites had no military service. That, for one, does not help temper the temptation to see the military as the first and not the last resort to national security challenges. The article also asked what would replace the unintended role of the armed forces as ladder into the middle class, especially for minorities, through the GI Bill and VA home loans. "It is right that America is reducing its military," I affirmed. "In its haste to do so, however, it needs to carefully consider risks as well as rewards. . . . Perhaps the greatest of these risks is that, as the military shrinks and becomes less familiar it faces the risk of isolation and estrangement from the rest of society."

The real reason for having the majority of Civil Affairs in the Reserves has been societal and psychological, mind-sets as well as skill sets. The best way to talk to civilians and understand them is to be one yourself, most of the time. Most of the civilian world is a complex, dynamic, indefinable place where a persuasive—or collaborative—style of leadership is the predominant way to win friends and influence people. It is a horizontal world. Like a lot of the government, in contrast, the military lives in a hierarchical (or vertical) world with more clearly defined rule sets for human behavior and where a coercive style of leadership—or a tactical or operational command-and-control management style—is more effective. The differences are more nuanced, and you can find plenty of examples of both styles in both worlds, but this sums it up.

Reservists well understand the complex, uncertain, transitional, and collaborative character of modern peace and security challenges, because that's more indicative of their world. "Human interaction in a complex environment is the key to our success in the future," retired general Raymond Odierno eventually put it in 2013 as Army chief of staff. This quality and competency already apparent in the Balkans would prove even more important in dealing with asymmetric challenges in the peace, stability, counterinsurgency, and counterterrorism operations in the Middle East, Central Asia, and Africa. It's why the more effective commanders in Iraq and Afghanistan tended to be those who had earlier exposure to what the Army now calls the human terrain.

The Reserves, however, were slow to change. Instead of wholesale mobilization, specialized Reserve forces like Civil Affairs were called up in partial mobilizations—by individuals, teams, or units—in the 1990s. As the decade wore on, the Army began to rely increasingly on the Reserves and Civil Affairs. But neither were keeping pace with the rapidly changing times.

Civil Affairs as well had been based on its military government or nation-building role. As late as the Haiti crisis in 1994, when it needed to restart the hydroelectric power grid there, our Civil Affairs command brought in a hydroelectric power plant manager from Upstate New York, or a district court judge from Philadelphia to restore the judicial system, or a managing board member of the New Jersey Turnpike Authority to bring back the road system, and so on. But this model of Civil Affairs was diminishing—there were now more civilians in NGOs, development agencies, and the UN better suited to do this stuff. Besides, there were fewer in Civil Affairs with cultural expertise in areas other than Eastern Europe or with the right civilian skills, such as management consulting rather than public administration—what was needed was less building and more art.

What it meant was that Civil Affairs needed to go back to school on the changing relationship between military and civilian actors. These civilians could no longer be seen as force multipliers. What was really slowly going on, I began to realize, was role reversal—the military was doing more to support rather than perform such activities, indirectly rather than directly. The business, however, was still about transition from war to peace and military to civilian lead. When deploying on Civil Affairs missions in the 1990s, I told every commander I reported to that our mission was to help him work himself out of a job—a rather unusual thing to say.

In order to help enable these civilians to take the lead for their tasks, you had to engage them and work with them. Most commanders I met back then pushed back on this. They saw civil–military operations as some kind of public affairs thing, without realizing how they were integral to their own operations, as I had already learned back in Germany. Many commanders embraced the mission creep they complained about because, while some began to realize civil engagement really was the mission, all of them wanted to control what was going on in their area of responsibility. Still, they had little patience to wait for the civilians to get their act together, whether the perception was justified or unjustified. During a discussion with an infantry brigade commander in the Balkans who saw all of our work as a sideshow, I asked, "Sir, can you name the last war when there were no civilians on the battlefield?"

What I was beginning to internalize but couldn't articulate until much later was that civil–military operations embrace the art of leveraging nonviolent means to achieve the same ends as violence. There may be no substitute for victory, but there are substitutes for the ways and means to achieve it. Civil Affairs is among the 1 percent of the US armed forces dedicated primarily to peace and stability operations—ending and preventing wars—through a people-centric versus warfighting approach to the mission. Getting the civil–military approach right was and remains the most important but toughest sell in this business.

Political sponsorship for Civil Affairs had always been thin, especially after longtime champions like Senator Strom Thurmond and Congressman Ike Skelton, who remembered the contributions of Civil Affairs after World War II, went away after the 1990s. It's hard to find friends on Capitol Hill when you don't have an air base or build submarines in their districts. Executive or congressional constituency for Civil Affairs has been episodic. In the conventional Army, Civil Affairs has been poorly understood—seen as a form of combat support. In Special Operations, it has been a redheaded stepchild—Civil Affairs doesn't do the sexy stuff that you see in the movies. Since 9/11, Civil Affairs has been employed in support of an enemy-centric focus on winning hearts and minds—in other words, getting to know the butcher, the baker, and the candlestick maker in order to help find the bad guys and kill them.

Another reason Civil Affairs was not being taken seriously was that it needed to better work with an Active Component professionalizing more rapidly than the Reserve Component. I had that vantage in my long deployments with the commands receiving Civil Affairs support. As someone who spent a lot more time on active duty than the average reservist then, I would coach and mentor my colleagues coming into that world by referring to the three-strike rule, as in baseball. "Strike one," I would tell them, "you're in the Reserves, the summer hires and second-rate soldiers on the visiting team. Strike two—you do this Civil Affairs stuff the infantry warfighter types hardly understand, would otherwise not do, and see as additional duty rather than part of it. They would rather you do it and leave them alone while they focused on the 'real' mission. Strike three," I would end, "is when you walk in the door and ask, 'What do you want me to do?' Now you've just told them you need a babysitter. Look," I would tell them in a privately held session before they joined up for the exercises, "you need to run faster, jump higher, and piss farther than these steely-eyed killers just to get invited to lunch."

Beyond the culture of the country of concern, the Civil Affairs reservists needed to be versed in the organizational culture and language of the Army and its Military Decision-Making Process (the military version of problem solving in its core management process of preparing and executing plans). Otherwise, they would be at best on the bench and not in the starting lineup.

In fairness, the marginalization of Civil Affairs has had as much to do with self-mismanagement as circumstances beyond its control. Civil Affairs struggled to keep pace with the professionalization of the practitioners of peace as well as of war. Its core transition management competency has not itself transitioned from being based on military government to being based on peacebuilding—from *national security* to *human security*, a term I first saw in the UN Development Programme's "Human Development Report 1994," which explained the increased importance of the security of people rather than just states but took me a few years to understand. As a result, many in Civil Affairs could not operate effectively in either sense—so many of us had as hard a time working in the spaces between war and peace as anyone else.

In the early fall of 1995, I was involved in a command field exercise, preparing the 173rd Airborne Brigade for numerous NATO-led contingency plans leading up to the deployment to Bosnia. I was on the Civil Affairs plan's team that the 304th Civil Affairs Brigade sent there, but as a junior major in a team of mostly colonels and lieutenant colonels. As the exercise peaked, the general staff briefed courses of action to the commander, Major General Jack Nix, a highly competent military leader whose demeanor set the tone for his staff.

Civil–military operations, of course, were last on the briefing agenda—after an endless retinue of presentations on intelligence, operations, logistics, and so on—and stood between all of them and the chow line. The colonels in charge of me, some out of shape, under-prepared, and with weak military bearing, shrewdly decided at the last minute to send up to make the pitch the fit and polished young major who did most of the Civil Affairs planning work and spoke the war-fighters' operating language. So I had to say something to grab the general's attention, the look on his face making it abundantly clear that I was on a very short leash.

"Sir," I said as I looked at him squarely, "everyone up to now has explained to you how not to get carried by six [as at a funeral]. I'm here to help you not to get tried by twelve." Then silence.

He cracked a thin smile as the chuckles broke out among his staff: "Go ahead, Major, I'm listening." From that point on, I was able to close the deal. He asked pointed and incisive questions that told me he was not only interested but sensed our part of the operation was no mere sideshow. He got the memo, and as a consequence, his staff took us more seriously.

Not all of the senior Army leaders were that enlightened. In fact, the deployment to Bosnia involved some of the worst examples of senior leadership I've seen in my career. Micromanagement and risk aversion in Bosnia were practically endemic. It was a mission with little popular support and at the direction of a commander in chief openly despised by some senior officers. The gaggle of general officers there routinely made decisions way below their pay grade, such as what the off-duty uniform would be on the base, a decision normally rele-gated to the post sergeant major. Given the overkill of overhead, it was almost all control but not much command. Staff officers were falling over each other to tell the generals what they wanted to hear rather than what they needed to hear, and those with the prettiest PowerPoint presentations won the day.

Zero defects was the term to describe it. Beyond the relentless pursuit of perfection was a reluctance to allow junior leaders to make mistakes or be outspoken. Anything perceived to be unprofessional, or in contravention with the warfighting ethos was a career killer. Peace operations, however, being more of an art of collaboration than conventional warfare, required much greater trust in junior leaders—and that meant allowing them to learn by doing and, more important, to work from principles rather than prescriptions. Essentially a learning activity, peace operations meant you had to venture into areas outside your comfort zone to figure out what might or might not work—and you had to do that with partners in the horizontal, civilian world you weren't used to working with and were definitely not part of your vertical command-and-control structure.

But with zero defects, there was no room for risk, let alone bad form. "The Army needs to make the realization that if mistakes are not being made, decisions are not being made," pointed out one captain in the *Army Times* in February 1996.

It was disheartening to see briefed that the Army's number-one mission in Operation Joint Endeavor was force protection. That basically meant that the purpose of the military was to protect itself instead of other people. Hungary at least was safer from terrorist threats than Germany, according to the G2 intelligence reports I was reading. Most of the people we met in Hungary or in Bosnia were quite happy to see Americans. After the fecklessness of the European Union monitors in "ice cream suits" and the United Nations Protection Force (UNPROFOR) in blue helmets, they thought that the forces of NATO in combat camouflage, led by the Americans, would finally sort things out—and that the Americans would be spending lots of money on their economy.

We delivered very little, especially on the latter. First, we created the most convoluted rules for routine Civil Affairs missions—for example, visiting the town mayor required four high-mobility, multipurpose wheeled vehicles (HMMWVs), the successor to jeeps, and at least one mounted heavy machine gun and lots of personal protection gear. We called it "battle rattle." The locals nicknamed the GIs "American Mutant Ninja Turtles," in reference to the then popular movie. Each mission required general officer approval.

Some of us tried very hard to get the leadership to understand how counterproductive all this was, and not just because they made it next to impossible for our small teams to get out and mix with the population; help people recover from the devastation of the fighting; find assistance for food, housing, and work; get the lights turned on and the water running again; or just explain to them why we were there—which after all was our job. But we could do little of that, hemmed in by all the risk aversion.

Our (in)actions, much more than our words, were communicating loud and clear to the locals some very unflattering messages. A few years later, in *Black Hawk Down*, I read how a Somali warrior confronted a captured US pilot and contemptuously observed that the Americans' weakness was that they were "afraid to die." With all the force-protection-on-the-brain, we were telegraphing this same vulnerability. More importantly, we were also saying that we really didn't care about these people, because we would do nothing for them that involved any risk to us.

With the reduction in force after the Gulf War, many of the Army's more creative and outspoken people had already left. That left relatively more officers competing for fewer promotions. The way to promotion in hierarchical organizations like the Army is not to buck the system. Exactly when you needed innovators, you got more conformists. No wonder much of the criticism in Bosnia was coming from Reserve or National Guard officers. "You know what the difference between guys like us and guys like you is, Sir?" one of my Civil Affairs colleagues quipped to a general in Bosnia who chewed us out for asking overly critical questions. "Guys like us have a life after this." In people-centric warfare, you have to worry about the tactical general as much as the strategic corporal. Now the US military has more than twice as many flag officers to manage a force one-tenth the size it had in World War II. In Bosnia as well as Afghanistan, it had one general officer for every hundred or so GIs—about the same number commanded by a captain in an infantry company.

Lost in all of this was the obvious reason we were there in the first place—to help people out. One of the truly gut-wrenching moments I had in Bosnia was when I and my good buddy and fellow Civil Affairs officer Major Tony Sherman—a balding, mustached Irish Catholic tri-athlete and history professor at Beaver College outside Philadelphia—were on a site visit in the contentious border town of Brčko on the Sava River between Bosnia and Croatia. Walking through the town, Tony and I turned the corner and abruptly stopped.

There we stood, face-to-face with a boy about ten years old hob-bling along on makeshift crutches, with almost one leg gone, obviously the victim of one of the millions of mines or unexploded ordnance strewn around the country. It put a lump in our throats, but we did our best to show a cheery attitude, chat for a while in our broken Serbian, and share some candy with him, while he tried out his English. Tony handled it better. He knew something about children with physical challenges, having an autistic child at home. We would later lose Tony in Iraq.

Lots of people think the fundamental troubles we're now facing—in terms of how we approach the world, peace, security, and the civil–military relationship—are a result of 9/11. The truth is, they go back to even before the fall of the Berlin Wall—but we failed to recognize or understand them because we were too busy congratulating ourselves. After all, we had won the Cold War, then the Gulf War, and then stood alone at the top.

Seeing familiar things in new ways was why I found my time at the Steinbeck museum in Salinas so helpful. Besides finding new insights since the first time I had read *Travels with Charley* as a young man, I also learned that Steinbeck, as a war correspondent, wrote *America and Americans*. After that inspiring afternoon, I rode on to Pleasanton, home of Bill and Grace Tiemeyer, close childhood friends of my father.

Nearly every day of my trip, wherever I was, I was on Skype with Rosa in Bukavu in eastern Congo, where she was with UNHCR, the UN's refugee agency. She was vicariously enjoying my riding adven-ture, following me in cyberspace. Knowing where I was going, she did some online research and picked out interesting facts about the next stop. Pleasanton, she discovered, was founded by John W. Kottinger, an Alameda County justice of the peace, and named after his friend, Union army cavalry Major General Alfred Pleasonton. A Postal Service typo apparently led to the current spelling. In the 1850s, it was "The

Most Desperate Town in the West," ruled by bandits and desperados, as in any failed state or ungoverned space. Main Street shoot-outs were common. Banditos like Joaquin Murrieta, who inspired the legend of Zorro, would ambush returning gold prospectors and then seek refuge in Pleasanton. Now it's a bedroom community for those seeking refuge between working in San Francisco or Sacramento.

Uncle Bill and Aunt Grace took me to San Francisco in their Cadillac DTS—the last of the big Caddies. We wandered around town and took in the usual sites as well as a stop at Mara's bakery for a cup of cappuccino and a piece of Italian pastry like I used to enjoy as a kid when we visited the previous generation of Tiemeyers in the Bronx. That afternoon I took on my old vertigo problem and walked across the Golden Gate Bridge, which I thought highly symbolic. It marked the apogee of my trip westward as well as symbolized crossing into a new future.

The last stop was Grace Cathedral, with murals depicting the 1906 earthquake that devastated San Francisco as well as the founding of the United Nations there on June 26, 1945, with the charter signed by the original 50 of today's 193 nations. Most intriguing was the eleven-ring labyrinth modeled after the one in the cathedral in Chartres, France—Joseph Campbell's favorite. I thought of him while Aunt Grace and I paced the labyrinth, which is believed to help quiet the soul. The fascinating thing about walking a labyrinth is that while you seem to be walking it at random, it turns out to have an order and symmetry to it in the end. I'm not sure how much that's true for others, but that's how a lot of things in my life have worked out.

As I turned away from the West Coast and continued pacing the physical and mental labyrinths of this cross-country trip, I reflected on how builders and artists have shaped the country, and what that may mean for the future. Years later, Michael Stipe, front man for R.E.M., one of my favorite bands in the 1980s and 1990s, best summed up what artists are and do in modern society in his April 2014 Rock and Roll Hall of Fame induction speech for Nirvana:

When an artist offers an idea, a perspective, it helps us all to see who we are. And it wakes us up, and it pushes us forward

*towards our collective and individual potential. It makes us—
each of us—able to see who we are more clearly. It's progression
and progressive movement. It's the future staring us down in
the present and saying, "C'mon, let's get on with it. Here we are.
Now."*

When I heard this, I reached out right away to my old history professor friend Miriam Haskett's son, Chris, who was the guitarist for
the Henry Rollins Band and recorded with David Bowie. "I realized
the connection between what people like you and people like me have
striven to do in our respective, parallel careers," I wrote him, recognizing the heroism in his and all true art. I thanked him less for the music
than his service and sacrifice in having given people like me something
to serve and sacrifice for.

In American culture there is an almost pointless tension between
art and science. In a commercial republic, science carries more
weight than art. And yet, the icons of our landscape—from the Statue
of Liberty and the Brooklyn Bridge to the Golden Gate Bridge (and
everything between)—reflect the triumph of fusing art and science.
Architects are among those who come closest to this fusion, but most
are on one side or the other.

Maneuvering in the spaces between soft and hard power and
between peace and war in the 1990s, I realized that many of the tensions
I was seeing on the ground had resonance with larger developments—
as below, so above. Due to the changing nature and balance between
these things and the fact that warfare was becoming more apparently
people-centric, my own profession of Civil Affairs was caught up in
the change and needing a greater emphasis on the art of leadership
than on the science of the use or control of violence, placing far higher
demands on our personalities than before. Civil Affairs and civil–military operations are, in truth, a form of leadership—and leadership is
more of an art than a science. You lead people; you manage things. But
that was hardly the conventional wisdom in the 1990s.

No matter our walk of life, however, as we maneuver between our
individual and collective lives, the spaces between are where it all happens. The state of being between things is often uncomfortable and

unsettling, full of risks and dangers, but it's where life is most vibrant and rewarding—and where innovation occurs. To deal with it, you need a self-discipline that helps center you and symmetry between your internal and external identities—as below, so above.

This became fully apparent to me when, at the age of thirty-one, I began to learn from my German friend Andreas Nickl how to play guitar. I always wanted to play when I was a teenager but knew then that I was not mature and patient enough to do it until much later on—of course, the epiphany came after I broke up with a girlfriend. Being German, Andreas first taught me about music theory and the basics of chord progressions, fingering techniques, and so on. It was all drill and practice until I played my first song, "King of the Road" by Roger Miller, some six months later. Music, I began to comprehend, is another language. But like all art forms, it serves as an expression of the connection (or a conduit) between our inner and outer selves. That's why art has such therapeutic value, collectively as well as individually.

This wasn't all I learned about art. Just a few months before my trip, I had come across a remarkable speech by John F. Kennedy given at Amherst and memorializing Robert Frost about a month before his own death. Along with his concept of the New Frontier, which he already recognized as more moral than physical, it's worth recalling that the foundation of American strength—and thus its power—is how well each generation lives the moral in the physical. But I never saw it put so eloquently:

> In America, our heroes have customarily run to men of large accomplishments.... The men who create power make an indispensable contribution to the Nation's greatness, but the men who question power make a contribution just as indispensable, especially when that questioning is disinterested, for they determine whether we use power or power uses us. ... When power leads men towards arrogance, poetry reminds him of his limitations. When power narrows the areas of man's concern, poetry reminds him of the richness and diversity of his existence. When power corrupts, poetry cleanses. For art establishes the basic human truth which must serve as the touchstone of

our judgment. . . . The artist, however faithful to his personal vision of reality, becomes the last champion of the individual mind and sensibility against an intrusive society and an officious state.

We often overlook the potency of our cultural strength and the role artists have played and must continue to play if the country is to remain strong and relevant in the world. In our endeavor to again make America anew, as Kennedy realized, we would be wise to strike a more conscientious balance between builders and artists—we need both to make our place in a safer and more prosperous world for generations to come.

Builders basically make things; artists basically make sense of them. Builders make things function in our communities; artists make them meaningful in our lives. Builders manage risk; artists manage expectations. Builders improve upon the past; artists create new futures. No doubt we need more builders who are artists as much as artists who are builders. But we also need far more ordinary people who can put more art in their lives than extraordinary people who can put life in their art.

Something to think about next time your local board of education wants to cut art and music classes from the school curriculum.

CHAPTER 9

THE NATIONAL PARKS: STRENGTH
AT HOME IS POWER ABROAD

While in California, during one of my Skype sessions with Rosa, I asked for her help in clarifying my understanding of Spanish, the language now clearly second to English in the United States, replacing German about a half century ago. My question was on the difference between *San* and *Santa* in place names in the United States (Santa Fe, San Francisco, and so on). Her explanation was embarrassingly simple: *San* is masculine; *Santa* is feminine.

"So, does that mean that Santa Claus is really a girl?" I quipped. And Americans thought other countries were strange: The United States, after all, is still the only place I know where you can park on the driveway and drive on the parkway.

The ride across central California's huge truck farms described in some of Steinbeck's novels, back over the aqueduct, and into the foothills of the Sierra Nevada was uneventful—mostly through the tracts of agribusiness. Passing through Modesto was like negotiating a maze, given all the detours due to construction in the town. The nature-based abundance I saw on those farms helped temper the impression I'd gotten of California when I initially entered over the Mojave Desert. My appreciation of the state's environmental diversity peaked as I rode along Route 120 into Yosemite National Park. About halfway through its bending roadways, I stopped to gaze from Olmstead Point at Tenaya Lake, half-covered in snow and ice, although it was June. By the time I left Yosemite, I had an admiration of the Golden State that I would never have obtained had I not taken this trip. Given both its human and natural variety, California is one of many horns of plenty in the American cornucopia.

Yosemite National Park was the first of the great national parks I would see on my way back East. The arrival of European-Americans in 1851 set in motion events leading to legislation to establish the national park system. The idea of setting aside a large expanse of land for the future enjoyment of everyone in society, regardless of standing, was something unprecedented in history. In the midst of the Civil War, President Lincoln signed a bill proposing its establishment as a natural preserve.

It was Yellowstone, however, that officially became the world's first national park in 1872. Administered by the US Army in its early years, it evolved as a land-use model from merely a pleasuring ground and wildlife refuge to a biosphere reserve and World Heritage site. Mostly in Wyoming but overlapping into Idaho and Montana, it has over a thousand miles of backcountry trails and more active geysers than Iceland or New Zealand. The area was formed nearly two million years ago by volcanic eruptions, the most recent spewing out 240 million cubic miles of debris over its 30-by-45-mile caldera (or basin) in the heart of the preserve.

The popularity of the national parks was in plain view when I later rode into Yellowstone. It was far busier than Yosemite, so it took me over an hour to go less than twenty miles from the park entrance. The burgeoning peak-season traffic backed up partly due to road construction as well as wildlife wandering along the road. Fortunately, the bison and bears were spooked by my rumbling two-wheeler. It's as hard to get into as Manhattan, I thought, but much more scenic and with far better air quality. As I sat there waiting, I also realized how uniquely democratic the idea of national parks is. Unlike Europe's attractions— the castles, palaces, and churches that are artifacts of aristocratic rule—America's greatest attractions are open to anyone, rich and poor, and belong to everyone. But I also realized how the national parks were the characteristic result of a long and difficult struggle against no one but ourselves.

A little more than a century ago, the momentum for a national parks system was gaining fast. The unrelenting rush to conquer and tame the West had come at a terrible cost. Forests had been devastated and entire species ravaged, all in the name of progress. I have read no better account of this than in "Americans and the Land" in Steinbeck's *America and Americans*:

> *I have often wondered at the savagery and thoughtlessness with which our early settlers approached this rich continent. They came at it as though it were an enemy, which of course it was. They burned the forests and changed the rainfall; they swept the buffalo from the plains, blasted the streams, set fire to the grass, and ran a reckless scythe through the virgin and noble timber. Perhaps they felt that it was limitless and could never be exhausted and that a man could move on to new wonders endlessly. Certainly there are many examples to the contrary, but to a large extent the early people pillaged the country as though they hated it, as though they held it temporarily and might be driven off at any time.*

Although this helps explain the callous attitude Americans have had toward their natural environment, it is also worth remembering that home ownership is a mark of identity for most middle-class Americans, many of whom also believe that nature is property— something that belongs to people, not the other way around. The vast tracts of thinly populated land were as much a curse as a blessing. "The merciless nineteenth century was like a hostile expedition for loot that seemed limitless," said Steinbeck. "It was full late when we began to realize that the continent did not stretch out to infinity; that there were limits to the indignities to which we could subject it. . . . Conservation came to us slowly, and much of it hasn't arrived yet," he wrote in the early 1960s.

Joseph Campbell's more philosophical thesis, in *The Power of Myth* a quarter century later, is that we inherited many of our attitudes from the Europeans, whose norms on nature are formed by the Abrahamic religions, which are essentially anti-nature. For many Jews, Christians, and Muslims, nature is seen as corrupting and sinful, starting with the chain of natural seduction from the snake to Eve to Adam in the Fall in the Garden of Eden. "You get a totally different civilization and a totally different way of living according to whether your myth presents nature as fallen or whether nature is in itself a manifestation of divinity," he explained. This inherent disdain of nature in the Puritan ethic has been a driver of the development of science as a mechanism to dominate and subdue nature, the love affair with technology, and a subordinate appreciation of art and artists (unless of course they have commercial value). It's one reason why conservation will not likely be the center-piece of any energy strategy in the United States for quite some time.

The Native Americans had an opposite reading of the same topography. Land for them was sentient; it had agency and personhood. As Campbell explained, they "addressed all of life as a 'thou. . . .' The ego that sees a 'thou' is not the same ego that sees an 'it.'" In contrast, Genesis reads, "Let us make mankind in our image, in our likeness, so that they may rule over the fish in the sea and the birds in the sky, over the livestock and all the wild animals, and over all the creatures that move along the ground." So, because European settlers saw everything in nature, including the natives, as an "it," there has been no guilt or shame in destroying something seen as detached and separate from oneself.

The creation of the national parks was a moment when Americans had the sense to act counter to their compulsive opposition to nature. Those advocating for the national parks innately understood that when we destroy external nature we destroy internal nature with it. On earth as it is in heaven: From our bodies and minds to the land and the people in it, what God has given us is God's gift to us; what we do with these things is our statement of how much we value that gift.

The national park system became official under the pen of Woodrow Wilson in 1916, just before America's entrance into the Great War in Europe and its rise as a global power. But it was Theodore Roosevelt who had the greatest impact. Before Wilson, he signed the Antiquities Act of 1906, which enabled Roosevelt and his successors to proclaim historic landmarks, historic or prehistoric structures, and other such objects of interest under federal ownership as national monuments. The first of these was Devils Tower, Wyoming. Then came the Grand Canyon in 1908. By the end of Roosevelt's two terms of office, he had reserved six predominantly cultural areas and twelve predominantly natural areas in this way.

Successive presidents also used the Antiquities Act as the authority for about a quarter of the more than four hundred areas composing today's national park system in every state but Delaware. President Barack Obama's declaration of more than 1,600 acres of beach, river, and forest lands along the California coast as well as the designation of 782,000 square miles of US-controlled areas of the Pacific Ocean as a nature preserve is among the latest applications.

Theodore Roosevelt ("TR") was among the first presidents to recognize that conservation was not just a moral act or an end in itself. It was also a matter of a broader sense of national security. In his seventh annual message to Congress in December 1907, he noted:

> [T]he conservation of our natural resources and their proper use constitute the fundamental problem which underlies almost every other problem of our national life. . . . As a nation we not only enjoy a wonderful measure of present prosperity but if this prosperity is used aright it is an earnest of future success such as no other nation will have. The reward of foresight for this nation is great and easily foretold. But there must be the look ahead, there must be a realization of the fact that to waste, to destroy, our natural resources, to skin and exhaust the land instead of using it so as to increase its usefulness, will result in undermining in the days of our children the very prosperity which we ought by right to hand down to them amplified and developed.

TR, whose attitudes toward nature as a younger man were as callous as anyone else's, grasped as president that the accumulated strength of natural and human resources was the basis of America's national power as well as its democracy. At the same time, the United States was witnessing one of the largest waves of immigration in its history.

I had always wondered why he was the fourth president to appear on the face of Mount Rushmore. Having seen much of his handiwork and understanding its far-reaching national strategic implications as I gazed upon the sculpture in the Black Hills of South Dakota, I now know why.

The national parks also showed me an example of what can be good about government. Currently, about 4 percent of the territory of the United States is managed by the National Park Service, assisted by about a quarter-million Volunteers-in-Parks, and with a budget of over three billion dollars. The parks draw about as many visitors as the US population, at the same time generating nearly thirty billion dollars of economic activity. TR's cousin Franklin further shaped the macro-managing role of government under the New Deal. The Civilian Conservation Corps, in addition to being a public relief program, helped preserve the natural treasures of the country as well as modernize its infrastructure. We could no doubt use such a program again, given, for example, all the destruction of wildfires

The national parks have also turned out to be a great tool of national diplomacy. About 30 to 40 percent of those who see the physical grandeur of the United States are from foreign countries, no doubt contributing to a more positive image of America. As soft power has grown in importance and it becomes more difficult to preserve the world's natural treasures in the face of urbanization, climate change, and resource demands, this comparative advantage Americans have taken for granted will be more prized and take on new meaning as the century wears on.

As a Civil Affairs operator in the 1990s, I was gaining firsthand appreciation of soft power. Just over ten days after I departed the Balkans in uniform in June 1996, coming off active duty, I returned as a civilian with the United Nations. I had essentially gone from an organizational culture that was ostensibly more about hard power to one that was more about soft power.

The UN was not in very good shape then. It had not done well in Somalia, failed to thwart genocide in Rwanda, and gained further notoriety from its disastrous attempt to keep a peace that hardly existed in Bosnia-Herzegovina—the most ignominious example being the

Yours truly with a fairly tame tatanka. I was a big Davy Crockett
fan as a kid and fantasized about being a frontiersman. So I bought
myself a coonskin cap and was a kid again, for the moment.

massacre in Srebenica. Less than a year later, I arrived in Vukovar, at
the far eastern edge of Croatia along the Danube River, and the site of
the outbreak of the war in Yugoslavia in the summer of 1991. The UN
Transitional Administration in Eastern Slavonia (UNTAES) resulted
from an agreement reached in the town of Erdut at the same time as
the Dayton Accords created the NATO Implementation Force (IFOR).
The UNTAES peacekeeping force consisted of Belgians, Jordanians,
Pakistanis, Russians, Ukrainians, and others mostly from Eastern
Europe. Its mission under UN Security Council Resolution 1037 was
"the peaceful reintegration of the region of Eastern Slavonia, Baranja,
and Western Sirmium in the Republic of Croatia."

When the war started and the Yugoslav army pushed out the
Croatians, the Serbs set about ethnically cleansing this border region
by reversing the percentage ratio of Croats to Serbs from about
80:20 to 20:80, with small minorities caught in between. Slobodan
Milošević repopulated Eastern Slavonia mostly with Bosnian Serbs

who themselves were then ethnically cleansed. Repatriating these unfortunate political pawns was not the answer. Under its strict two-year mandate, UNTAES had to stabilize the area, transition governmental control from Belgrade to Zagreb, re-register the population, hold an election, and begin rebalancing ethnic ratios, while helping the economy likewise transition from command to market mechanisms, including the money system. It was quite a tall order, considering the complexity of the situation and the UN's track record to date.

Once again, I found myself in transition. I had started the year as a (military) Civil Affairs officer helping military logisticians and finished it as a civilian logistician working with (civilian) Civil Affairs officers. I had first belonged to a national military contingent, with some civilians, in support of an international peacekeeping effort and then joined an international civilian organization, with a military contingent, in support of peacekeeping in a single country. It was exciting to be involved in a start-up operation and see it all the way through to completion, as well as to be involved in a truly multinational effort to bring peace to a war-torn area.

It was also a bit of a surprise for me to wind up as a logistics officer, as I had applied to be a UN Civil Affairs officer, considering my obvious background. UN Civil Affairs officers are basically civilians appointed to UN field missions with the job, as the UN Civil Affairs manual reads, of "cross-mission representation, monitoring and facilitation at the local level; confidence-building, conflict management and support to reconciliation; and support to the restoration and extension of state authority"—not far from what I had done in uniform.

Upon arrival at the UN logistics base in Klisa, near Vukovar, I reported to Peder Cox, a just-retired Army Special Forces logistics officer. Youthful and energetic, with salt-and-pepper hair and a no-nonsense attitude, Peder had served in uniform with the UN mission in Haiti and was now the (civilian) UNTAES chief logistics officer. Not expecting me, he asked for a copy of my UN résumé and my letter of appointment.

"Jesus Christ! What the hell are you doing here?" he blurted as he read it. "You're an Army Civil Affairs officer! You ought to be down in

Vukovar with the political staff at the mission headquarters and not here on Klisa Base with the loggies."

"Well," I explained, "UN headquarters [in New York] told me that the reason I got diverted here is because my qualifications don't match their requirements for Civil Affairs. They have enough [UN] Civil Affairs officers already and I'm more needed here."

"Really? Okay. Hell, I'll be more than happy to take you. Welcome aboard!" Peder eventually found out that the head of UN Civil Affairs at UNTAES was not that anxious to have someone working for him who was as well qualified as he was—office politics was apparently the real reason.

Serendipity being what it is, I turned out to be quite effective from my position at the Joint Logistics Operations Center at planning and implementing a lot of the initiatives that UN Civil Affairs headed up but knew little about how to implement. Among these were setting up the national ID card and voter registration offices around the area, running and coordinating security support for key population movements, putting on the municipal and national elections, and other like tasks.

It was challenging, frustrating, and fun, with all the different nationalities represented there, civilian and military. Then, after a few months into our start-up operations, as the bureaucrats from UN headquarters began moving in, coordination became more odious. It became harder to get things done. Rather than a phone call, a quick e-mail, a note, or a chat and a handshake, procedures had set in. I always asked new people in the mission where they were from because I was curious and excited to meet all these people from different countries. More of these increasingly well-dressed staffers answered, "New York," which I know is a very cosmopolitan place, but it still struck me as odd. What they really meant was that New York was synonymous with UN headquarters. From then on I introduced myself, with just a touch of characteristic sarcasm, by saying, "Hi, I'm Chris Holshek and I'm *really* from New York!"

Like most of the international civilians there, I was a mission appointee. My contract with the UN was subject to renewal every year or so, much as my Army job in Heidelberg was. In those days, the UN, much like the State Department, had little to no operational culture—not a lot of people with field savvy and street smarts. People came in and out as needed, so there was little continuity, and many civilians were less professionally accomplished, except those willing to wander from mission to mission, appointment to appointment. It's far better now, but back then I described the UN as "the world's largest temp agency."

The other advantage of two years at UNTAES was that I could do something I couldn't dream of doing in Army Civil Affairs but always thought made great sense—live among the population. Not isolating myself on a base enabled me to derive the benefit of vital local street smarts. I took a small apartment in the home of the Makivic family, Serbs who were part of the original 20 percent in the village of Dalj (pronounced "dye") along the Danube just north of Vukovar.

It didn't take long to become part of the family, with Mama adopting me as her third son, after Milan, a tall, dark-haired, dark-eyed, easygoing fellow who spoke English that was far better than my Serbian, or *Serbski*, and Nicholas, his shorter, younger brother, who was already working for UNTAES. In many traditional extended family structures, while men dominate the public domain, women take charge of the interior spaces of the household, and the same was true among Serbs. Milan had one small daughter, Dragana, whom I coached with her English while she taught me some *Serbski*. Milan and Mama would be waiting for me when I came in from work, around seven or so each evening. Mama would beckon me into the kitchen: "Christopher, *kafa!*" Then she served me nuclear-grade coffee that kept me up for hours past bedtime. I drank it out of politeness for a time, until we became familiar enough that I could ask for a beer—*pivo*—instead.

Nearly every day, I joined Milan, his wife, Jasna, Dragana, Mama, and Vlado—a heavyset, white-haired patriarch, whose main job was to kill and butcher an occasional pig and whose main form of recreation was to go fishing in the Danube, then make a delicious fish soup—for a *pivo* and supper. I got better at *Serbski*, while they got better at English.

Then one day Milan, while sipping on his red wine, told me he and Jasna were going to try to have another child. "What do you want this time?" I asked, to which Milan responded unequivocally: "A son, *par da!*"—of course. So, knowing how folkloric Serbs are, I relayed some wise council handed down from my Slovak great-grandfather. "Milan," I said looking at him earnestly, "you know that the man determines the sex of the child. So if you want a boy, you have to drink *pivo* [beer] before Jasna gets pregnant." Knowing I was being a bit facetious, Milan of course kept drinking his wine each evening.

Nine months later, Jasna gave birth to a beautiful little girl, Milica. From then on, it was the running joke in the family—"If you only had listened to Christopher!" Mama would chide Milan. A few years later, I met Milan, Jasna, the two girls, and their infant brother in Vancouver, Canada. Milan told me right away, "Christopher, this time I drank *pivo!*"

We were very dedicated to each other and took great care of each other (Mama was always trying to find me a Serbian wife). It was heartbreaking when I eventually had to leave—the Makivics had nearly half of the village of Dalj at my farewell fest. I had been their main source of income—and brought a lot of food and other gifts—while they provided excellent room and board. We also provided each other security. As Croats began to move in, some with vengeance on their minds and the intent to throw out the Serbs regardless of whether they were part of the original population, my presence at their home was a deterrent to any ill will that might come their way, including forced eviction or harassment through vandalism.

It also worked the other way around. Driving home one night in my careworn white Nissan pickup truck with "UN" painted on the doors, I cut across the farm roads and found myself held up by an illegal patrol toting AK-47s. In my broken *Serbski*, I mentioned that I lived with the Makivics. One thuggish youth brightened up and said their families were close. They let me pass after a few more minutes of chatter. I had no intent to turn them in but warned them that they were in a business with little future. They explained, like many, that they were in dire economic straits. We eventually got one of them a job working in one of the kitchens for the troop units. As in many war-torn or underdeveloped places, when one person has a job, the whole family has food and shelter.

Some months later, when setting up the national ID and voter registration offices, we ran into a snag trying to gain access to a building that Jacques Klein, as mission chief, had picked out for that purpose. It was in a rather sensitive area just outside of Vukovar, under the control of the same kind of resistance group whose patrol I had run into. (Klein picked it out specifically to break the power the group held over that community.) The building custodian was predictably refusing to hand over the keys to the UN Civil Affairs officer, mainly as a delaying tactic but also to test the resolve of the UN. On the appointed days, I would show up with the engineer crew and others to set up the place, with the unfortunate UN Civil Affairs officer negotiating unsuccessfully for the keys. After the third try, I drove over to the mission headquarters building and entered Klein's front office, where his personal assistant, an Army Reserve officer, jealously guarded access.

"I need five minutes with the Old Man, Jackie," I told her in military slang.

"He's busy," she muttered back.

"He's always busy. This is urgent *and* important," I responded, poking a bit of fun at the overuse of the word *urgent* among UN staffers. I had to wait for a while but got my five minutes and gave the boss a quick verbal, military-style decision briefing on my plan.

"Go ahead," he told me.

The next day, I showed up with the usual construction crew, but right behind me was a squad car of Serb Police (funded and equipped by UNTAES) and then UN civilian police, in this case Austrians. Farther back, but still in view, was a Belgian army armored fighting vehicle with a squad of infantry that happened to be on patrol. Our Serbian logistics officer and I walked up to the building custodian waiting for us outside the front entrance. After we exchanged some pleasantries for a while, I turned to the custodian, put my hand on his shoulder for a moment, and looked directly into his eyes (a very important thing to do when speaking with Serbs to let them know you're sincere and serious).

"Look, I know, you've got your instructions. I've got my mine, too. So I understand," I said to him a bit like a mafia don. "Here's what I propose: I'm going to go over there and smoke a cigar. In a little while, the Serb Police will ask you for the keys." Then I wished him luck in Serbian.

An hour later we were in the building. Face was saved. We all sat around, drinking *kafa* in a strange sense of celebration, as if there had been no problem in the first place. I gave the custodian a carton of cigarettes for his trouble. I sometimes called tokens like that "wampum."

Not everything went so smoothly or successfully, though. Like a third-string quarterback, I inherited the chief logistics officer post from Buddy Tillett, who got it from Peder Cox. Soon afterward, things were getting out of hand at the fuel point run by the Russian airborne battalion on the logistics base. The battalions were actually rewarded this as R&R from their combat rotations in Chechnya. Unsurprisingly, they ran prostitution, arms smuggling, and drug rings in concert with their Serb allies. Among these rackets was one to siphon off diesel fuel from our fuel point to sell on the black market, for which they obtained a freshly stolen car. About fifteen hundred liters got you a used VW Golf and at least twice that a BMW. When the battalion rotated every three months or so, a convoy of twenty or so of these stolen vehicles, driven by their new owners with forged plates and documents, departed the base, heading for Russia via Belgrade and Bulgaria.

Over time, the losses in fuel were becoming intolerable. So we got together with an NYPD detective serving with the UN Civilian Police and asked her to set up a sting operation to catch them in the act and gather the evidence. About a month or so later, we had our proof and showed it to the chief administrative officer. I read the riot act to the Russians: Effective immediately, they were off the fuel point—the civilian staff would run it instead.

Unfortunately, I couldn't cover the diplomatic tracks—those were way above my pay grade. The battalion commander got back to the Russian Ministry of Defense in Moscow, and the Russian mission in New York filed a protest to the UN Security Council. We had to let them back on the fuel point, although we won a small concession in that it would be run and secured jointly (meaning both civil and military in UN parlance). Fuel losses resumed but at much lower levels.

In spite of issues like these that make most people roll their eyes about the UN, UNTAES turned out to be a rare and much-needed "win" then for the organization. It completed its mandate successfully, on time, and under budget, thanks to the hard work of many dedicated civilians, military, and police working as a team. I contributed to the UNTAES end-of-mission report by writing the key lessons on logistics, which up to that time were little mentioned in UN mission reports that usually focused on the political side. After coming home from Croatia, I briefed Benjamin Gilman, still then our congressman in New York and at that time chairing the House International Relations Committee. The UN could be an effective indirect instrument of US foreign policy, I told him—if properly organized, resourced, and backed by Washington. In other words, when done the right way, multilateralism is preferable to going it alone.

My experiences in the Balkans helped me realize that hard power should be something you use only when soft power has reached its limits, as a last resort, and clearly in a supporting role. When in uniform, I saw the presence of the United States in these operations as particularly catalytic. While the multinational nature of the international presence communicated an example of collaboration and cooperation as well as the seriousness of the world's concern, the presence of forces from our multicultural society sent a very powerful, demonstrative

From peacemaker to peacekeeper: At Klisa Base in Eastern Slavonia.

message. Although the impacts were uneven, hard to measure, and not immediate, you could still see them over time.

After my stint in Eastern Slavonia, I returned to my drilling duties at the 304th Civil Affairs Brigade in Philadelphia while trying to see if I could get a job at the UN headquarters in New York. Meanwhile, I took up a job with Airborne Express as an area manager, just a few blocks from the World Trade Center, while living on the Upper West Side. That didn't work out either. Working with the unionized labor force there was a nightmare. Unlike soldiers, they were not self-motivated and had no trust of management. The coup de grâce was when six-month bonuses came out based on productivity improvements. I was in line to receive about two thousand dollars, not bad then. But when my immediate supervisor took 25 percent of that, while his boss—a domineering corporate clown—took another 25 percent, I tendered my resignation.

That experience fueled real doubts in me about American-style laissez-faire capitalism. I began to see some striking civil–military comparisons, having gotten firsthand exposure to the obsession with the bottom line of many corporate leaders. The short-term, tactical mind-set that dominates the policies I saw played out in the field is the same one that seems to have prevented businesses from looking beyond the next quarterly profit-and-loss statement, at least when I was working in private industry. The transactional line-management style of traditional corporations, where everyone colors inside the lines of their own job description without thinking holistically, independently, or collaboratively, parallels the hierarchical, stay-in-your lane, and risk-averse culture of the government and the military I had seen.

My experience at Airborne Express suggested that too many businesses still see labor as a cost and not an investment, management–labor relations being more adversarial than collaborative. Firms now seem to be finding out what many in the military have held sacred: Trust is vital to organizational success. Superior leadership also works better than improving profit margins through mergers and acquisitions, downsizing, rightsizing, and other, less imaginative measures. Even in business, humans are more important than hardware.

Beyond adaptability, the success of the American socioeconomic model has been seen in the robust American middle class and its upward socioeconomic mobility. The erosion of these advantages should be a critical national security concern. As the military has begun to learn in community-based operations in wars of late, corporations seem to be likewise learning that the communities that comprise their markets are codependently prosperous. Yet since World War II, corporate profits as a percentage of gross domestic product are at their highest level while wages are at their lowest level of national earnings, adjusted for inflation, since then.

It's also essential to recognize that the other secret to our success is in innovation—which is why it's as important to teach and honor the arts as much as the sciences and cultivate rather than curb our immigration–assimilation culture. Science and management improve productivity, whereas art and leadership spawn innovation.

After quitting Airborne in late 1998, I went to work as the head-quarters company commander at the 304th Civil Affairs Brigade. I prepared the Brigade to send out more teams to the Balkans, while introducing innovations in the management of a Reserve Civil Affairs headquarters that the brigade commander, Colonel Fred Jones, suggested the Army Civil Affairs command review. Our turn came soon: War in Kosovo broke out in the early part of 1998, bombing began in early 1999, and the 304th began deploying teams there. I went in early 2000 with the second rotation, six months after the war ended.

While serving as the NATO Civil–Military Cooperation (CIMIC) liaison officer to the UN Mission in Kosovo (UNMIK) in the capital city of Pristina in 2000, I attended a meeting at the US base at Camp Bondsteel between the Kosovo Force (KFOR) headquarters and the US task force there. The task force commander at the time was a one-star general named Ricardo Sanchez, and his operations officer was an exceptionally competent lieutenant colonel named David Hogg. As the US officers talked off-line after meeting, Hogg questioned the US presence in Kosovo, reflecting a lot of public opinion back home. "It's not our fight," he argued, a lot like my dad. "This is for the Europeans. I don't know why we have to be here at all." He had a point, but I gave in to the temptation to offer another perspective, working at the time with mostly non-Americans.

"Sir," I spoke up. "We're here so that everybody else can be here, because if we don't come to the party, they won't either. Things just won't get done here unless we get involved, and none of us could do it ourselves. We shouldn't forget that."

Another thing I began to realize, being part of a NATO deployment, is how advantageous it is to have allies from smaller nations that don't carry our political baggage or superpower profile. They also have the benefit, in their smallness, of being more nimble in coordination, less weighed down by our huge bureaucracies. "Interagency coordination for a lot of these guys," I would report back to my American colleagues, "is often a matter of just walking across the hallway." This is an advantage of multinational operations we've often overlooked.

One of the things I set up at the UNMIK headquarters building was a CIMIC Liaison Office, well located just around the corner from the UN café. We turned it into a very attractive place for people to come for a visit—in addition to information about what was going on in the security area with KFOR, we were always well supplied with chocolate chip cookies and other goodies like magazines that I was able to purchase from the American PX (Post Exchange) at Camp Bondsteel. Of course, it also enabled us to build relationships and get information that would improve our situational understanding. Our CIMIC reports, in turn, were read by everyone. "Build it and they will come," I said, taking a line from the movie *Field of Dreams* as I briefed the KFOR CIMIC chief when proposing the center.

We even delivered. I had been having a difficult time getting an appointment with one of the key UNMIK financial and economic advisors to figure out how we could phase out KFOR's role in the distribution and security of civil-service payments around the countryside. His Filipina secretary jealously guarded access to him, but I eventually wore her down with a bit of charm and attention to a decisive detail. Being a transplant from the UN headquarters in the world's most convenient city, she casually complained that one of the creature comforts she most missed was American toilet paper.

A week later I showed up with another form of "wampum"—a whole case of TP that I picked up at the PX, where the UN staff members were not authorized to go. Three days later, I had an appointment with the advisor and was able to help get things moving along again. Soft power, indeed.

We were a pretty effective team, able to buzz around town like bees cross-pollinating among people who would otherwise not share information or coordinate with each other, mentioning in casual conversation things like the guy over in this or that office is working this or that, and you might want to get with him. My pal Tony Sherman and I worked to great effect in helping to synchronize the two key pillars of civil administration (run by the UN and where I was liaison) and institution building (run by the Organization for Security and Cooperation in Europe, which Tony covered). This kind of "facilitating" (a favorite Civil Affairs term) helped pick up the pace of international recovery operations.

One of the proofs positive that this work required a mind-set as much as a skill set was in the two opposites within our own CIMIC team. Among the most effective civil–military officers I have had the pleasure to work with was Air Force Lieutenant Colonel Scott "Doc" Holloway. A strapping, blond-haired former Nebraska University football player who became a B-52 navigator, Doc never had a day of civil–military training in his life. Yet, he was a natural at his job, due to his great interpersonal and social skills and easy, affable manner. In contrast, the Civil Affairs colonel from Boston back at KFOR headquarters obviously didn't get it—a bit of a curmudgeon, he spent more time lecturing us on what we couldn't do instead of what we should be doing.

Just as I was preparing to go home after more than nine months, I received an offer I couldn't refuse from some of my UN friends and came back a month later to become one of the people I liaised with in uniform. As the political reporting officer of the mission, I enjoyed a bird's-eye view of the mission and its activities and a comprehensive understanding of the issues it dealt with. The political reporting officer had the job of researching and writing daily, weekly, monthly, and quarterly situational and mission reports for the special representative to the secretary general—for much of that time Bernard Kouchner, an effervescent and accessible leader and the founder of Doctors Without Borders (Médecins Sans Frontières) and later French foreign minister.

Although it was not the most exciting of jobs, requiring long hours of writing and revision, it made me one of the better-informed people in the mission—and I got to work with many interesting personalities. Information being power, it also gave me a pretty good vantage point to affect what was going on in Kosovo. I got to know a lot of people from many places in and out of UNMIK. While I enjoyed this post immensely, it was cut short by two things in quick succession. In the late summer of 2001, I learned I had been selected to take command of a Reserve Civil Affairs battalion in Buffalo, New York. Then came September 11.

The 1990s as well as the twentieth century ended for me on that day. What I had seen and done up to then had prepared me well to comprehend this unexpected event, above as well as below. I thought I had seen enough paradigm shifts after leaving Germany in 1993, when my exit paralleled the wholesale withdrawal of the US military from Germany and Europe and the "operations other than war" in Rwanda and the Balkans. But not long after the September of my second year in Kosovo, in 2001, my sixteen years of service in Europe would soon seem like another era—which, of course, in many ways it was. Yet, in some ways, what I learned in the 1990s would become a kind of experiential capital I would draw upon for what was to come.

Given that first exposure to the protected wilderness of the United States, I could begin to see how the country's physical grandeur and diversity alone make Americans a truly fortunate people. But I also realized that outer nature was only one source of strength and power. We must understand, as TR did, that the wellspring of our power abroad—economic, military, diplomatic, and so on—is in our inherent strengths at home, be those natural or human. Strength is the source of power, whereas power is the manifestation of strength. Identity is in how that strength, in action, gives you power. This I learned innately through all my years at work abroad. But that understanding never came home to me—until I saw the national parks.

CHAPTER 10

FROM WEST TO EAST: CONTROL OR CONNECTIVITY?

A lot of times it's better to look at an experience from opposite the way you went through it in order to gain a greater understanding of it—even though, as Søren Kierkegaard advised, "life can only be understood backwards; but it must be lived forwards." The value of history, after all, is in knowing where we are and may be going by knowing where we've been. For a few years after graduation from high school, I went back there several times precisely for this reason—to regain my bearings in an azimuth check, referring to Army land navigation training as well as my orienteering days at NMMI. But after a while, I no longer had to do that, for I had found my footing in an updated identity that worked in the new paradigm in which I found myself.

As I was riding west to east, I realized a similar opportunity to enjoy a unique perspective in my continued search for personal and national identity. As I had been able to look at my homeland from the outside in terms of space, I was looking back at the development of the United States from the opposite direction of its path of advance, yet going forward along a passageway I had never been on. It was simultaneously new and old, offering a retrospection and introspection that deepened my understanding of America and its place in the world as well as helped me process my personal experiences of and roles in that larger dynamic.

After leaving Yosemite along a fifteen-mile, steeply declining road winding along the cliff sides, I rode up Route 395 past Mono Lake, California, and stayed at a great little western-style motel. It was curiously named the "Virginia Creek Settlement" and was run by a husband-and-wife team with—among the most important prerequisites to any long-lasting romance—a great sense of humor. "Every man needs a wife," one plaque in the breakfast room read, "because many things go wrong that can't be blamed on the government." They put me in the John Wayne Room, decorated with pictures of the Duke, especially in his roles as a cavalryman, flashing me back to my formative days in uniform on mechanized horses.

From Bridgeport, California, the next day, my own mechanized horse and I meandered up the scenic valleys along the Sierra Nevada Mountains, leading us through Carson City and Reno, Nevada, where we turned decisively eastward along Interstate 80. This route converged with the Truckee River outside of Reno. It was also the path of the iron horses of the Central Pacific Railroad, where thousands of laborers hacked through the Sierra Nevada from Sacramento (where Interstate 80 also begins, or ends) in the building of the Transcontinental Railroad.

As I began the long way back East—the second four thousand miles of my trans-America trip—I slowly reviewed two of the most significant endeavors in America's breach of physical frontiers. Both the Lewis and Clark expedition and the Transcontinental Railroad helped form the United States as a continental power. By looking at both from the reverse direction, I could see them as part of a continuous flow rather than episodic events, as in my own career and life path.

When crossing the Mississippi on my way westward, I remembered how Jefferson's Louisiana Purchase and the ensuing survey of the West opened the way for the United States to secure its dominance of North America. In *Nothing Like It in the World*, author Stephen Ambrose picked up on the stream of consciousness he described in *Undaunted Courage*—how Lincoln initiated the Transcontinental Railroad less to consolidate Jefferson's territorial ambition than as an emphatic act of confidence in a country in existential crisis. (At the same time, Lincoln purchased Alaska from Russia as if to complete the inexorable process of Manifest Destiny.)

These two critical national infrastructure projects, by the way, are prime examples of what the second floor of the West Point Museum calls "the Army's contributions to the growth of the Nation." About 90 percent of the displays are about operations other than war. Lewis and Clark, of course, were Army officers performing a strategic reconnaissance mission at the behest of their commander in chief, whereas a great many of those who led and managed the building of the Transcontinental Railroad were Civil War veterans. It's hard to overestimate the impact of the railroads on the economic and social development of the country and its rise as a continental power in the nineteenth century, just as it's hard to overlook what the Eisenhower Interstate Highway System did for the physical and socioeconomic mobility of Americans in the next century, or what the Internet is doing now.

From the 1830s on, a national rail network rapidly took shape. When the Civil War broke out, the United States had thirty-one thousand miles of rail, more than in all of Europe. However, almost all of it was east of the Missouri–Mississippi basin, and two-thirds of that was in the North. But the idea of a transcontinental railroad didn't come from there. By 1862, the young Californian engineer Theodore Judah, following his own plan, surveyed a route over the Sierra Nevadas. He then persuaded wealthy merchants in Sacramento to form the Central Pacific Railroad. Congress authorized it to lay track eastward when it chartered the Union Pacific Railroad of New York to begin along the route of the Mormon Trail, with the eastern terminus in Omaha, Nebraska.

The Central Pacific broke ground first, in January 1863, and the Union Pacific that December. Neither made much headway, despite loan subsidies of sixteen to forty-eight thousand dollars per mile (between one and four million dollars today) as well as ten sections of land (a section is ten square miles) surrounding each mile of laid track. With the country's attention and investors' profit incentives, labor, and material diverted to military contracts, little progress was made until the two railroad companies, in the freewheeling business ethics of that time, vigorously lobbied (or, perhaps more accurately, bribed) key members of Congress. Soon, a second railroad act of 1864 doubled the land grants. Once the war was over and huge pools of unemployed laborers, managerial know-how, and capital were freed, work picked up steam and speed.

Central Pacific crews faced the rugged Sierra Nevada barrier almost immediately, its mostly Chinese workers hammering out tunnels through mountain rock sometimes at an agonizing eight inches a day. With eight flatcars of material needed for each mile of track laid, logistics were a nightmare, especially for the Central Pacific, which had to bring in every rail, spike, and locomotive fifteen thousand miles from the industrial eastern United States and around Cape Horn (which later served as a case study to justify the building of the Panama Canal).

Meanwhile, the Union Pacific—drawing on Irish, German, and Italian immigrants; Civil War veterans from both sides; ex-slaves; and even some Native Americans—set out from Omaha to cross easier but far longer terrain. They faced severe winters, blistering summers, violent thunderstorms, and incessant Sioux and Cheyenne raids, leading to the use of contract security forces—like those employed nearly a century and a half later in Iraq and Afghanistan. If the 24/7 media existed then, the project might not have been completed at all, or at least not as it was. No one knows for sure, but estimates run between one thousand and two thousand as to how many workers perished. One of the reasons labor unions later formed was the volume of workers killed and maimed in industrial accidents in the late nineteenth century.

By mid-1868, these polyglot work teams, drilled for precision track laying by their mostly ex–Army officer team chiefs, invented a pace far faster than their civilian bosses originally thought—an innovation in productivity. Driven by the land-subsidy incentive, the railroads kept going past each other for about two hundred miles until Congress finally intervened to declare Promontory Summit in Utah to be the point of connection, at the suggestion of the railroads, which were driving on as much as ten miles per day absent government direction. When it was over on May 10, 1869, the Central Pacific was credited with laying 690 miles of track, the Union Pacific with 1,086.

While stopping off for fuel along the Central Pacific's route at Lovelock, Nevada, I met up with two Air Force veterans, Charles Price and Chuck Carbon, who were likewise looking to overnight in Winnemucca before heading to Salt Lake City the next day. We decided to ride together. Winnemucca (Shoshone for "one moccasin") has a large community of immigrants from the Basque region of Spain. We shared a lively family-style dinner at one of their restaurants. I told my temporary traveling companions about the ride, and they suggested I continue with them to meet up with their friend Toby Wolf (nicknamed "the Wolfman") in West Wendover, the last casino town in Nevada at the border crossing into Utah and where Interstate 80 diverges from the pathway of the Central Pacific.

The crest of the highway entering the town offers a stunning vista over the salt flats to the mountains masking Salt Lake City, visible more than a hundred miles away on a clear day. That view helped me truly appreciate the vastness of the West and see how easily city dwellers can become disoriented, like a pygmy suddenly coming out of the jungle into the Serengeti or German soldiers losing their way in the vastness of the Eastern Front.

Toby, a tall and well-built fellow with a salt-and-pepper goatee, who was a banker by day and a biker at any other time he could get, invited me to stay with Charles and Chuck at his home. "Anything for a veteran," he told me. I found it a bit unusual for someone to

The Wolfman leads the way, with Charles in trail. The Oquirrh Mountains, masking Salt Lake City, are still about sixty miles away.

invite a total stranger to his home but accepted it for what it was—exceptionally gracious.

The Wolfman led us over the salt flats, his hands on high handlebars and his rain slicker flapping through the jet stream behind him like Dracula's cape. Not far from where ground rockets broke land-speed records approaching the sound barrier, we sped along at a mere eighty-five miles per hour. While sailing over the former ocean floor, I peered toward the horizon, not able to tell where the earth ended and the sky began. Distances are not the only thing hard to judge in the desert.

When we got to the Wolfman's home in Jordan, just south of the state capital, we parked our bikes among the other two Toby had in the triple garage of his spacious single-family home. Toby offered us beers while he and his wife, Chris, prepared us a barbecue feast. We then met the rest of the household—a collection of mixed-breed dogs named Ricky, Lucy, and Fred (Chris said she was still looking for Ethel to round out the canine cast of the iconic 1950s sitcom *I Love Lucy*).

After dinner and lots of storytelling around a small outdoor fire, Toby said to me, "I want to show you something." Then he took me downstairs to a small room in the basement dedicated to his father, a highly decorated Special Forces soldier who served multiple tours in Vietnam. The room was carefully adorned with pictures, uniforms, medals, and other memorabilia. It was a fitting tribute. I told him my story about Uncle Randy and how Vietnam veterans deserve as much recognition for their service as people who went to Iraq or Afghanistan. "People like your dad did not come home to a grateful nation. Thank you for honoring me by letting me see it."

"Dad would have been honored to know you as well," Toby said. His father had passed away only months ago. Now I knew why it was so easy for him to invite me to his home. Still, his hospitality and open-heartedness were inspiring, as immense as the landscape, and something for which I'll be eternally grateful. We all stay connected on Facebook.

I was on the road again the next morning. It was time to be alone once more. After casing the city center, I edged the Dyna along the Great Salt Lake, then pushed slowly upward into northern Utah to take

Standing between two engines of connectivity.

a look at Promontory along a hundred-mile diversion I was happy to make. Seeking this point of intersection on land felt for me as critical as locating one on a ship—it would help me find balance, if not buoyancy.

The Golden Spike National Historic Site was in the middle of nowhere. On the wall of the visitor center was a poignant quote from Frank Leslie's *Illustrated Newspaper* in 1869: "The journey across the plains was a great undertaking that required great patience and endurance. Now all is changed. . . . The six months' journey is reduced to less than a week. The prairie schooner has passed away, replaced by the railway coach with all its modern comforts."

It wasn't just this excerpt that began to stimulate something stirring longer and deeper in my mind. At the final linkage point, I stood between the Central Pacific's Jupiter and the Union Pacific's 119, facing each other on the same track where the golden spike was driven. While having my picture taken, I realized I was standing between two engines of connectivity.

I then took the twenty-mile access road back down the hills and again registered the enormity of the landscape. I noticed all the barbed wire, rusted out, stitching the landscape, and sensed the abandonment. Barbed wire was the other great development that led to the closing of the frontier in 1890, at least a century faster than Jefferson had prophesied when sending out the Corps of Discovery. It was a revolutionary technological breakthrough because it allowed great tracts of land to be claimed by settlers—nature taken as property, away from the natives.

In addition to the Transcontinental Railroad and barbed wire, what really enabled the rapid and roughshod conquest of the West was the Homestead Act of 1862. The act provided land grants for farmers and ranchers, along with the railroad land grants and those to establish universities and colleges in the West. The unparalleled number, diversity, and quality of the US university system are largely the result of those grants and a tremendous source of national strength and soft power as foreign students continue to flock to American universities.

As the miles slipped beneath the wheels on Interstate 15 northbound, a critical piece of the cognitive puzzle of my American identity was falling into place. I wandered into Idaho's rolling expanses, on my way to stay in a small motel in the little western town of St. Anthony. Just after sunrise, I resumed along US 20, lumbering alone past the Grand Teton Mountains into West Yellowstone and then into Wyoming and the park. In the cool, fresh air that morning, I began to think again about the dualistic struggle in the American soul. The push of the pioneers across the frontiers of the North American continent was, of course, another link in a chain of endeavors in the American journey. But then I realized that in the first century of the history of the United States, these frontiers were essentially physical; by the end of the twentieth century, they had become predominantly psychological—more moral.

John F. Kennedy, in his acceptance speech for the Democratic nomination the summer before my birth, advised us of that still largely unexplored human domain:

> [W]e stand today on the edge of a New Frontier . . . a frontier of unknown opportunities and perils—a frontier of unfulfilled hopes and threats.
>
> . . . Beyond that frontier are the uncharted areas of science and space, unsolved problems of peace and war, unconquered pockets of ignorance and prejudice, unanswered questions of poverty and surplus.

What Kennedy was telegraphing then was that we ourselves are the ultimate frontier—human nature, right here as much as out there. Then I thought about the moment I stood between those railroad engines of connectivity and something else hit me.

In the early twenty-first century, the United States is confronted with the opportunities and perils of globalization. As I traversed this country that is in many ways itself a continent, traveling the path of its development in reverse, it dawned on me that all of these past endeavors constituted an integral series of events—the result of not just the impulse to surmount an obstacle or respond to a challenge (and Americans are indeed at their best when challenged). Rather, each of these events seems also to have been an answer to a compulsion to connect as much as to conquer, confront, or control—to unite or attach one person or place with another or the past with the future.

America's quest for frontiers has not only been about expansion for its own sake. It has also been about reaching out to something more elemental, even if it seeks constant redefinition. In exhausting its geographic frontiers, the United States transformed itself into a transcontinental power to reconnect with the larger world it once rejected in revolution. In fact, the history of the United States is the history of a country that, in many ways, has become the world's engine of connectivity—in space, in time, and most importantly in the world of ideas. From its very inception, with the signing of the Declaration of Independence, the United States was put on this trajectory. This is America's foremost place in the world, its most basic identity as a nation. And each generation must decide if it is up to the task.

The fate of this nation of nations is, in this way, inextricably linked to the fate of the world, and vice versa. What happens over here matters over there; but what happens over there also matters over here. The tension between control and connectivity still plays out well beyond our borders, which at times explains the clumsiness of our foreign and security policies. Control is a dispensation of power; connectivity is an exercise in gathering strength. One is more about coercion, the other about persuasion. Whenever we act upon the more vertical Old World compulsion to conquer, subdue, overwhelm, annihilate, or control, we belie and betray the promise of the more horizontal New

World opportunity to connect, engage, unite, reconcile, or collaborate. It's what we connect with and to that gives us our exceptional identity.

As I forged ahead, my mind continued to expand as if to match the geographic dimensions in which I now found myself. I realized I was on the verge of greater perspective about what happened in my own experience of 9/11 and what happened after it.

September 11, 2001, was one of those generational moments, like Pearl Harbor or the JFK assassination, when everyone can vividly recall where they were and what they were doing the moment they heard about it. For me, I was leading an Army Civil Affairs team at a field exercise in Hohenfels, Germany. We had just started when the message came over the radio that the exercise was abruptly suspended. We packed into the briefing room to hear the blow-by-blow description of the attacks. When the operations chief, talking about the World Trade Center, said matter-of-factly that the "towers had collapsed," I could hardly register it until we shuffled into the mess hall to watch on TV the surreal images of the planes crashing and the cascading buildings, over and over again. Then there was a moment of eerie silence.

I felt compelled to fill it but could only succeed in thinking, "Welcome to the twenty-first century. The world has come to America—now America must come to the world." But it was with the open hand, I had meant, not the clenched fist.

I believe if we would have responded far differently to 9/11—following the urge to connect rather than control—we would have avoided the strategic blunders that were to come. Terrorism has since bedeviled us because we are suckers for its theater of provocation and media play. Whether driving airplanes into buildings or beheading people, its intent is to incite overreaction. It's bad-guy baiting—and every time it rears its ugly head, we seem to take the bait, responding primarily in a global game of whack-a-mole that degrades our international stature and ultimately our moral power. We get played by responding to the violence with more violence and succeed mostly in alienating the very people we say we're trying to help—only to make the terrorists' case for them.

When I came back from Kosovo in early October, I took up a spacious upstairs apartment owned by a Swedish-South African couple in

Jersey City, New Jersey. They lived downstairs and were professional clowns. To make matters more bizarre, just after bringing down my things from storage in Upstate New York, the day before New Year's Eve, a midnight chimney fire destroyed much of the house and a good many of the things I had just placed in it, including about half of the books I had collected since I was a kid. Good-bye to all that, too.

A couple of weeks later, after searching desperately around the Jersey City waterfront, I saw a high-rise apartment building directly across the Hudson River from the site of the World Trade Center with a banner posting a phone number to call for rental. "To hell with that," I thought, "I'll walk right in." Two weeks later, I had moved into a one-bedroom apartment with a view of the Statue of Liberty about a half mile away—talk about living in metaphors.

A few days before going up to Buffalo to take command of the 402nd Civil Affairs Battalion at the end of January 2002, I watched President Bush, in his Axis of Evil speech, look directly into the television camera and say, "We will deal with Saddam Hussein."

"Oh, shit," I said audibly to no one but myself. "We're going to war."

That is what I told my battalion after the change of command: "We're going to war: Get ready. I'm not sure if it's Afghanistan or Iraq, but before this year is out, we'll know and we'll be going." It was not exactly the most upbeat thing for a new commander to tell his troops, but for a Reserve unit that met one weekend each month and with two or three weeks of annual unit training, there wasn't much time. Actually, they already realized it as much as I did, but there are some things you just have to say anyway.

Most people have little notion of the difficulty of managing a Reserve unit to meet 80 percent of the readiness requirements 10 percent of the time. Reservists have done, or been required to do, things many others would find hard to accept. We have traveled to and from our duty stations at our own expense, purchased things like small two-way radios or GPS devices because the ones issued to us were ineffective or we didn't have any. We have performed a lot of work and training while not on duty—unpaid. For the ten times I had to travel from Jersey City to Buffalo before we mobilized, I paid for my own airfare, rental car, lodging, and so on, with what amounted to about half my drill pay. I also

paid my way to attend command and staff meetings at our higher headquarters outside Washington, DC. If I were ever compensated for the
extra time and expenses in the service of the Army Reserve over thirty
years, I would be at least a hundred thousand dollars richer. Many others could say similar things. And despite the Department of Defense's
Employer Support of the Guard and Reserve office, established in 1972,
unemployment rates for returning Reserve and National Guard members has been two to three times as high as those who leave the active
services. So, although you may question the proficiency of these citizen-soldiers, you can hardly question their dedication.

The job of any commander is to structure his or her people for
success. My first order of business was to get the battalion to understand that things were not going to be as they were in the Balkans,
where about one-third of them had been. Many felt we should deploy
as a whole battalion, but Civil Affairs units were often sliced and diced
rather than sent as a whole. And this time, the teams would have to
operate remotely as part of combat units in geographic areas much
larger, less developed, and more hostile than in Europe.

So my focus was on building these small teams and training them
hard. "I can't guarantee you that we'll deploy as a battalion," I told them,
"but what I can do is my best to make sure the person you're training
with now will be the one you share the foxhole with when we go to
war." I further explained in our newsletter how being in the Reserves
had really changed:

> *Being a Reserve soldier is now a full-time part-time job. Training*
> *and readiness don't just take place during drills, but also*
> *between them. On a personal level, this means, for example,*
> *making sure you are maintaining physical fitness and adminis-*
> *trative readiness, being attentive to current events and reading*
> *up on CA doctrine, and attending schools, language training,*
> *and any other kind of training that improves your readiness to*
> *support the mission. . . . Being a CA soldier is also a job that*
> *requires a high degree of professionalism. In conducting our*
> *mission, we will be judged from many angles—as Reservists, as*
> *members of the military, as Special Operations soldiers, and as*

Americans. How we do things as well as what we do will greatly influence how we are perceived by friend and adversary alike, as well as affect our mission legitimacy.

The other thing I explained to our family support group was how our spouses and families were going to be part of this fight—taking care of the "six" (meaning "six o'clock," or rear area) of our soldiers at home would enable them to concentrate on the "twelve" (meaning "twelve o'clock," or front) of the battlefield. In a complex and dangerous environment, any distractions from that focus on the twelve o'clock position could have dire consequences.

The 402nd Civil Affairs Battalion, whose unit motto is "Provide Order," did a remarkable job to ready itself, working with little guidance and support from the rest of the command or the Army. The noncommissioned officers (NCOs) in particular worked hard to ensure that soldiers were in good physical and medical shape, were well trained on tactical skills and survival techniques, and had their security clearances and other administrative requirements updated.

By August 2002, we had managed to improve our Army readiness rating from about 50 percent to nearly 80 percent in just over six months (or really twelve days, considering we drilled one weekend each month). So, when I then briefed Major General Herbert Altshuler, the commander of the US Army Civil Affairs and Psychological Operations Command, I was able to say with a straight face that, with the battalion readiness exercise we were calling "October Order," we would have the only deployable Reserve Civil Affairs battalion available to his command. That may have rung impressive, but it was actually rather bad news—it meant the rest of the command was in even worse shape. Once we invaded, demand would overtake the Army's—and thus the nation's—capabilities to transition from war to peace and from military to civilian control, because Civil Affairs had not been very well managed over the last few years through the post–Cold War transition and all the deployments in the Balkans. The closer we got to the end of the year, the more it felt like we were paddling up increasing rapids with one oar.

Just before our October exercise, I was at the Fletcher Conference, an annual national security seminar held in Washington in the Ronald Reagan Building. A lot of heavy hitters in the national leadership were there, including cameo appearances by the vice president and the secretary of defense. Chairman of the Joint Chiefs of Staff Richard Myers sat with us at lunch. I also got to meet Army Chief of Staff General Eric Shinseki—who showed remarkable moral courage by telling Congress the truth about how much and how long it would take to stabilize Iraq, then was shown the door to retirement for telling his political masters what they didn't want to hear.

The next morning, there was a panel discussion on whether unilateralism or multilateralism was the best way to approach the world. Congress was about to authorize the use of force in Iraq, so the discussion quickly revolved around whether we would go it alone or obtain a UN Security Council resolution as President Bush's father had. During the discussion, someone had the temerity to ask, "What happens after we take down the regime? What do we do then?" One of the panelists answered, "I think it's premature for us to consider that right now," which drew a few gasps. During the break, I explained to a group why some of us found that response so disturbing by telling them the story about how modern Army Civil Affairs got started.

"Once upon a time there was a guy named Roosevelt and a guy named Churchill, and they had a series of meetings that ended up in the summer of 1941 with the Atlantic Charter, which listed the war aims of the Allies in World War II. Two of them were US contributions—one was the UN and another was 'unconditional surrender.'

"The War Department, as it was then known, did what we now call mission analysis. If there's going to be unconditional surrender, they assumed, then there's going to be an occupation and, with that, military government similar to what had been done after the war with Spain, and then in Germany at the end of the last war with a colonel named MacArthur, as explained in the manual they wrote in 1925 based on what they learned. So they got out that manual, updated it, and started writing the plans for how we were going to administer the occupied areas of Europe and Germany. And they started looking around for people with public administration backgrounds who spoke French,

Italian, and German and trained them up in places like Camp Detrick, Maryland; Camp Rucker, Alabama; and Camp Ord, California.

"And this all got started a few months before Pearl Harbor," I told my astonished listeners, other attendees who knew next to nothing about Civil Affairs.

"Folks, we are in a lot of trouble, because we're only a couple of months or so before the president pulls the trigger. I guess we just don't do what his dad called 'the vision thing' anymore. And I understand someone [meaning the SecDef] said we live in uncertain times, so we can't plan that far ahead. Well, if I were a Las Vegas bookie in the summer of 1941—with Hitler at the gates of Moscow and Britain on its knees, with the Japanese holding China by the throat, and with only one major, vibrant democracy left in the world—I wouldn't have put my money on the Allies. I would say those were pretty uncertain times, too."

Shaking my head as we returned to the conference, I repeated: "We are in a *lot* of trouble."

After a couple of false starts to be prepared to mobilize for Afghanistan, the unit administrator called me at the end of the day before Thanksgiving. We had received the prepare-to-deploy order, with less than half the regulatory thirty days to have the unit at its mobilization station at Fort Bragg, North Carolina. The mission was going to be in Iraq.

From top to bottom and start to finish in Operation Iraqi Freedom, we weren't structured for success. After we got to Fort Bragg, staying in World War II–era barracks at a remote location we called Splinter City, we were shoved through routine "check-the-block" force-protection training that a lot of us also called "cover-your-ass-chicken-shit." We were being processed but not prepared. To make matters worse, although the 402nd was the first Army Civil Affairs battalion to mobilize and deploy for war in Iraq, only half the battalion was initially brought forward—sliced and diced—as part of the initial Civil Affairs task force, because the Army did not prioritize Civil Affairs among the troop units it was sending first into Kuwait under the Time-Phased Force Deployment List (TPFDL, or "tip-fiddle").

For some time, our higher Civil Affairs headquarters had been raiding the battalion for everything from weapons to vehicles to some of our best NCO leadership. This went on right up to before the start of the war. I fought a lot of this, mostly behind the scenes. Sometimes I won; sometimes I lost. But Brigadier General Jack Kern, our Civil Affairs task force commander, eventually got the point: He was taking away critical tactical leadership of troops that were going to be exposed to a lot more of the fighting than his. So he finally had his staff ease off.

After nearly two weeks at Fort Bragg, the Army Special Operations commander held a town hall meeting with the first group of Army Reserve Civil Affairs preparing to go to Iraq. He got an earful, including a barrage of complaints about things like the shoddy check-the-block treatment, or why we hadn't received the same late-model body armor as other Special Operations soldiers. I sat and listened. Then, when things hit a peak, I raised my hand.

"Sir," I explained to him, "I think what these people are asking you to do is make a key decision. Either Fort Bragg is a no-shit mobilization station for Reserve Component Special Operations Forces, or it isn't. If it is, then you have to commit the right kind of resources to that capability. If it isn't, then you should send us to places like Fort Dix [New Jersey] or Fort McCoy [Wisconsin]. They mobilize Reserves there for a living. That's the message here." He thanked me for the point, then quickly left. Then we got an ass-chewing from our own chain of command. As we broke, I asked General Altshuler if I could have a word with him on the side.

"Sir, you know me well enough to know that I don't pull any punches. Do you remember our briefing in August, and what my 'Issues' slide said? It had only one thing on it—'Mission Clarity.' Give us some idea what country we are likely going to be in, Iraq or Afghanistan, what Civil Affairs missions we might have—anything to help us focus our training. You couldn't tell me then but just got finished telling us now how we should have been doing country and cultural and other 'battle-focused' training, because as you know we're hired by the Army, more than anything, to provide the commanders we support with an understanding of the places we're in. Well, the other day, I went over to the training officer at the [Army

Just below the border between Kuwait and Iraq about three weeks before the start of Operation Iraqi Freedom. Note the sign.

Special Operations] schoolhouse here to get someone to provide us the classified country and cultural briefing on Iraq, and he told us he didn't have time."

Altshuler was less than pleased with the calling out. But I shared my soldiers' frustration. We had done our best to get ready to go to war, but it was clear at that moment that it was far from enough. We had not been structured for success. We were heading into a real mess, and I knew it but could do little about what would impact us greatly on the ground but was more and more beyond our span of control. And I knew that with foresight rather than hindsight.

In Iraq, we were not looking to connect, consider what had happened to us on 9/11, and understand what we were doing in that part of the world. Reaching out with the closed fist rather than the open hand, we responded instead to the primordial urge to control what we feared by annihilating it without first comprehending what we intended to destroy. It was vengeance, not justice, that we were really looking for—an unexceptional act by an exceptional people. As Goethe put it, "Nothing is more terrible than to see ignorance in action."

Conquest and control are illusory and temporary. Connectivity and compassion are liberating and lasting. The first demands physical bravery, the second moral courage. Real connectivity is more psychological than physical. Technology can only enable and enhance it, because it ultimately comes from human interaction. Civil–military operations are a process of synthesis more than analysis—it's about bringing things together rather than breaking them down, fusion rather than fission. As in nuclear physics, that is ultimately more powerful and generates more desirable effects, but it is much harder to do. It is far easier to divide than to bring together.

Neither peace nor war is an imperative. They are choices. In going out to smite monsters more invented than real, we succumbed to fear and anger rather than exercise courage and foresight. In doing so after 9/11, we heeded the lesser angels of our nature instead of facing up to them.

Waiting patiently in vain for a full eruption of Old Faithful, I climbed back on the Dyna. Storm clouds were gathering, so I donned, for the first time during the trip, my rain suit. I was hoping to get through Yellowstone before the storm hit, but it was too late: Man and machine were caught in a torrential downpour as we crossed the Continental Divide.

CHAPTER 11

THE GREAT PLAINS: REAL AMERICANS

After leaving Yellowstone, I followed a circuitous and sometimes treacherous route along US 212 over the Rocky Mountains in Wyoming. As in Yosemite, it was not quite what I expected in June. As the Wide Glide pulled higher and higher into the cool, clear mountains, the road narrowed, laden heavier with ice and snow. By the time I reached the summit looking at the Bear's Tooth at over twelve thousand feet, the meter-high snowbank on the twisty little roadway narrowed to one lane, then a few feet. At various points along the switchbacks, I glanced down sheer drops of up to a thousand feet, feeling a trace of vertigo. But the scenery I gained access to was breathtaking: I could see through the peaks of the Rockies as far as thirty to forty miles to other mountain ranges.

Gradually negotiating the twists and turns coming back down for nearly eighty miles until reaching the wide open spaces of Montana, I limped, exhausted, into Billings. The next morning, my filthy filly ran us beneath prodigious cloud formations filling the Big Sky and dumping more rain. I aimed that day for Deadwood, South Dakota, after stopping to take a look at Devils Tower, called Mato Tipila by the Sioux and arguably the greatest of natural sculptures. I took great pleasure in reading the Lakota legend on how Mato Tipila was formed as a place for the natives to find refuge from bears as well as a place to worship the Great Spirit in solitude.

Then I drove along windy roads through nearby Sturgis, where every August thousands of bikers gather at the largest bikefest in the world. In Deadwood, I had a chance to clean up and catch up, mentally and physically, especially after what I had just seen and experienced.

Before all that, I had stopped off at Little Bighorn Battlefield National Monument to punch a popular history ticket. It had turned out to be much more than a ticket punch.

Most of us know the story. On June 25 and 26, 1876, Lieutenant Colonel George Armstrong Custer and five companies of his 7th US Cavalry Regiment were routed at the hands of the Plains Indians—a combination of warriors from the Sioux, Cheyenne, and Arapaho tribes who hunted, fished, and gathered all year rather than stay on the reservation in winter, refusing to depend on US government handouts for their livelihood.

The battle on the bluffs and ridges overlooking the Lakota encampments on the Little Bighorn River became the iconic event of the long struggle between European and Native Americans, entering into folklore as a sort of Wild West Armageddon. Often thought of on a deadly scale of thousands, the battle actually claimed the lives of about 260 US cavalrymen and 60 to 100 Native warriors. As the group I joined gazed out into the open fields where the battle took place, we received an illuminating presentation from a park ranger, who brought it all to life with his blow-by-blow rendering of events and colorful descriptions of the personalities. More captivating, however, was his insightful explanation of the larger circumstances leading to this inevitable encounter.

Understanding the Battle of the Little Bighorn as a link in a chain of events helps us understand the complex history of a centuries-long clash of civilizations that peaked after the Civil War, when settlers resumed their vigorous westward movement, driven on by the railroad, the Homestead Act, and fresh waves of immigrants mostly from Europe. The US government signed a treaty at Fort Laramie, Wyoming, with the Lakota, Cheyenne, and other tribes of the Great Plains in 1868. A large area in eastern Wyoming and western South Dakota was designated a "permanent" Indian reservation. Thought of as "bad lands," they had no apparent value at the time—there was no gold, no oil, nor could they be farmed or used for grazing cattle.

As long as the tribes stayed put, the government claimed it would protect them "against the commission of all depredations by the people of the United States" as well as provide food. The slogan that it was "cheaper to feed than to fight the Indians" masked the intent to make them comply with the government's terms. Food insecurity was also frequently a favorite tactic to control, manipulate, or subjugate populations in the Balkans, Iraq and Afghanistan, and Africa. "If you control the food supply, you control the population," the tall young guide explained.

The arrangement with the Great Plains tribes did not last long. In 1874, as the country plunged into the Long Depression after the collapse of an overheated postwar economy, gold was discovered in the Black Hills, the heart of the reservation, drawing thousands of eager prospectors. Undermanned in the wake of postwar demobilization and with no police forces on the frontier, the US Army was unable to stave off the encroaching settlers. Efforts to purchase the Black Hills from the tribes (whose culture had no concept of contractual land ownership) met with failure. In growing defiance, the Lakota and Cheyenne left the reservation and resumed raids on white settlers, partly out of anger and partly out of desperation for provisions—most of the buffalo and other wildlife they used for more than food were eradicated. In December 1875, the Commissioner of Indian Affairs ordered them to return to the reservation before the end of January—in the middle of winter—or be treated as hostile forces. President Ulysses Grant (who knew more about war than diplomacy) ordered an expeditionary cavalry group to enforce the order. The rest, as they say, is history.

The Army's defeat at Little Bighorn occurred as European Americans celebrated the centennial of their own independence. Called a massacre in the press, it sent shock waves throughout the country, eliciting a military response eventually leading to Wounded Knee in 1890. Custer, a flamboyant and popular war hero, was promoted three grades posthumously to major general and martyred with his men. "It was a kind of 9/11," the guide said in his Texas drawl. As occurred a century and a quarter later, Americans experienced media-hyperbolized shock and anger. "We asked the same thing then as now—how could this have happened?'"

There are, of course, major differences. For one, the militaries were dissimilar. As at the Alamo, 44 percent of the nearly nine hundred poorly fed, poorly trained, ill-equipped, largely illiterate, and poorly motivated cavalry troopers at Little Bighorn were foreign born. A plurality was from Germany. Over one-third of the US military in the nineteenth century did not speak English, making it hard to communicate orders. The military force responding to 9/11, on the other hand, was highly professional. Even though it was also a voluntary force, it was the total opposite in training and equipment, technical and tactical proficiency, logistics, and motivation. Whereas the Indian Wars could be described as a counterinsurgency campaign, the US Army possessed clear superiority to an enemy who could not run and hide on the Great Plains, as Al Qaeda did for years in central Asia's vast mountain matrices.

Besides, in the nineteenth century, the United States considered the entire Native American population the enemy. It was total war, thus invoking a strategy of annihilation. It was only a matter of time until the US government would get around to subduing the tribes. The Indian campaigns, in fact, affirmed the American way of war in the use of firepower to destroy everything, including the civilian base, as Sherman had done in Georgia and the US Air Force would later do in Germany, Japan, and North Vietnam. Given the lack of moral restraint in public and global opinion back then, there was no need to employ hearts-and-minds tactics or precision-guided munitions, even if they were available.

The US approach also owed to cultural chauvinism. Most European Americans felt Native Americans were primitive savages who needed to be civilized and Christianized, although more enlightened Americans like George Washington thought white men could learn a few things from these nature-loving peoples and should integrate them into American society. But this was not to be: Native Americans had an even lower status than black slaves—despite the 14th Amendment— until the Indian Citizenship Act of 1924. Before that, they were not even considered persons, let alone citizens.

In such extreme forms of superciliousness, nonwhite Americans have been perceived as morally if not physically inferior. Just as epithets like *rag heads* and *hajjis* provided a convenient caricature for Islamic jihadists after we had dispensed with the Soviets, *blanket niggers* provided a bogeyman to unite the nation after the defeat of the South. A dynamic of hate makes it easier for one race or group of people to justify destroying another. Mark Twain was appalled by all the unabashed bigotry: "There are many humorous things in the world, among them the white man's notion that he is less savage than the other savages."

One reason Americans have struggled to manage their narrow-mindedness is because of their dualistic thinking and obsession with bad guys—and not just those abroad. What has stood most in the way of progress or right-mindedness at critical times is a lack of public self-honesty. That requires moral courage—and we were certainly short of that as we looked to lash out in 2002–2003 much as we did in 1876. Then again, truth is always the first and greatest casualty of war. Many politicians and pundits love demonizing fellow citizens who don't share their worldview—even accusing them of not being real Americans. It stirs up public passions, detracts from the real issues (as well as one's own shortcomings), and is low in intellectual overhead. It puts the accused on the defensive, guilty until proven innocent, with little or no real evidence. At best, it's reckless.

When your own identity is in doubt, as Pope Francis noted, you look for affirmation by discrediting other people. Real identity, he said, "comes through transcendence, diversity, and vision"—a list to which I would add humility and the willingness to step outside of yourself, especially by taking that mental journey and connecting with and learning more about the world around you. Ignorance-based beliefs are not a form of identity but a cheap substitute for it. They're just an empty attitude. Identity, in turn, is not something that's given or recited—it's learned and earned.

This tendency to demonize anyone we don't understand explains a lot of the overwhelming groupthink leading up to the war in Iraq. Anyone who didn't think we should send out the posse to bring down bad guys like Saddam was just not a real American. Yet, my gnawing sense was that we weren't thinking this thing all the way through.

Like ghosts returning to the plain, the Indian Memorial at
Little Bighorn came about 120 years after the monument to the
7th Cavalry, as if to remind us of another heritage.

"It ain't what you don't know that gets you into trouble," Mark Twain advised. "It's what you know for sure that just ain't so."

For the first two months at Camp Arifjan in Kuwait, we endured a sort of *sitzkrieg*—a sarcastic pun on blitzkrieg that Allied troops used while waiting over six months for the Germans to attack France in 1939–1940. We were doing whatever we could to prepare ourselves, mentally and physically, for what we knew was coming. We trained and trained some more. We went on power runs, wore body armor in the sun to acclimatize ourselves, checked and rechecked equipment in numerous precombat inspections, and held chemical attack drills. Having no other sources of training for our own Civil Affairs work, we researched, prepared, and gave ourselves classes on everything from desert health and hygiene to Iraqi and Islamic culture, Arabic, and the use of interpreters. We rested and read books, in part to escape our unshakable uneasiness.

One book I reread was Barbara Tuchman's *The Guns of August*, about how the Great Powers stumbled into World War I. I noticed

Twain's rhyme between how European statesmen and commanders were trapped in their own military mobilization timetables in 1914 and how enabler units like Civil Affairs, crucial to winning the peace, were chewed up by the TPFDL. The manipulation of the TPFDL was to deploy the maximum combat forces to deny Saddam time to prepare his defenses and get off as soon as possible to what General Tommy Franks called a "rolling start." So we waited for war from late January, through February, and into March 2003. Things took on their own momentum, and Civil Affairs once again was more and more a side-show, even though Franks listed civil–military operations as a key line of operation for Operation Iraqi Freedom.

Whenever the war plan was briefed, the planners gave a politically correct pitch on Phase Four—post-conflict stability and reconstruction. In addition to predicting that the Iraqis would hail us as liberators after only brief hostilities, it said we would turn over all responsibilities to the Office of Reconstruction and Humanitarian Assistance and the new Iraqi government, lean on Iraqi oil exports to fund reconstruction as well as the UN Oil-for-Food program, and go home—the same kind of short, sharp war narrative heard in 1914.

"Yeah, right, sir," I leaned over and whispered into General Kern's ear. "And the Great Pumpkin is going to rise up over the pumpkin patch and bring toys and goodies to all the children," I continued, referring to the Charlie Brown Halloween movie.

I had been reading the plans for Phase Four, which we were told we weren't going to execute (and many later claimed didn't exist). I also read classified reports from various agencies warning of an insurgency to follow after the fall of the regime—the training of irregular forces called the Fedayeen Saddam who were loyal to the Ba'athist government of Saddam Hussein, the deliberate flooding of the marshes in the south where the Marsh Arabs lived, the wholesale release of more than fifty thousand prisoners from jails, and the proliferation of small arms just before we invaded. All of these actions were taken in order to wreak havoc and instability for the invaders.

In one of my sidebar discussions with the planners, I surmised that "Saddam is a consummate survivor as well as a consummate son of a bitch. He may be an evil bastard, but he's smart enough to know he

can't take us head-on and win. He has something else up his sleeve—
he's learned something from the last war. After we take him down, he's
going to make holding the ground very costly. That's what we ought to
be paying attention to—what happens after we've done regime take-
down." Others thought the same, but to speak up about it was heresy.

Then came the most damning example of what some of us realized just wasn't so. In the Oktoberfest-size mess tent at Camp Arifjan
on February 5, we sat transfixed to the live broadcast of Secretary of
State Colin Powell's speech making the case for war in Iraq before the
UN Security Council. After a few minutes, I blurted out, "He doesn't
believe what he's saying."

"Why's that, sir?" one of the younger officers asked.

"I've spent many years with Toastmasters, and I can say he is not
speaking with conviction. His body language is giving it away. Look at
how his eyes are shifting, as well as his body weight, back and forth.
He's also perspiring. He's nervous. That's what amateur speakers do,
and Colin Powell is no amateur. Besides, his case for war doesn't even
square with his own doctrine."

More than most others, the American soldier needs to know the
reason why he or she is fighting. I was still in desperate search of it
until our last meeting with the assembled half battalion, before it split
again to link up with the British and Marine units they would go to war
with. One of our sergeants came up with it, plain and simple.

"Sir, we've come here to give these people their country back."

That became our tagline, to which I elaborated, "I know we don't
have a very explicit mission order—we're doing nation-building-on-
the-fly here, but you all have been in Civil Affairs long enough to figure out what to do. Just go out there and help these people take care
of themselves and turn things over to civil organizations and local
authorities as soon as you can. Do your best—that's all I ask." Recalling
what I had learned as a lieutenant, I added, "You have to do only two
things and I'll have your back 100 percent—focus on your mission and
take care of your troops." A few days later, Operation Iraqi Freedom
commenced.

After the docent's presentation at Little Bighorn and walking the
grounds for a short while, I climbed back on the Harley, mentally and

Even in the midst of war, I exhorted the troops to maintain physical as well as mental fitness because "this will be a marathon, not a sprint." Here I set the example at our makeshift camp gym at Tallil Air Base, in southern Iraq, in early April 2003.

emotionally agitated by what it all brought back. As we did in response to Little Bighorn, in the Global War on Terror we sent out the cavalry to chase down the Indians. What this former cavalryman witnessed in Iraq was now making more sense—I was connecting the dots between my own experience with the collective experience of my country. The steady pace of the Wide Glide on the twisty, breezy highway in Montana leading into Wyoming was somehow tempering the velocity of onrushing thoughts and memories from the first few months of the war. With hardly anyone else on the road, I was again alone with my recollections, as if the Dyna were acting like a time machine.

Our men and women were right behind the combat units as they hurtled forward, sometimes finding ourselves mixed up in the fighting with the Saddam Fedayeen and others whose handiwork some of us saw up close. During the Battle of An Nāṣirīyah, the Fedayeen herded women and children into fire zones to be caught purposely in the crossfire and used for propaganda value against the invaders. The scenes made the maiming of the young boy Tony Sherman and I saw in Bosnia look innocent in comparison.

For the first six months the 402nd was in three places in southern Iraq—in Basrah with the British 1st Armoured Division (which included the celebrated 7th Armoured Brigade, known as the "Desert Rats"); in An Nāṣirīyah, halfway to Baghdad; and farther north in Al Kut (the last two with the 1st Marine Division). My sergeant major and I went back to Kuwait to pick up the rest of the battalion two months later, integrating old and new faces into the operation. We jury-rigged the third detachment for Al Kut, mostly by gutting the headquarters section, to cover the ground we were assigned. Command, control, and communications were feckless. The detachments and teams worked independently, hardly seeing each other—just as I thought they would, except worse.

I camped out with the detachment deploying to An Nāṣirīyah at the foot of the Ziggurat of Ur, a huge, capped-off pyramid that is one of the world's great treasures and is located in one of the first cities in history (and a source of the word root for *urban*). The complex also contains the site of the House of Abraham, the founding father of three of the world's religions. It seemed ironic that we were there to try to help the Iraqis reestablish something their ancestors started before any of us, more than four thousand years ago—civilization as we know it today.

After waves of combat units passed through An Nāṣirīyah, with Task Force Tarawa pushing out the last of the Fedayeen fighters, we did our best to help deal with civilian casualties. Then we settled down with Marine Reserve units like the 2nd Battalion, 25th Marine Regiment in "An Nas," comprised mostly of first responders from New York. A group of NYPD cops was helping to reorganize and train the local police—exactly the right kind of guys. We and the Marines were working hard under harsh and dangerous conditions to help stabilize things, but we were more in the minority as troops whose mission had nothing to do with engaging the population poured in. We had what the Army called embedded media, including CNN, Fox News, and major newspapers during the first month or so. They dwindled as the combat operation wound down in May, even though I told Scott Pelley of *60 Minutes* that "our work has just begun."

We knew we were in a honeymoon period with the Iraqis, and if we didn't show them signs of improvement in their daily lives pronto it would be over soon. I expressed that concern to *PBS NewsHour*'s Elizabeth Farnsworth. Standing in front of our civil–military operations center (CMOC) in An Nāṣirīyah, tapping on my Soviet-era tanker's watch, I said to her off camera, "Elizabeth, the meter's ticking. We're wearing out our welcome here, and when these people figure out they're not going to be driving Cadillacs to the 7-Eleven in six months as they seem to believe, they'll be pissed off. And they're going to take it out on my kids."

"What do you need?" she asked.

"I need the rest of my government to show up. Tell the American people the military can't do this job by itself, nor should it. We need help with reconstruction. Lots of it. Now."

Too few of us understood what was at stake at that moment. To double the distribution of electricity in southern Iraq, our detachment took it upon itself to find a way to hook up a seventy-ton distribution transformer from the largest power plant in southern Iraq and miraculously found relatively intact on the other side of An Nāṣirīyah. Although the Iraqis could get our hands on two thirty-five-ton cranes to lift it, the only thing sturdy enough to transport this gigantic box was one of the Army's Heavy Equipment Transporters (or HETs). As our little dirt camp at Tallil airfield sprouted into a huge, built-up logistics base, dozens of these half-million-dollar tractor-trailers began running in and out, sometimes with nothing on them. Surely we could get one for at least a day or two.

It turned out to be a much more daunting feat than we thought. When we first occupied Tallil, the only other Army unit there was the 377th Area Support Command, a Reserve logistics unit commanded by Major General Jack Stultz, who would later command the Army Reserves. Stultz got it. He understood our mission and its importance. At the morning and evening stand-up meetings in a dusty old Army tent, I identified opportunities to deliver humanitarian supplies or perform some kind of infrastructure work, like fixing a collapsed road or canal. He would simply turn to one of his staff and say, "Get with Colonel Holshek and see how you can help him out."

Unfortunately, after the 377th had gone to the north, as I saw in Eastern Slavonia, the administrators had moved in. The HETs could only be used for "mission essential" work (although the combat phase was over). It meant getting authorization from a one-star general back in Kuwait whose sole purpose was to lord over them. So I arranged a small convoy to drive us nearly four hours to give him the "Captain Kangaroo" briefing explaining the obvious: We get the HETs; we get the transformer hooked up. We double the electricity in southern Iraq; we make a lot of people happy. Happy people don't shoot at soldiers or support those who do.

Once again, we were turned away. It was not "mission essential." Risking insubordination, I hammered the general with questions: "Sir, what the hell could be more 'mission essential' right now than stabilizing Iraq?" Finally, in exasperation, I asked him, "Are we soldiers or just bureaucrats in uniforms?" He threw us out of his office and told us never to come back.

For nearly three months, we kept trying. Ironically, we found a heavy-enough equipment transporter in Basrah, owned by an Iranian contractor. We got an NGO to finance it.

There are dozens of stories like this, but they all point to the same thing: As seen in Bosnia, the World's Richest Government with the World's Most Powerful Military was sending a clear message to the population, transcending language and culture, that we really didn't care about them. As in Bosnia, it was about us and not about them. Ours were, at best, sins of omission.

By that point, the US military was starting to wear out its welcome. The narrative that we were occupiers and not liberators was taking hold. By then, the radical young Shi'ite cleric Muqtadā al-Ṣadr was stirring up trouble around areas like ours in Iraq, exhorting his followers to rise up against the invaders and kill them, while Sunni insurgents roused in other nearby areas. The die had already been cast. The insurgency would have probably happened regardless, because of the paucity of governance below the Baghdad level, the divisiveness among tribes and sectarian groups, and Arab distrust of Westerners, but not to the intensity it eventually reached. Those first few months were the war's most decisive time, not the surge a few years later. What we did—or failed to do—cost both Americans and Iraqis horribly, and it was not all the fault of the politicians, as some in the Army had said about Vietnam.

Fortunately, things were still relatively stable in our area because we had been making a bit of progress in many of the other public service areas I mentioned. We had managed, in our partnership with the Iraqis, to get the police, firefighters, and courts back to work, the streetlights turned on, the markets and banks open, the garbage picked up, and provincial and municipal governments working, with the help of the TV station.

A couple of weeks after our arrival in An Nāṣirīyah, it became apparent to me that I had to reach out to the one person to whom most Iraqis looked for information and guidance, especially in times like these. In a Shi'ite province like Thi Qar, that would be the imam. To understand the sectarian division in Islam, you need to understand that, in essence, Sunnis believe in the caliph, the Islamic leader decided upon by consensus of the faithful, while the Shi'ites believe in the imam, his divinely ordained counterpart from the family of the Prophet.

After a few weeks of seeking an audience with Shaikh Muhammad Baqir al-Nasiri through the networking of my local assistant, Adel, I had my first meeting at his residence. An elderly, white-haired, bespectacled gentleman, he reported directly to Grand Ayatollah al-Sayyid Ali al-Husayni al-Sistani, the senior imam in Iraq and caretaker of Shi'ism's holiest of shrines in Al-Najaf. The imam understood some English, but his son spoke it quite well. I noticed the many books on many different subjects and languages on the shelves. These were learned people.

At our first meeting, I explained to Shaikh al-Nasiri that the reason I came to him was that it seemed to me that the greatest damage done by all these wars—with Iran, Desert Storm, and Saddam's reprisal after that, and of course this one—was not physical but psychological. This was a traumatized population. Their minds were where most of the rehabilitation needed to take place. "No doubt these people will eventually rebuild their homes and towns," I told him. "As you are the caretaker of these people's souls, however, I must seek your advice on what we can do in our limited capacity and short time here to help these people begin to rebuild their lives. At the same time, I think it's right and best to keep you informed of what we're doing."

"Yes," he replied, "I've seen you on An Nāṣirīyah television, telling us to be patient and of your confidence that, as the people who built Ur, we can rebuild our homes and towns. But it will take time. The people know you as *Shway Shway* [Arabic for "step by step" or "slow down"] because you're very fond of using those terms when you talk."

"Yes, sir," I replied, "I think that managing expectations is our most important task at hand right now. There seems to be the perception, as people are saying here, that being the people who put a man on the moon, Americans have 'the staff of Moses' [a local metaphor for omnipotent power]. If their expectations are too high and we can't deliver what they think they want when they want it, then they will be disappointed, and it could bring even more unrest and suffering. This is where I think we can help each other."

In this way I was empowering him—but he was also empowering us. The imam shaped public opinion there by what he said at his sermon every Friday afternoon. Over time, he and I developed a relationship of trust through open, honest dialogue. Even if we occasionally did not share the same political opinions, we agreed on humanitarian and development matters. The whole of the province soon knew that every Tuesday evening at seven o'clock we met at his residence. We chatted amiably, and I made it clear that we had no interest in cultural conversion or installing American-style democracy. Our message was simple and in two parts—"We have come here to give you back your country; once you take it, we can leave." I avoided discussing religious issues, until one day he casually asked about my personal beliefs and my view of Islam.

I showed him my dog tags—"Roman Catholic"—then recounted a speech by John Paul II at the UN Economic and Social Council (ECOSOC) in 1995. Calling for greater tolerance of and by religions as well as dialogue among them, he noted in an unprecedented remark that there are many paths to the truth. I also recalled being in Jerusalem ten years earlier with my friend Father Gregory, standing within a mile of the Wailing Wall, the Dome of the Rock, and the Church of the

Holy Sepulcher—three of the most sacred sites to religions followed by nearly half of the world's population. Despite how close the sites were in mythological as well as physical terms, so many followers couldn't get past the literal meanings of their symbols, causing much unnecessary tension.

"My personal opinion," I shared with him, "is that if you are a true follower of your faith, then your path to the truth is as legitimate as mine, and we all wind up in the same place. Besides, all the great religions teach the Golden Rule—do to others as you would have them do to you."

In a sense, it was the same kind of message Chief Seattle may have conveyed in his storied letter to the Great Father, President Lincoln: "There is but one god; we are brothers after all."

A few days later, Adel came to me at our CMOC with a look of astonishment on his face. He told me he had just received a phone call that the imam would appreciate it if I could join him at Friday prayers. "I've never heard of such a thing," Adel (who was Sunni) told me.

Sitting at the imam's right hand in front of thousands of worshipers, I heard him refer to me as a "brother in faith." It was one of the most exhilarating and moving moments in my life.

Then Adel presented me with a dare: "If you or any of your soldiers were to go out on the streets, to the market, and get out of your vehicles, take off the body armor, and simply walk out among the crowd, nothing would happen to you. And if anyone tried to do something, the people would form a wall around you, to protect you." So the sergeant major and I went to the weekly market and did just that. We were greeted as if we were celebrities, people coming up to shake our hands and, of course, tell us their problems. We continued to do it until we left.

After returning to the States, I told this story to a colleague with the Defense Science Board conducting a summer study on force protection. Then I asked, "Josh, have you ever thought of civil–military operations as the most cost-effective form of force protection?" He didn't think that was going to fly, because it was too hard to measure the effects.

Just as we were gaining effectiveness in southern Iraq by building relationships, we received orders to turn our areas over to our NATO allies, the Italians and the Poles, right away and wait for further orders. That did not go very well—not due to any fault of our allies, but the Iraqis there had learned to trust us, with great effort on both sides. It takes a long time and a lot of interpersonal work to build trust; it takes time to transfer it. Trust is the most important commodity in a people-centric war, humanitarian work, or peacebuilding. Without it you can't restore or build civil society.

For some of us in the battalion, the wait for what came next went on for more than a month. With no mission clarity, the burgeoning question for our soldiers in the field and their families back home was "When are we done here?" The weight of this question reached obsessive proportions and presented a major leadership challenge, which was understandable, considering what we had already gone through. We didn't know what was coming up next and what our mission really was or what the "end state" looked like. We were attached to other units but not really part of them. And we didn't know when we would be done in Iraq.

So we sat around again—more sitzkrieg—but this time in the combat zone. In my personal experience monograph about my command of the 402nd written at the Army War College a few years later, I estimated that of the approximately 36,500 man-days that the battalion spent of its year of boots on the ground, more than 12,000, or about one-third, were spent waiting on or between operational missions. No wonder mission focus was hard to maintain.

By the end of August, with disciplinary problems breaking out, I went all the way up the chain to General Ricardo Sanchez, Combined Joint Task Force 7 (CJTF-7) commander, through Brigadier General Kern in Baghdad, and stated that the battalion should redeploy to home station if it had no real mission. CJTF-7 had ordered units like ours to freeze in place as it considered what next to do with us. I recommended that—regardless of whether the battalion would go home or to another mission in Iraq—the most prudent course of action would be to reconstitute as each detachment came off-line, in order to bring the battalion back up to full combat effectiveness. We needed to reorganize, replace, service, or issue new equipment; refresh combat and other tactical skills; and address long-neglected personnel issues like pay problems. Some needed stress counseling, but everyone needed a rest. The most logical place to do this was Kuwait, where the facilities we needed for all of these things were located.

My simple charts notwithstanding, the proposal must have made too much sense. Three times it was rejected. We eventually got orders to move north to support the 2nd Brigade Combat Team of the 4th Infantry Division north of Baghdad. After more wasted time, we hobbled into Camp Arifjan in September, where we had started in Kuwait, and were told to reconstitute in three weeks. Morale was now at rock-bottom. This was made-up work as far as the troops were concerned, and of all places it was in "Indian country"—Diyala province, the Triangle of Death of rising sectarian violence and insurgency. For my soldiers, going into strange territory to perform what was now one of the most dangerous jobs on the battlefield for only three months was madness. Conspiracy theories and dissension sprouted like weeds. Although mission focus was still the priority, these self-generated issues turned out to be a great distraction.

As Rob Schultheis wrote in *Waging Peace*, about Civil Affairs in Iraq, "CA is all about continuity, building up personal relationships and building lasting institutions that will survive far into the future, and you can't do that when you use CA teams as QRFs, quick reaction forces, plugging them in wherever things got bad and then pulling them out and sending them somewhere else as the fortunes of war shift." This was the greatest abuse and biggest misunderstanding of Civil Affairs. This short-term, mission-order, tactical approach to its employment is likewise detrimental to any attempt to win the peace.

When we first arrived in Kuwait, General Kern and others, including yours truly, proposed that Civil Affairs be employed under a "terrain management" model. The CA brigades and battalions would be assigned geographically by region and province for the entire duration of their deployment, regardless of which maneuver units came and went. This would focus the Phase Four operation on addressing the causes of conflict instead of the bad guys and enable us to build relationships and trust with the population and many players there.

We would also become resident area experts who could help stabilize things. We drew this idea from how Civil Affairs was used in postwar Germany and Japan.

Instead, Civil Affairs was simply thrown in with all the other combat-support operations done by force multipliers. Even NGOs were seen as force multipliers, as enunciated in Colin Powell's statements about them in Afghanistan before our deployment to Iraq. My experience suggests that the real problem with Army Civil Affairs is that it has not been optimally organized, populated, trained, educated, and resourced to perform its increasingly strategically relevant mission—and much of that has been self-inflicted. "For the sake of the young CA soldiers who have done and continue to do magnificent work," I later wrote in a War College paper, "in spite of and not because of their stars, senior leaders in the CA community need to do more to structure them for success and reinforce rather than punish their good deeds."

Contemplating what happened in Diyala Province, I rode into the Black Hills—the last home of the Plains tribes and where Mount Rushmore is dedicated to the European American "Great Fathers." At Deadwood, I conducted my own, two-day reconstitution before resuming operations across the Great Plains. In 1876, the thriving frontier town of about two thousand offered many conveniences normally found in bigger towns back East. Named for the dead trees constantly sliding into its gulch, Deadwood was an illegal settlement until Little Bighorn. After the battle, General George Crook's pursuit of the Sioux took pause there, while gamblers and prostitutes moved into the town. It's rather gentrified today, with numerous specialty shops and upscale restaurants instead of saloons and bordellos.

After a short look at Mount Rushmore, I began to make my way toward what I forecasted to be a long and uneventful ride over the prairie—wrong again. South Dakota's landscape unfolded slowly but with surprising variation over the four hundred miles from the foothills of the Rockies in the mountain time zone, across more predictable and nearly endless steppes, then to lush, hilly areas in the central time zone. In just one day, I had gone from a western landscape of open, dry prairie to a greener, lusher topography that was decidedly eastern. As impressed as I was with the hushed, uninhabited enormity of the

Rocky Mountains, the territory once known as the Great American Desert was no less awe inspiring, not really because of its immensity as much as its surprising richness. The Great Plains are anything but plain.

As I took in the expansive grassland home to many of the greatest Native American tribes, I rewound more of my year in Iraq. The 2nd Brigade Combat Team (BCT) made us feel at home in Diyala. For the first time, we enjoyed the full conveniences of an American military base. At Camp Warhorse, just outside Diyala's capital at Baqubah (meaning "Jacob's House"), we lived in containerized "houches," with heating and air conditioning, greeting it all much as I'm sure Crook's cavalry troopers probably saw the modern conveniences at Deadwood. Considering the aforementioned distracters to mission focus, the state of morale, and our relatively short stay in Diyala, the battalion performed remarkably well. This was again due mainly to the excellent NCOs and enlisted soldiers in the battalion. The priority was to support establishment of local security forces. Then came the economy and jobs, internally displaced civilians, preparations for fall 2004 planting, and local diesel and other fuel distribution, education projects, power generation, and water treatment—pretty ambitious expectations for a brigade combat team.

Colonel David Hogg, whom I first met in Kosovo, was the BCT commander. Though a very competent military leader, he was emblematic of the kinetic mind-set dominating the Army. There were some things I took issue with right away. The first was, after taking a look at the CMOC in the center of Baqubah, where one of our detachments lived and worked, I noticed two Tactical Human Intelligence (HUMINT) Teams (THTs) also living and working there. I brought this up during one of the occasional bull sessions we had outside the operations tent after the evening battle update briefing. We both smoked Cubans bought from Iraqi suppliers.

"Bad juju, sir," I told him, taking a puff.

"Why's that?" he asked in surprise. "I get my best intel out of the CMOC."

"Sir, I get that," I said, taking another. "I understand that more than half of your HUMINT comes from operations like ours. But CA can't be seen as intelligence operators—we do information, not intelligence. That's for force protection reasons as well as for reasons of trust and credibility with the population and our civilian partners. Of course we collect information that becomes intelligence, but it just can't be that obvious. It's no wonder we're taking an RPG [rocket-propelled grenade] in the CMOC every week. The word on the street is that the 'CIA' [which is what Iraqis called anyone in the intelligence business] is in the CMOC. Let's keep it discreet: Have the THTs posted here at Warhorse, and we'll make sure our guys debrief them each day, behind the wire, here."

"No way," he shot back. "They're staying put."

Less than a month later, just before Thanksgiving, a truck bomb went off at the police station downtown a couple hundred meters from the CMOC. It cratered a huge hole, flattened an area the size of a football field, killed nearly twenty police officers, and injured a few of our people from the percussion, flying debris, and shards of glass. It made the evening news back home. Two days later, at the morning update, the brigade intelligence officer reported that the primary target of the truck bomber was not the police station. It was the CMOC. Because concrete barriers had gone up a few days before, the truck couldn't maneuver to the entrance. So it went to its secondary target—the police station. I was standing in Hogg's peripheral vision. He glanced over at me and I shrugged my shoulders, as if to tell him, "What can I say?" A couple of days later, the THTs vacated the CMOC.

Another issue I had was how we were responding to the mortar men—insurgents launching mortar rounds from the backs of pickup trucks into our bases in hit-and-run fashion from the villages just outside them. Hogg's response to them was classic firepower—counter-battery fire from 155 mm howitzers or, when available, thousand-pound bombs from fighter aircraft if they happened to be loitering in the area. At another cigar-smoking bull session, I suggested this tactic was counterproductive and that there might be a better way without infuriating half the population.

"Sir, let's get the CA teams to get out on the ground with the infantry platoons and local Iraqi security forces on presence patrols. They can stay out longer, including at night, establish good relations, and show how we can deliver better security than the bad guys. Eventually, they'll tell us when and where the bad guys will be, and we can take them out or round them up."

Hogg first felt it was too risky, which puzzled me. I thought what we were already doing was far riskier. I had already taken three or four dives into a bunker to avoid mortar rounds coming down as close as fifty yards away. Walking across the compound at night to relieve yourself or take a shower had become an adventure more real than any "reality" show. After going back and forth on it during another smoking session, I asked Hogg a simple question: "Sir, what is the battle space?" He gave the standard answer—key terrain, key leaders, and so on. And, of course, the bad guys.

"Not exactly, sir," I replied.

I went on to explain, as Tom Ricks recounted in his book *Fiasco*, "The Iraqi people were the prize in this fight, not the playing field." Because we were no longer in major combat operations and in counterinsurgency, the operational environment had shifted from being predominantly physical to being predominantly psychological. The civilian population was now the center of gravity, and the key terrain was now the five and a half inches between the left and right ears. It wasn't about killing bad guys. "You can kill all the bad guys you want," I told Hogg. "Bottom line is for every bad guy you kill today there will be two more tomorrow. Look, sir, I'm not out here selling Girl Scout cookies—I'm also here to keep our soldiers from getting killed."

I explained how we needed to work within the cultural space: "Two o'clock in the morning, your door bursts open. A bunch of infantry guys rush into the private space of the house—in a society where family honor is the most important thing. They lay you out, as the man of the house, down on the floor with plastic cuffs on. Even if they say, 'Oops, wrong home,' in this society you have no other choice but to seek restitution. So you'll set up a roadside bomb for a hundred bucks—a whole month's salary, but more importantly because your family honor has been compromised, to put it mildly." A lot of times, when we were shot at and missed, it wasn't because the Iraqis were bad shots, as we thought, as much as because they were just trying to balance the honor ledger. As they say in the mafia, "It's nothing personal—it's just business."

But it wasn't our presence in Iraq that was losing hearts and minds—it was our attitude. Again, to channel the proverb "Manners make the man," how you comport yourself in a foreign culture communicates far more—and far more authentically—your attitudes toward locals than even whether you speak their language. *USA Today* and *New York Times* polls taken not long after we had left revealed that majorities in Iraq felt the behavior of American soldiers in Iraq was "arrogant" and "insensitive." As I wrote in a 2004 Cornwallis Group paper:

> *Such troop tactics and behavior, void of cultural sensitivity, were generating "POIs"—"pissed off Iraqis." By early 2004, more commanders were concluding that POIs accounted for many if not most of their casualties, not the "bad guys." Add to this that, while scores of Iraqis were killed, for example, during protests in Fallujah in August 2003 or during the raid in Samarra three months later, hardly any troops were publicly disciplined. This not only made the US look hypocritical on human rights and the rule of law. It implied that Iraqi lives were neither respected nor valued. Then came Abu Ghraib.*

Hogg was a stubborn negotiating partner, but he was no dummy. He eventually adjusted his tactics. Later on, I went with him up to the 4th Infantry Division headquarters in Tikrit (Saddam Hussein's hometown) for a meeting with Major General Ray Odierno, who, like Hogg at the time, was rather kinetically minded. I liked him, and not just because he had the same haircut as I did and was a New York Giants fan. Like Hogg, he listened.

On December 13, 2003, not more than about twenty miles from our location, Operation Red Dawn resulted in the capture of Saddam Hussein. We thought that would be a game changer, but it didn't turn out that way. We weren't too far from finding out when we would be going home, so beyond focusing on our mission and taking care of our troops, the main goal was now just getting everyone across the finish line in the vertical position. That hope was dashed a week later, as the Serious Incident Report read:

> *At approximately 0930 19 Dec 03, while on a logistics/adminis-*
> *tration mission en route from Baqubah, Iraq, a three-HMMWV*
> *convoy from the 402nd Civil Affairs Battalion was involved in*
> *an accident and apparent hostile fire incident. The trail vehicle,*
> *an up-armored two-seat HMMWV, conducted a sudden eva-*
> *sive maneuver, hit a deep cut in the road, causing the vehicle to*
> *flip twice on the pavement. . . . All three soldiers were casual-*
> *ties and evacuated to the local Combat Support Hospital. . . .*
> *SPC Charles Bush, who was thrown from the vehicle, was pro-*
> *nounced dead of massive physical trauma caused by multiple*
> *wounds.*

The news was devastating to morale—six days before Christmas and about three weeks before our exit from Iraq. Specialist Bush's death and the news of our redeployment order, however, pulled us together long enough to limp back home. His memorial service was first-class, put together entirely by his enlisted buddies and with the help of Hogg's brigade and other units that showed their support and respect. In my remarks, I cited St. Paul's Epistle to the Romans, 12:5: "We who are many form one body, and each member belongs to all the others." E pluribus unum.

Like every commander who loses soldiers in combat, you take such a loss personally. Regardless of what caused it, it's a feeling of respon-sibility unlike any other except parenting. It's why a lot of commanders call their troops their kids. That's also why, after the drive-by, fly-by change-of-command at 1:00 a.m. in the waiting tent at the air base in Iraq, I struggled to take the first half of the battalion all the way back to Buffalo. I wanted to make sure they got home all right.

After the battalion was greeted by hundreds of family members, well-wishers, and media at Niagara Falls Air Reserve Station, I qui-etly slipped away, checked out of the unit the next morning, and then visited the home of Bush's father to spend a couple of hours talking with him about his son. It was my final act as the departing battalion commander. It was also the most humbling experience of my life, as I struggled to provide this unfortunate man perspective on his tragic loss. As a last gesture, I delivered the case of beer I promised Charles I would provide as a result of a bet he and I had made on that year's Bills–Giants game. Then I got on a plane and flew to Newark, New Jersey, where my own family was waiting for me.

A couple of weeks before Bush died, I was at my final appearance at the monthly Civil Affairs command conference in Baghdad. It occurred to me, with all the new faces around the table, that I had the rare privilege of having commanded the first Civil Affairs battalion to deploy in support of the operation as well as to have conducted both joint and multinational tactical civil–military operations. I had also commanded it through the entire Reserve cycle of pre-mobilization training and preparation, mobilization and deployment, operations in theater, and redeployment and demobilization. It gave me valuable insights for that War College paper.

At lunch, General Kern, who had changed command and was on his way out, came up to me, looked me right in the eye, and said, "Holshek, of all the commanders I had out here, you were the biggest pain in my ass. I damn near fired you twice." Then he shook my hand. He later wrote in his evaluation, "This guy drove my staff nuts, but he was right. So I backed him."

Despite being structured for everything but success, the battalion performed extraordinarily well, a tribute to the young men and women who filled its ranks. With little more than 120 soldiers, including two dozen women, and with more than a one-third shortfall in officer strength in the unit, the 402nd Civil Affairs Battalion earned more than forty Bronze Star and fifty Army Commendation medals in addition to Army and Navy Meritorious Unit awards.

As the Dyna rolled harmoniously across the plains, I felt a greater sense of peace with this less-than-glorious time in Iraq than ever before. Like those who served in Vietnam, we tried to do the right thing, if under the wrong circumstances. In the fall after my return from Iraq, an Apache tribesman gave my father and me a sunset tour of the Grand Canyon. Seeing his faded and torn Vietnam-era fatigue shirt with a 1st Infantry Division patch, I shook his hand and thanked him for his service to his country. That somehow had felt like righting a bit of an old wrong. Other than African Americans, Native Americans have served in the military in proportionally higher numbers than any other demographic. Yet both groups have been systemically treated the worst by the societies they defended.

Spotting a billboard on Interstate 90 as the Dyna droned eastward, I made an unplanned stop at the small, privately run Wounded Knee Museum in Wall, South Dakota. Wall is about ninety miles to the north of the site of the final destruction of the Indian tribes as an independent civilization on December 29, 1890, among the greatest of atrocities committed by the US military against civilians. I found it disappointing that the US government has national historical sites and national parks for practically everything, including the nearby Minuteman missile site, but hadn't designated land to commemorate anything like Wounded Knee. "The Canadians," Stephen Ambrose contended, "have managed to live peacefully with their Indians. It is a disgrace that the United States has not done the same. "

Signs remain of lingering prejudice and failure to reconcile with this and other darker moments in our national history. The wide use of Native American symbols among American sports teams, cars, and even weapons is one example displayed in the museum. Many Native Americans object to this: for one, because they were never really asked; for another, because some of the names or symbols were often offensive epithets; and not least of all, because these adaptations are not about them as much as commercial exploitation. Identity theft isn't just for individuals.

We cannot embrace the better angels of our nature unless we face our demons. Among these are racism and indifference—structural, if not attitudinal or latitudinal, and born not out of blind ignorance as much as a choice that chooses ignorance. Steinbeck confronted this during his trip more starkly than I did, but it's still clearly out there. Martin Luther King's dream will never be anything more than that until most Americans stop pretending that it's already fulfilled. We cannot find redemption for our faults, our sins of omission as well as commission, in any other way except to reach out in compassion in the service of others. And when we help others, we help ourselves.

Diversity is threatened by division and paradox by irony. The docent at Little Bighorn pointed out that, to the original inhabitants of the North American continent, European settlers were the illegal immigrants, made poignant by a quote from Chief Crazy Horse posted at the Indian Memorial: "We did not ask you white men to come here. The Great Spirit gave us this country as a home. You had yours. . . . We did not interfere with you. We do not want your civilization!"

Just as we treated Native Americans as foreigners in their own land, too many of us want to close the open door to the latest people that have come here to find opportunity—just as most of our own ancestors did. This attitude threatens to make a nation of immigrants into a country of ingrates, forming an identity based on privilege rather than inclusion, subtraction rather than multiplication. Given the fear of Muslims among our latest national phobias, if we have no confidence that our culture of inclusiveness can withstand its inherent risks, then we might as well hang it up and join the rest of the world—and most of that is not a very pretty place.

Is this the American character we wish to invoke as our collective identity for the times in which we now find ourselves? If this is the path we have chosen, then how can we go around claiming how great and exceptional we are, when we lack the moral courage to walk that same talk? Whether as individuals, communities, or a nation, what makes you special is not who you are or where you come from but what you've done with what you've got.

Thinking more about this as I left Wall, I figured that if the Germans have been able to face up to the commitment of some of the worst affronts to human dignity done in their name through communal self-reflection, then so should Americans. If there can be a Holocaust Museum in our nation's capital for something America had little to do with, there ought to be national monuments to commemorate Wounded Knee, the Trail of Tears, and other shadowy moments in our own history. It's not just about museums and monuments: If we want to see our society as inclusive, we must do the same with our past—all of it and not just the parts we like. We cannot move forward into a brighter future if we cannot live down our darker legacies.

Both journeys—spiritual and physical—across the Great Plains helped me reach a new lucidity about what being an American means, or at least should mean. While in the Balkans, Iraq, and Liberia, my experiences in helping broken countries taught me that the most successful, powerful, and enduring societies have an inclusive sense of identity. Those who don't get that risk banishment to the ash heap of history. United we stand, divided we fall.

As an American soldier deployed in the face of far more morally complex situations than those of past generations (and probably less than those that will follow), I have often contemplated the small patch on my right shoulder (with the blue field on the right, facing forward into battle), and the special privileges and burdens placed on those who wear it. Indeed, we are not on a level playing field, held to a higher moral and ethical standard for the encouragement of friends, the dissuasion of foes, and the deliberation of the nonaligned. It is perhaps unfair—we are no better, no more or less human than any other citizens of the globe. But we and no one else put ourselves there, so we are called to that higher level of humanity.

I came face-to-face with this reality as a citizen-soldier, which my friend and fellow retired Army Special Operations officer Wayne Long told me is "the defender of the social contract, of which he is also a stakeholder." As public servants performing the ultimate community service, we either accept that task or move on to another job. As the citizenry that soldiers defend, we must similarly either answer our personal call to service, for community or for country, or adopt a lesser moral standard. Otherwise, we have no right to send our young men and women into harm's way on our behalf, wearing our flag, to represent what we believe is good for others but cannot live up to ourselves. We are either all real Americans, or none of us are.

As the Dyna drifted into the increasingly verdant landscape of eastern South Dakota, leaving behind the Great Plains, I recalled the quote from Black Elk I read at the Little Bighorn museum:

Know the power that is peace.

CHAPTER 12

THE HEARTLAND: LEADERS AND CITIZENS

After a long day's ride across South Dakota, I turned directly south from Sioux Falls to pick up the Lewis and Clark National Historic Trail in Iowa. The catharsis from all the intense introspection during the long prairie ride and the emotional visit to the Wounded Knee museum had left me mentally spent. I was looking forward to a quiet, relaxing stay at a (yet unknown) hotel in Sioux City.

I knew something was awry when I saw about fifty motorbikes parked downtown in front of the Holiday Inn. As I charmed my way into getting the last room available there, I discovered I had happened upon Sioux City's eleventh annual Awesome Biker Nights only a few blocks away. "Historic 4th Street" had become a pedestrian zone bordered with streetside beer bars, burger joints, souvenir vendors, and a handful of hypercharged rock and metal groups on high-tech stages. Their crashing rhythms competed with the din of Harleys and "crotch rockets" trying to out-rev each other as they crawled among the crowds. Boys, toys, and noise.

It was fun until I got up the next morning with my ears still ringing. Hopping back on the Harley, I made my way farther south along the route of the Corps of Discovery, down the Missouri River Valley, stopping off to take a look at a full-scale model of a collapsible river boat being readied for the new museum at Lewis and Clark State Park near Onawa, Iowa. It impressed me how it could have been dragged for hundreds of miles overland. In Omaha, Nebraska, I toured the Durham Museum (once the Western Heritage Museum). After chatting at the information desk with a charming French lady who had become a naturalized US citizen, I wandered through the displays that carefully laid out Omaha's role in westward expansion, including the eastern origins of the Transcontinental Railroad and the Mormon pilgrimage to Salt Lake City. They showed me how, due largely to geography and its location as a major hub and industrial center for the railroad and inland shipping industries, Omaha was really more a gateway to the West than was St. Louis.

On the way out of town after lunch, I passed Johnny Rosenblatt Stadium, in its final year as the venue of the national college baseball championship. Finding a vantage point on high ground, I looked down into the stadium as South Carolina—Uncle Randy's home state—won its first National Collegiate Athletic Association (NCAA) team championship in any men's sport. (The game was taking place in Nebraska due to the NCAA's ban on South Carolina as host for sanctioned championship events, which ended after nearly fifteen years in 2015 following the decision to remove the Confederate flag from the state's capitol grounds.)

The Harley cruised down Interstate 29 along the river, and as I rode on it dawned on me that I was seriously southbound for the first time since the start of the trip. Then the vast cornfields and grain farms rose up to embrace me on both sides of the roadway, as if welcoming me into the American heartland. In many ways, now, a number of circles were beginning to close.

For instance, one of my goals for this trip was to take my Wide Glide to its place of birth at the Harley-Davidson factory just outside Kansas City. As it turned out, my timing was a bit off. Being a Saturday, there were no factory tours. Fortunately, I ran into one of the supervisory staff, an amiable young man with prior service in the Marines who was kind enough to take my picture with the bike in front of the factory. That mission accomplished, I found a nice place to stay and treated myself to a delicious steak dinner, some great live blues music, and easy chatter with other patrons. From this point on, the trip was ad-lib.

As I embarked early the next morning for St. Louis, I made an unscheduled stop at the Harry S. Truman Library in Independence. After the Reagan Presidential Library in Simi Valley and Mount Rushmore, I thought I had seen enough of presidents for this trip, but I liked Truman. He seemed fairly honest—or honestly fair, a rarity among politicians. It turned out to be well worth the diversion. It also became apparent that I had not really finished my thinking about leadership in general and American leadership in particular.

Truman was an underrated president. He may not rank with those on Mount Rushmore, and even his predecessor, Franklin Roosevelt, who steered the country through the Great Depression and then World War II, overshadows him. However, while America has been fortunate to have had iconic leaders like Washington, Jefferson, and Lincoln at crucial times, it has been just as fortunate to have had a number of them like Truman. Starting out in FDR's footsteps, the thirty-third president encountered one crisis after another in a time of great transition. They included the decision to use the first atomic bomb, the division of Europe, the rebuilding of Germany and Japan, the unprecedented establishment and stationing of large standing peacetime military forces overseas, the Berlin Airlift, the National Security Act of 1947, the Marshall Plan and the Cold War strategy of containment, the founding of the United Nations and NATO, the "fall" of China, the Korean War, and the sacking of General MacArthur.

Amid this parade of crises and turning points, Truman fiercely defended his convictions. His commonsense wisdom came from his frontier-family roots and his heartland values. Until coming to Independence, I had also not known much about his role in the initiation of the civil rights movement, beginning with the desegregation of the military. Truman's stand, in fact, led to the split of his party when southern Democrats walked out of the 1948 national convention. He won an improbable election that year, as if in defiance of a political cartoon that jabbed, "Would you rather be right or be president?" Turned out he was both.

Truman left history to be his eventual arbiter. "The truth is all I want for history," reads the inscription on the wall at the Trumans' gravesite. Amen, Harry.

In many regards, learning more about Truman helped me to better understand the president most emblematic of my own lifetime. Poll after poll reveals that if there were to be a fifth likeness of a chief executive at Mount Rushmore, it would be that of John F. Kennedy. I was born the Friday before Kennedy was elected president and barely three years old when he died.

There are moments in history that loom larger in our lives than any other single event, when communal and personal experiences flatten to the point of becoming one and the same, connecting us all in mythic proportion. More than 9/11, the assassination of the thirty-fifth president transcends human divisions as well as time and space. The paradox was that he was able to unify Americans and the world in his sudden and tragic death in a way he could never have in life. The Kennedy gravesite is the most visited at Arlington National Cemetery, as if the funeral that began over a half century ago still goes on, for more than just the man interred there. JFK, in memory, is a metaphor of what most people find good about America—youthful exuberance, idealism in action, and the ambition to do great things.

For many, the United States appeared to have been at its apogee in 1963. Perhaps the greatest casualty since that event was the faith of the young in government. "There has been a loss of morale, a loss of confidence among the American people toward their own government and the men who serve it that is perhaps more wounding than the assassination itself," opined Walter Cronkite a few years later. That was probably one of the reasons why Lyndon Johnson, in his own brilliant stroke, saw the passage of the Civil Rights Act as so vital.

But then came Vietnam, Watergate, and the untimely, violent deaths of one hero of hope after another—Robert Kennedy, Martin Luther King Jr., John Lennon, and others like Anwar Sadat, Yitzhak Rabin, and Benazir Bhutto. All these events have eroded belief in government and thus public service and politics with it—and not only in America. Our public discourse has not only become leaner in logic but also meaner in message. And Americans have set themselves up for this letdown, in good part because they seem to expect far too much from presidents and government.

After visiting the Truman Library, I thumbed again through Steinbeck's *America and Americans*. On the paradox of American presidential leadership, Steinbeck wrote:

> *In reviewing our blessings, we must pay heed to our leadership.*
> *. . . Not all our Presidents have been great, but when the need has*
> *been great we have found men of greatness. We have not always*
> *appreciated them; usually we have denounced and belabored*
> *them living, and only honored them dead. Strangely, it is our*
> *mediocre Presidents we honor during their lives.*

Then I read this next part:

> *The relationship of Americans to their President is a matter of*
> *amazement to foreigners. Of course we respect the office and*
> *admire the man who can fill it, but at the same time we inher-*
> *ently fear and suspect power. We are proud of the President,*
> *and we blame him for things he did not do.*

And Steinbeck might as well have been writing this today:

> *The President must be greater than anyone else, but not better*
> *than anyone else. We subject him and his family to close and*
> *constant scrutiny and denounce them for things we ourselves do*
> *every day. . . . We give the President more work than a man can*
> *do, more responsibility than a man should take, and more pres-*
> *sure than a man can bear. We abuse him often and rarely praise*
> *him . . . he is ours, and we exercise the right to destroy him.*

Myths being public dreams and dreams being private myths, the truth about our personal bonds with any president lies somewhere between how good we think things were when he was in power and how bad they seem to be now. Kennedy, a flawed character, was a man of great vision—as all presidents should be. But he was a realist as much as an idealist. His ambitions were grounded in practical truth and a call to action; he challenged Americans and the world to ask not what others could do for them but what they could do for and with others—the polar opposite of the self-indulgence and narcissism that afflict our cultural consciousness today.

The Cuban Missile Crisis was a turning point in his presidency. As a leader, Kennedy matured exceptionally quickly from his first year of faux pas with the Bay of Pigs invasion, his initial meeting with Khrushchev in Vienna, and the Berlin Crisis. By his last year, it was clear who he was and what he was about. His last few months in office were especially rich in examples of a rare ability to exercise and express pragmatic idealism. Kennedy understood the relationship between hard and soft power—he is credited with starting both the Special Forces and the Peace Corps. In his speech in Berlin where he showed himself a citizen of the world, he had already sensed what we should have sensed on 9/11—that the security of people and not just states abroad was linked to our own, that what matters over there also matters over here.

A little more than a week later, Kennedy acknowledged in Philadelphia something we still struggle with—that our relationships with Europeans and others must be based on partnership rather than patronage, in order to form "a nucleus for the eventual union of all free men." That Fourth of July, Kennedy envisioned a more collaborative world enjoined by a "Declaration of Interdependence." In announcing the start of a generational series of nuclear disarmament initiatives, beginning with the 1963 Nuclear Test Ban Treaty, JFK called not for an "absolute, infinite concept of universal peace and good will of which some fantasies and fanatics dream." Rather, he exhorted, "Let us focus instead on a more practical, more attainable peace, based not on a sudden revolution in human nature but on a gradual evolution in human institutions. . . . not toward a strategy of annihilation but toward a strategy of peace."

Like any great leader, many of his ideas on peace and security and civil society have not yet found their time. Or have they? If JFK was so far ahead of his time, like so many great presidents, then perhaps his death was really not all that untimely—for his life and legacy point toward opportunity more than tragedy, if we choose to see it that way.

Continuing with Steinbeck:

> *It is said that the Presidency of the United States is the most powerful office in the world. What is not said or even generally understood is that the power of the chief executive is hard to achieve, balky to manage, and incredibly difficult to exercise. It is not raw, corrosive power, nor can it be used willfully. . . . The power of the President is great if he can use it; but it is a moral power, a power activated by persuasion and discussion.*

In other words: soft power, which makes even more sense today. This idea of presidential power as essentially and primarily moral has even greater relevance when it's becoming clear that American power, as a whole, is essentially and primarily moral. At home as well as abroad, it's more about the power of ideas and how they can be made to work in people's lives—identity achieved through action.

Our government in general and our elected officials in particular are, in many ways, a reflection of what we think they ought to be. That's what votes communicate. Not voting is still a choice—silence may not be approval, but it is abstention from the democratic process, leaving matters up to others. So why should we expect more of our elected leaders and less of the citizens they serve? If we want responsible government, after all, we need to provide responsible citizenship. The truth of the matter is that it wasn't a wacko with a mail-order gun that killed the JFK we've come to immortalize. We've been killing his vision and inspiration through our cynicism and indifference. Government has failed us because we have also failed it.

Kennedy's call to action was most importantly a call to citizenship—local, national, and global. It was a call to embrace the promise of American reinvention and renewal. By pointing out that the new frontiers we face are more moral than physical, at home as well as abroad, he reminded us that the path to a more perfect union and a more peaceful world lies within ourselves. This is ultimately an even greater challenge than walking on the moon.

It's up to us today to decide whether more than Kennedy was killed that day, and what and how much of his myth is reality. That begins with each of us before it can be for all of us. As we consider that which can bring us together positively instead of divide us negatively, we must find our own personal profiles in courage. We weren't ready for Kennedy's messages then. Perhaps we're ready for them now.

As I learned at the Reagan Presidential Library, no president can succeed if he or she cannot connect or communicate on a moral level with the American people. The most effective leaders in history, the sinister as well as the saintly, have been effective communicators. Many, such as Churchill and Lincoln, were also great storytellers. As the late American professor of human–computer interaction Randy Pausch has explained about leadership, "Do not tell people how to live their lives. Just tell them stories. And they will figure out how those stories apply to them."

Even before I got to the US Army War College in Carlisle, Pennsylvania, in the summer of 2005, it was apparent to me that strategic leadership was mostly about moral courage and the ability to connect and communicate, or in more contemporary terms, to shape the narrative.

The year at Carlisle was a welcome excursion from short active-duty stints to help successive generations of Civil Affairs soldiers prepare for Iraq and Afghanistan while, as a consultant, also helping think tanks in Washington, DC, consider lessons from the War on Terror. Only about a dozen of the class of over three hundred were drilling reservists. So I relished every day there with enthusiasm. It was hard to believe that I was being paid full-time to think and learn and would obtain a master of science degree in strategic studies to boot. An inordinate number of my Regular Army classmates, however, saw it as a distraction from their "real jobs." Many struggled with the transition from tactical to strategic thinking. Despite how things were obviously changing in the world, the institutional inertia of the Army, grounded in the tactical and the physical, was holding them back. For this reason more than any other, I believe strategic leadership must be taught much earlier in an officer's career—long before they get to the War College, when junior leaders likewise must have a strategic as well

*With my Army War College diploma after receiving it from retired Air
Force general Richard Myers (upper left). Note also the 1st Marine Division
patch, worn as the combat tab on the shoulder of my uniform.*

as operational understanding of the situation at hand. Besides, you
change a culture by educating the younger generation in a way that
anticipates the future while still drawing on the past.

Among my own experiences with bottom-up strategic leadership,
one could be described as how to deal with being at what one general
officer described to me as "the long end of the whip"—when you're at
the business end of decisions made much higher up that swing you and

your people to and fro, putting you and them in absurd predicaments. Just a little motion of the hand of senior leadership can jerk you and them around widely and wildly, which is something good senior leaders don't forget when they get to the top.

I certainly got a good sense of this in Iraq. While holding a meeting with the newly formed governorate council at our civil–military operations center (CMOC) in downtown An Nāṣirīyah, Iraq, in mid-May 2003, a disturbed-looking Marine lieutenant came into the room.

"Gentlemen," he said to me and Lieutenant Colonel Bob Murphy, the 2/25th Marine Regiment commander, "we've got a big problem outside."

Waiting for us and nearly surrounding the CMOC were about two thousand men of various ages, some with weapons, in an advanced state of agitation, chanting slogans. They were POIs—pissed off Iraqis. The lieutenant in command of the platoon that was our security force asked whether we should call for help. I turned to Murphy: "Let's see what this is about first."

Thinking I must have seen this in a movie somewhere, I removed my "battle rattle," donned my soft cap, and marched straight toward the center of the group with my assistant, Adel, at my side. Some of the Marines in their firing positions stared at me as I stepped outside the gate.

"Okay, who's in charge here?" A handful of more senior members of the group, introducing themselves as "General" and "Colonel" stepped forward and introduced themselves as the Iraqi army leadership council in the province.

"What's going on?" Adel translated for me.

"You mean you don't know?" they answered. "Mr. Bremer just fired us."

What they were talking about was Coalition Provisional Authority (CPA) Order Number 2, which the new CPA chief authority, Paul Bremer, had issued only days after taking office. It disbanded the entire Iraqi army, all four hundred thousand of them, and mostly Sunnis (many of whom later joined the "Islamic State"). In Order Number 1, he had banned the Ba'ath Party, but he forgot to tell any of us on the ground about it first. The word got around faster with the Iraqis, despite all our modern communications. In people-centric operations, it's the informal power structures and systems you have to understand and appreciate in particular.

My tone having softened in some embarrassment, I invited them in for tea and talk. We had one of our water trailers sent out to give people some fresh water in the sweltering sun, and eventually we set up some awnings to provide shade. For three days, we held counsel with them, explaining our regret that we were still waiting for guidance from the 1st Marine Division Headquarters in Al Hillah, south of Baghdad. Meanwhile, the POIs had doubled in number and restlessness. Finally, in a brainstorming session with the governorate council and the Iraqi army leadership council, Murphy looked at me and said, "We need to do something, now."

So I asked Major Bill Broderick, one of our Civil Affairs officers helping out with courts and finances in An Nāṣirīyah, to tell me how much money we had left in captured cash funds, having just helped the council draft its operating budget for the next six months in another exercise of nation-building-on-the-fly. I scribbled that amount on the whiteboard and asked the Iraqi army representatives, "You said you have about thirty thousand men in our province, right, about three thousand of them officers?" They nodded.

"Adel," I asked, "how does 'honor payment' sound in Arabic?"

"Very good, sir," Adel replied.

"So, here's what I propose: We release uncommitted funds to you, the Iraqi army leadership council, to provide your people with an honor payment. After all, it's the people's money in the first place. We use your rules—they have to present an ID card, you have to manage the lists, et cetera. We'll work side by side with you to make sure everything is done in as accountable and transparent a fashion as possible. It won't be coming from our hands but yours," I explained.

"The honor payment," I continued, looking directly at the veterans, "is just that. It's to recognize you all for your service to your country, the hardships you and your families are going through right now, as well as your cooperation thus far with the Coalition. It's not back pay, a pension payment, or baksheesh [essentially a bribe]." The Iraqis chuckled. "Heck, it's only around a hundred bucks for the officers and half that for the men. But it's a small gesture, until such time as your new ministry of defense and veterans affairs agency is established. Make sense?"

Everyone around the room nodded. "Go ahead," Murphy said to me. "Get it going as fast as you can. And write me the report to send to division headquarters." A couple of days later, we got started with the honor payments. But word spread like wildfire around the rest of Iraq. Similar groups in other provinces were asking their Coalition force units in similar circumstances why they weren't receiving an honor payment.

A day or two later, the 1st Marine Division headquarters in Hillah sent a message that the commander, Lieutenant General James Mattis, was on his way in his helicopter—and he was less than happy.

"My career is over," Bob moaned. "He'll relieve me in place."

"Well, Bob," I told him, "if you go down, I'm going with you. It was my idea more than yours."

Mattis sprang out of his helicopter, chatted with some Marines and soldiers for nearly an hour, and then went with us behind closed doors. He was hot under the collar and proceeded to dress us down, like R. Lee Ermey's Marine drill sergeant in *Full Metal Jacket* if he had been a Fulbright Scholar. We had gotten out ahead of him and the other commands. Bob and I glanced at each other, still at attention, waiting for him to sack us.

He suddenly relaxed and asked in a more moderate tone, "So how the hell are you doing it?" Later that day, I flew back with him to brief his staff.

A little less than five years later, in early 2010, at the (now defunct) Joint Forces Command (JFCOM) in Suffolk, Virginia, we held a brainstorming session with the JFCOM commander General James Mattis. I was there to help with the stability and multinational operations parts of the Capstone Concept for Joint Operations—the mother of all US military doctrines. I had not seen Mattis since Iraq.

After some time, when I raised my hand to answer a question he posed about what metrics to use in stability operations, the now four-star general recognized me immediately.

"Soldier!" he exclaimed, immediately noticing the 1st Marine Division patch on my uniform. "How the hell are you? What have you been up to?"

After answering his question on metrics, he called for a break and we held a fifteen-minute public reunion, reminiscing about the war in Iraq, including the honor payment episode.

"We were sweating bullets, at our wits' end," he told me. "We knew all you guys out there were in trouble." Bremer and the CPA had tied his hands while he waited to pass guidance on to us. When we forced everyone's hand with our own initiative, the pols in Baghdad were, to say the least, not amused that some little guys down south were jerking back on that long whip. But Mattis took the heat from Bremer and gave us cover instead of hanging us out to dry. "You guys saved a lot of lives by what you did," he told me when we met again in Suffolk.

In addition to trading war stories, I thanked General Mattis on behalf of the troops I had once commanded for going to bat twice against the Army bureaucracy to get us authorization to wear the 1st Marine Division patch as our combat service tab, which I was wearing proudly on my right uniform shoulder. It was a highly unusual thing to see Army soldiers wearing Marine patches on their uniforms—even Marines don't wear their own patches on their uniforms.

A few days later, back at my cubicle in the Reagan Building, a small handwritten envelope appeared on my desk. It turned out to be a "four-star note," handwritten:

14 Feb 2010
Dear Chris,

It was good seeing you again, still contributing with good ideas. We had a great team in Iraq and it was good to see the combat patch on your right shoulder, soldier. Thank you for your service, then and now.

Semper Fi,
Jim Mattis

I treasure this note as much as many of my medals. Between what he told me that day and in his note, it was especially helpful to hear that our actions in Iraq had made at least some difference—and how we were able to jerk back on that long end of the whip. With my career nearly over, it felt like vindication for some of the less glorious things that had happened to us in Iraq.

At the time of my reunion with Mattis, on my last, yearlong tour of duty, I was fortunate to be serving for another great senior leader, Admiral James Stavridis, Commander of the European Command and Supreme Allied Commander Europe (SACEUR). Even though my official job was as his representative at the US Agency for International Development, Stavridis took a very strategic view of my role there. That included agreeing (based on my persuasion) to be the first geographic combatant commander to visit the new USAID administrator, Dr. Rajiv Shah. In further demonstration of support, in his testimony to Congress, Stavridis explained that cuts to foreign aid in his theater didn't just hurt USAID's mission—they hurt his mission and US national security. He enthusiastically supported many things that I was doing that did not fit neatly into my job description, including the work at JFCOM.

When the earthquake hit Haiti in January 2010, the tiny military liaison staff in the Reagan Building was overwhelmed with the need for coordination between USAID and the Pentagon. As I explained to Stavridis, it was all hands on deck to help USAID stand up the National Response Center in the Reagan Building. Stavridis was most supportive of many other activities that were not exactly in my lane, such as the Capstone Doctrine or helping the UN write its policy framework on civil–military coordination, based on my experience back in Liberia. "No one else can do what you're doing, Chris," he told me later while he was visiting USAID. "It's in our greater national interest to help make the UN as effective as we can."

Like all great senior leaders, Stavridis could cultivate people who could contribute way above their pay grade for the greater good. It was incredibly gratifying to be working for someone like that and providing bottom-up leadership as my career was ending.

One directive Stavridis gave me was to be an interested observer on his behalf with the Project on National Security Reform (PNSR) to get a better understanding, show his support, and then help in any way I could. At the same time, given my background, he approved USAID's request to have me help with the first coherent long-term plan for USAID and the State Department in the Quadrennial Diplomacy and Development Review (QDDR), so the United States could find a more balanced approach between hard and soft power to foreign and national security issues.

I was one of the few uniformed military officers meeting regularly in the QDDR's civil–military working group The topic du jour was which agency should be in the lead in stability operations and when. I was amazed at this, although I understood why: Neither State nor USAID had the wherewithal to be the lead agency for such complex operations. I started to get edgy. Finally, I put my hands up to signal a time-out.

"Hold on a minute here, folks! With the possible exception of major combat operations," I professed, "and even then every military philosopher from Sun Tzu to Liddell Hart will tell you that the object of war is a more favorable peace—the military is not in the lead of nationally directed operations. It is always in support. Even if it brings most of the boys, toys, and noise, the Defense Department is not the lead agency. What that means, however, is that our discussion should be about what capabilities State and AID need to lead, not whether they should."

Astounded that it was taking a member of the military to give a civics class to a group of civilian government leaders about the fundamental democratic principle of the primacy of civil authority, I ended with, "And if anyone doesn't understand what I'm saying here, please take out a dollar bill, look on the back, and tell me which way the eagle is looking."

What I was referring to was something I learned about twenty years earlier in Campbell's *The Power of Myth*, which made more sense as my experiences accumulated—the obverse of the Great Seal of the United States. The main function of any state (the eagle) is to deal with matters of peace (the olive branch) and war (the quiver of arrows), both of which are choices. Strategy, after all, is about making choices now that shape the future. The olive branch also represents soft power, persuasion, civil power and authority, and so on; the quiver of arrows also represents hard power, coercion, the military, and so on. The eagle is looking at the olive branch, which is what makes all the difference in our national priorities and our exercise of power at home as well as abroad, in practice as well as policy. This is our ordering principle about how we are to engage the world and of course our civil–military relationship.

Most important, it is what we say, as a country, that we are most about. Peace is not merely the absence of war. Peace is a process, as Kennedy alluded, and not some lofty goal. It includes social, political, and economic justice. It includes stability and order—security—as a base requirement for peace. Most of all, it includes conciliation among disparate groups together in accord for a larger purpose—democratic civil society, which is the path the founders were setting us on to achieve a more perfect union.

The strengths of our national identity, civil society, and soft power should be leveraged widely and continuously in multifarious ways, especially at the personal level of connectivity. Military power should be used sparingly. A last resort, it is most effective when implied rather than applied. Every time we go for the gun—which we sometimes must do—we must first understand the full costs and risks, as the Powell Doctrine professed. Among these is an admission of failure in diplomacy and other forms of noncoercive engagement. Everything we do that is true to the ordering principle of the Great Seal makes all our strength and power that much more unbeatable; everything we do that detracts from it makes us all the more vulnerable.

"The core challenge of the twenty-first century is to construct a peaceful and prosperous world," PNSR colleague Ed Corcoran wrote in *Threats and Challenges: Strategies in a New Century*, "based on the universality of basic American values of the worth of the individual and the importance of freedom." That sounds more like building peace rather than taking down enemies is really the core business of the United States of America.

But you wouldn't think so by just looking at our nation's organization and resources. We spend about a dozen times as much on the quiver of arrows as we do on the olive branch. As I said at one appearance a few years ago on Capitol Hill: "If you want peace, you have to plan, organize, and most of all resource for peace." Talk is cheap: There is no paradigm shift until it reflects in programs, budgets, and operations—not just speeches and policy papers. In truth, we live mostly in the space between peace and conflict, not entirely within one or the other.

That's what PNSR was about. Its main purpose was the obvious need to update our foreign policy and national security operating software that is still rooted in the Cold War. By doing so, the United States could maintain its leadership role in the world and its way of life by more effectively using its strength and power. The project's success also could have led to a more effective national government. But PNSR closed down from a failure to find six-figure financing in a town that thinks in twelve or thirteen figures. At PNSR's last meeting in January 2012, I explained the directional dissonance to my colleagues there by saying that the United States is running the wrong way, as in the famous NFL blooper where a player recovers a fumble and runs into the wrong end zone, scoring a safety for the other team rather than a touchdown for his own. Uncle Sam is still running the wrong way. We left a legacy of our work online at www.pnsr.org, knowing one day Washington will at least not have to start entirely from scratch.

One thing I also learned throughout my career is that peace is for professionals. Winning the peace is much harder than winning a war. The tandem lesson is that you can't win the peace at gunpoint alone. Building peace is a complex and collaborative process of setting people on a course of political, social, and economic change, from the bottom up as much as the top down. Peacebuilding is applied national strategy and bottom-up strategic leadership. If we understand that, then it's not just the White House and Congress that must treat the profession of peace as seriously as the profession of arms—it's also the citizens that send these professionals there.

I learned at the PNSR that "It takes a nation to fix a government." Later I also learned from my good friend Lisa Schirch at the Alliance for Peacebuilding the difference between *government* and *governance.* Besides one being an instrument and the other a process, governance is values based, starts with identifying with your community as well as your country, and prioritizes ethics and common sense.

Thinking of that need to get to basics as I crossed back over the Mississippi and walked under the Gateway Arch in St. Louis, I decided it was imperative for me to learn more about the formative years of the greatest of presidents, Abraham Lincoln. Rather than go to Springfield, Illinois, to see the Lincoln Presidential Library, I rode through the farmlands and wooded areas along a more southerly path to visit his boyhood home in Indiana. If the presidency is mostly about moral leadership and the ability to connect with people, then what other way to better understand Lincoln than to go where he spent his formative years, between the ages of seven and twenty-one, when his character was forged and his core values formed?

Situated about twenty miles south of Interstate 64 and near nothing other than the nearby town of Santa Claus, the Lincoln Boyhood National Memorial is among the most thoughtfully laid out national presidential sites I have seen so far. Beginning with the five relief sculptures depicting Lincoln's life and nine of his trademark quotes, you can walk through the woods the young future president wandered through, reaching the cabin-site memorial that approximates his home and, perhaps most important, well conveys his rather humble beginnings.

It was a quiet day at a less busy time of year. So I was fortunate to spend nearly an hour sitting on the stoop of the cabin discussing the sixteenth president, and presidents in general, with an exceptionally dedicated park ranger. He had read about forty books on Lincoln, who he said read about a tenth that many while living there. One was the Bible. David Ramsay's *Life of George Washington* and Ben Franklin's autobiography ignited Lincoln's interest in politics and provided early role models. *Aesop's Fables* and *Pilgrim's Progress* helped develop his moral compass, optimism, and knack for storytelling. These early literary influences are reflected in Lincoln's speeches.

After a fascinating conversation, I paced the Trail of Twelve Stones marking significant milestones or phases in Lincoln's career, reflecting on his life and legacy, then climbed back on the Harley to resume the route to Kentucky, the state of Lincoln's birth. A pit stop at a mom-and-pop shop turned into another impromptu conversation, this time over a sandwich and a cold drink with the owner, Jean, who seemed to pick up where the docent had just left off. I mentioned to her what I learned about Lincoln and presidents in general during the trip.

She believed that most presidents and a lot of politicians are well intentioned and more competent than we credit them for, that there's continuity as well as change between them. Jean argued that we are at our best when we move to the center and find balance and the win–win solutions for which Americans have been famous. "Couldn't agree with you more," I affirmed as I finished my iced tea and put on my helmet.

In a country like ours, only good citizenship can ultimately engender good leadership, morally grounded in an ethos of personal and social responsibility, service to others, and living the values we say we uphold. A fusion of the real and the ideal, American leadership is citizenship from the top down, whereas American citizenship is leadership from the bottom up—strategic in both senses. Both are a form of service and responsibility to others. Leaders are never bigger than their business—be it sports, corporate leadership, education, politics, or foreign policy and national security. I think Goethe had it more right than Jefferson, though—the best government is not the least but that which helps us to govern ourselves. It's the same with leaders. If you want great leaders, you have to be a people worthy enough of great leadership. As below, so above.

As I headed to Kentucky, I remembered a conversation I had with Joey, one of our doormen at the apartment complex I lived in on the Jersey City waterfront. While getting ready to deploy to Iraq, I would have long chats with Joey. He was so moved watching the Twin Towers come down right across the river that he desperately wanted to do something—join the military, join the police force, firefighters, something, anything. But he was in his late thirties and physically unqualified for such work. He was despondent.

Shortly before I left for Iraq, I had another talk with him. "Joey," I told him, "you know what the best thing is that you can do for your country?"

"What's that?" he asked.

"Just be a good citizen."

"What's that mean?"

"First of all, vote. Exercise that basic right of political expression that so many around the world would love to have and for which people like me put our lives on the line. I don't care who you vote for—just vote, each and every time you can. It's your civic duty anyway.

"Second, take an interest in what's going on around you and keep yourself informed. Read the papers instead of just watching the news. Learn about all the places and things they're talking about. And get all the points of view. The more you know about what's going on in the world around you, the more power you have over your own life.

"Third and most important," I told him, "do some kind of community service. Find something that appeals to you—help a homeless person find a shelter, tutor or coach kids in an underprivileged neighborhood, help an old person go shopping or get to medical appointments, or just take a CPR class at the Red Cross. You know, I saw on some notices downtown that Jersey City is looking for volunteers to help restore the parks. There are hundreds of things to do. Find out what works best for you.

"What I'm trying to say, Joey, is that what you do over here makes a big difference to what we do over there. So what I'm asking is this: Help give us more of a great country worth defending. Besides, being a great American is nothing more than being a great human being."

Joey was later able to help out at the volunteer ambulance corps. I wasn't surprised, after I came back, to see he would find something both fulfilling and valuable. That's because I knew he understood that patriotism isn't just something you feel—it's something you do.

CHAPTER 13

THE HOMESTRETCH: IS THIS A GREAT COUNTRY, OR WHAT?

In Louisville, Kentucky—home of the championship boxer Muhammad Ali—I enjoyed a great seafood dinner on the Ohio River. Then I pushed on to Fort Knox, site of the US Bullion Depository containing more than 368,000 four-hundred-ounce gold bars. But Fort Knox was no longer the home of Armor and Cavalry, where I went to basic training and obtained early officer schooling. It was now the home of the newly formed Army Human Resources Command. There was nothing really to go back to, even though it was now about humans more than hardware.

A sense of emptiness had begun to creep in. As the machine droned steadily past the pleasantly arrayed horse farms of northern Kentucky along the Bluegrass Parkway and neared West Virginia, the man maneuvering it was becoming progressively bereft.

For one, I was slowly surrendering to fatigue, both physical and mental. The interlude in Liberia had compressed the second half of my stateside sojourn, resulting in only one day off the handlebars from otherwise continuous riding since I had left California nearly two weeks prior. I had really wanted to take more time—probably at least another week—and spend less of it on the interstate. Like summer thunderstorms, the epiphanies had pretty much blown past. Not able to keep up with the posts I had been writing for the PNSR blog, I had resigned myself to the fact that the rest of my qualitative reflection would have to happen after the trip.

The other reason for my mounting funk was the realization that two lifetime adventures were coming to an end at once. I felt I had missed much more than I should have on this cross-country ride. I felt like little more than a tourist—I had sampled more than seen America. Dozens of places and things I could have, would have, or should have seen or done flashed through my mind. As I've done many times, I began to mentally list missed opportunities, big and small.

I was also beginning to come to grips with the reality of military retirement. It was more than the end of one profession; it was the end of a lifestyle of living in the spaces between two worlds and somehow finding a sense of balance in that gap. It's hard to let go of anything that has defined the core of who you are, a vocation you invested so much in, enjoyed, and did so well, especially if you still have much to give. Now I was just Bruce Wayne—no longer Batman—but certainly not as rich.

You have to realize when it's time to move on, to close one chapter in order to open another. Some people stay too long in one place for no other reason than that they know nothing else, fear what may come next, or delude themselves that they're somehow indispensable. It takes as much fortitude to end a life-defining adventure as it does to begin one. As with parenting or any other vocation involving such commitment, the ultimate purpose is to prepare those who follow you to take your place, and with any luck move things further along. Then you must bow out gracefully. In many ways, it's the hardest but most necessary part of the process.

As for Steinbeck with Charley, my travels with Harley seemed already over. With the last few hundred miles slowly spinning on the odometer, I struggled between simply getting it over with and making the most of rapidly fading opportunities. But in the negative as well as the positive, life is what happens to you while you're busy making other plans. From several deployments in danger zones, I learned the most perilous part of an expedition can be the homestretch. Your mind may already have gone home, and you're weary, so you struggle to maintain concentration. On this last leg, I had to devote more of my remaining psychic and physical energies to "keeping the shiny side up and the rubber side down" rather than on simply enjoying the experience.

Traveling through Kentucky and West Virginia was like riding in a postcard—nice, even idyllic, but not arresting in the same grandiose way as the West. Like someone with attention deficit disorder or Churchill at his reputed last breath, I was becoming "bored with it all." As I picked up US 50 north of Charleston, the last major roadway directly back to my point of origin, tawdry trailer homes and cheap prefabs speckled the Appalachian landscape. Then some God-given irony showed up in the form of a stolen highway directional sign on the side of a barn: "Orlando—Disney World—Left Lane."

At Cool Spring Park, privately owned, I stopped off to look at a haphazard collection of nineteenth- and early twentieth-century railroad cars, locomotives, farm tractors, and other early industrial-era artifacts that had the effect of a sculpture garden. "One person's junk is another one's treasure," I thought as I moved on. As I neared Virginia, the landscape began to sprout McMansions, signifying the approaching suburbs of the Greater Washington area, now a knowledge-based part of the transforming yet still-sputtering American economy. The DC area is more diverse than when I first lived there in the early 1980s, when the federal government was the largest employer. Instead, management consulting, high-tech, and biotech are now the leading industries.

My last roadside lunch stop was at Shirley's Diner in Romney, West Virginia. A modest, family-owned eatery with simple, homemade fare, it seemed a border outpost between two worlds. Feeling nostalgic, I had meat loaf with mashed potatoes and steamed vegetables, with apple pie for dessert. As the sun began to descend westward, I guided the Wide Glide along the switchbacks coming down from the foothills of the Blue Ridge and was uplifted a bit by the panoramic views of the horse farms as I approached Winchester, Virginia. US 50 rolled through remarkably pictorial horse farms and colonial villages, but I took no pictures. I had seen these roads before.

The trip, however, seemed to want to end on its own terms. The last sixty miles of the homestretch took more than two and a half hours as

I ran into more traffic lights than I had seen in the last two states. Held up in one-hundred-degree heat and humidity over scalding pavement and a cooking ninety-six-cubic-inch V-Twin engine, I twice sought refuge in an air-conditioned service station and rehydrated, conscientious after having survived a severe case of heatstroke in Iraq.

The Wide Glide finally eased into its parking garage space in my apartment building at Montebello, in Alexandria, just before sunset of the first full day of summer and the longest day of the year—but also the beginning of the decline of daylight hours. At the same spot where I had started forty-nine days earlier, the trip odometer read one-tenth of one mile short of 8,061. For five minutes or so I stared at it, wondering how to make sense of all of this. Rather than the two questions I started out with, about personal and national identity, only one now hovered in my mind.

Is this a great country, or what?

Americans are more worried and anxious about the future than ever. Sure, every generation seems to think, for one reason or another, that the place is going to hell in a handbasket. This time, it appears to be a unique convergence of a number of things.

The first is what Samuel Huntington saw as a neurotic American tendency to always fear decline. At the moment, America is in decline because it's broke, because Washington is dysfunctional and corrupt, and because it's drawing back from a world it no longer can or wants to lead. Or maybe it's because Americans are obese, lazy, addicted to sugar and prescription drugs, reality TV, social media, and the sound of their own voices. We are ignorant and ill educated and we don't read. Or maybe it is because we are gun-crazy and violent, narcissistic, misogynistic, puritanical, hyped up on religiosity, and turning against science, math, art, and history. The American Dream is dead because today's children will be the first who must expect to have less rather than more than their parents had. Given all that, it's a wonder how we became the country we are.

This time, Americans sense the country is in real and not just relative decline. Their way of life is changing for the worse, and there's very little they can do about it—national insecurity. We are a nation unhinged by a midlife crisis, coming to grips not only with profound local and global changes. Frontiers have become limitations.

But America's relative decline should be no surprise, really, considering our psychological point of orientation. In 1945, we dominated as no other nation had in history. No wonder that era is thought of so nostalgically. We lived in a more dangerous but more predictable world until the Berlin Wall came down and the Soviets went out of business. How could we think this singular episode in world history could ever last? Nature seeks balance, especially in tumult, and the irregularity of a unipolar world has been seeking, as they say in the stock market, correction.

We are not only just recently in relative decline—we have been for a long time. In the cycle of Great Powers, we have gone from a rising power to a status quo power, with profound effects on our psychology. Yet, when the wall came down in 1989, we failed to see we needed another national conversation about who we are and what we're about as a changing nation in a changing world. So we muddled along, searching for the next big idea to help us figure it all out. Because the United States was the sole superpower, we had no sense of urgency about that national dialogue, though things were changing more rapidly than we realized.

That's because in good part we were too busy being triumphant, convinced that the way we did things was universally good whereas the way others did was not. An American Foreign Service officer told me in Eastern Slavonia, in 1997, after a meeting with the UN, "If we do absolutely nothing, no one will even come close to us for another fifty years." Maybe he was right, but his bravado scared me. We became enamored with our power, a growing sense of entitlement extending to our position as Chairman of the Board of Planetary Management, and it was to the detriment of our strength. In our complacency, we have constantly called ourselves the greatest country in the world without wondering what that really means. In our national narcissism, we still call our top sports teams world champions in sports that only compete on American soil.

A status quo power is more conservative and risk averse. Real reform is nearly impossible because too many people who profit from the system have too much of a stake in things as they are. Meanwhile, the rest have decided it's more comfortable and gratifying to be consumers than citizens—just give me a tax cut and go away until I need you again. So we dumbed ourselves down. Our attention spans shrunk with our mental bandwidth. We have, as Carl Sagan said, adopted a popular culture that is "a celebration of ignorance." Or as an article by Jonathon Gatehouse in *Maclean's* phrased it:

> *If the rise in uninformed opinion was limited to impenetrable subjects that would be one thing, but the scourge seems to be spreading. Everywhere you look these days, America is in a rush to embrace the stupid. Hell-bent on a path that's not just irrational, but often self-destructive. Common-sense solutions to pressing problems are eschewed in favor of bumper-sticker simplicities and blind faith.*

Some of the evidence of all this is in the content of our media and television. Our ability to compete with the rest of the world is another. From science and math to history and civics to language and literacy, students and adults in America score consistently lower than the international average. We don't educate people, certainly not in the classical sense. We train them to get jobs, and not very well-paying ones at that.

While on that final stretch of road, it came to me that before I was born in 1960 we had never really lost a war. Since then we have hardly won any. That's no coincidence. The world has been changing in ways in which our national business model has been increasingly ineffective. In most areas of national competitiveness, we've been losing ground. If we are the greatest country in the world, it looks more and more as though that's because of where we've been and not where we're going. We're living more on a legacy and less on a promise.

We have become the New York Yankees of the international affairs league, covering bad front office decisions and a weakening farm system by throwing money at problems. Our formula for foreign success continues to be, as they say in sports, "Sometimes it's better to be lucky than good." We jump from crisis to crisis, thinking we can play catch-up because we're so rich; have dominated the scene for so long with our military, technological, financial, and economic power; and have taken for granted the appeal of our ideals and values.

America has globalized just about everything but itself, which accounts for much of Fareed Zakaria's "rise of the rest"—the idea that other countries are catching up more than the United States is falling behind. The world we largely created is now closing in on us, and we don't like it very much—it means we have to change our profligate ways, get out of our comfort zones, get in the global sandbox and play nice with the others, and compete and collaborate according to rules that suit everyone and not just us. The latest seismic signs of this megachange are 9/11 and the Great Recession—the end of our splendid insularity along with our dominance. These signals will keep coming in installments. The more we ignore them or fail to understand them, like climate change, the more extreme they will become. What goes around, comes around.

It's not the national debt. If America is in real decline, it is in its middle class—its relative size, standard of living, and quality of life. The slow recovery from the Great Recession is rooted in the inability to grasp that the problem goes beyond the usual business or election cycles. As with our political malaise, it's a structural problem that has less to do with Wall Street and K Street and more with Main Street. We forget too often that America changes most and best from the bottom up rather than the top down—but only if there's a bottom from which it can rise through opportunity and not be stuck in structurally.

We are doubtless a country of winners and losers. But if more and more of us are either stagnant or losing ground, social cohesiveness and stability will begin to wither, and with it our strength and power. Other Great Powers such as Rome did not have a perpetually improving middle class as its core strength. The United States does. If it loses that, it loses its greatness.

Along with the loss of upward mobility in a stratifying society, the other main threat to our future is in the barriers to collective problem solving. Politics in America have always been complicated, messy, and vexing—to greater levels than in most other places. "When you lose the tension of polarities," Joseph Campbell reminded us in *The Power of Myth*, "you lose the tension of life." Divisiveness, in moderation, can be positive—except when the centrifugal forces of self-interest out-weigh the centripetal forces of common sense.

With a central legislature calcified in gerrymandering and monied politics, however, every issue of public conversation is hyperpo-liticized, permitting what is common in failed or fragile states—the rule of elites rather than the rule of law, the disproportionate sway of hard-liners over disassociated moderates, institutionalized corruption, and an overarching narrative in which "passion never fails to wrest the sceptre from reason." We careen from election to election, thinking it's the other party's fault and ours will fix it, focusing on wedge issues like abortion or turning immigration into a weakness instead of a strength. Yet, without the gravity of common sense pulling us toward modera-tion and progress, "things fall apart; the center cannot hold," to channel Yeats's line at the demise of the Eurocentric world order a century ago.

Our self-inflicted problems will continue until the fundamental power relationships somehow shift back toward moderation. The bad news is that it will probably get worse before it gets better. The good news is that our fate is still very much in our own hands—but not for much longer. The more our political bipolar disorder goes on, the more it costs us irrevocably, and the fewer and worse our collective options become. Our irresponsible political behavior is accelerating national decline faster than anything else. We have met the enemy and he is us.

The growing gridlock is more an indicator than an indictment. The Tea Party, after all, is a reactionary movement feeding on the under-standable fear of a long-established mainstream constituency losing its demographic and political supremacy. In many ways, it represents the denial and anger of a psychological process perceiving decline and loss. Rather than go forward, these contemporary romanticists seek refuge in the good old days of a distant mythological republic. Theirs is not the only ideological entrenchment.

On the central issue of wealth disparity, many on the Left argue that the solution is to just transfer wealth from the rich to the middle class, but that is an artificial solution. Like tax cuts, it is feel-good but doesn't get to all the structural economic challenges. The Right argues that allowing the market to function freely will fix things, but that's what got us into so much trouble in the first place. The free market doesn't guarantee social outcomes, merely economic ones.

This is why we have government to temper the excesses of capitalism—as long as government itself does not become excessive. As Ginny and I acknowledged back in Mississippi, the dangers of an overly powerful central government are why the framers of the Constitution went to great lengths to create an inefficient federal system and its complex checks and balances. Freedom, not security, is the traditional default of our national operating software. The sentiment of many on the Right is valid about government overreach, yet we have as much if not more to fear from Big Business as from Big Government (we can at least vote the latter out of power), especially when they are in collusion, which is why all the money in politics is so dangerous—it leaves out the little guy and favors patrons more than patriots.

Conservatism and liberalism have always been intrinsic inflections of the inherent variety of voices and opinions of disparate citizens navigating the relationship between the individual and the state. Neither party's conventional solutions grasp the magnitude or the complexity of the problem. It's neither the government nor the private sector that has the solution. It's both, as we're already seeing in many municipalities across America and described in the book *The Metropolitan Revolution: How Cities and Metros Are Fixing Our Broken Politics and Fragile Economy*. Besides, Adam Smith and David Ricardo, two of the deans of capitalism, rarely used the term *economy* alone. They talked more about the *political economy*.

America, however, will need a new liberalism as well as a new conservatism, both bringing the country back towards a more pragmatic center from its ideological extremes. That, however, is not going to come from a single politician promising one thing or another. It will come, as all great movements, from the bottom up—from an electorate that has finally understood the value of engagement over ignorance and works from the common core of American identity based on its singular, most powerful formula: E pluribus unum.

Standing most in the way of America's future, however, is its paralyzing angst. Since 9/11, the fear factor figures into just about every aspect of our social psychology. For a country whose founders and greatest personalities displayed remarkable moral courage and vision, the United States has become increasingly afraid of the future and reverent of the past. Too many have bought into a narrative of decay, despair, decline, and cynicism.

Nothing embodies this more than our obsession with terrorism. Spoiler alert: Terrorism is not, nor has it ever been, an existential threat to the United States of America. You have about as much chance of getting killed by a terrorist, even in Washington or New York, as I have of getting a date with Angelina Jolie. You have more chance of winning the lottery or getting struck by lightning. Besides, we murder almost four times as many of our own people *each year* with firearms as we lost on 9/11, according to the Center for Disease Control. Human life is human life. If we're willing to take chances with mentally deranged gun toters in our own front yards for the sake of personal rights, then why not with equally deranged foreign terrorists a few time zones away? Or, as George Carlin advised in his rant about airport security, "Take a fucking chance, will ya?"

Carlin was right—terrorism is the ultimate reality show. The shock and awe of the 9/11 attacks and videos of Islamic State beheadings in their own theater of provocation have come at a time when the violence on movie and TV screens has correspondingly risen to capture our dwindling attention spans. Our media loves the drama because we do. We don't watch guys make continuous left-hand turns at NASCAR races for three and a half hours because we enjoy watching them go like two-hundred-miles-per-hour lemmings. We watch them for the crashes.

Sure, we fell victim to a spectacular attack on September 11— mainly because we weren't paying attention. It took down some buildings, but not us. In fact, considering how much blood, treasure, and international standing we've lost since, you could better argue that it has been our response to terrorism more than terrorism itself that's really been doing us in.

Even though America is as safe and secure as it has ever been, the fear factor seems to drive everything. We still see the world predominantly in terms of threats—buying into a superficial narrative that "if we don't get them there, they'll get us here." We persistently pursue a highly costly strategy of global dominance, of intervening because we have monsters to destroy. The more we respond to the world out of fear, the more imperious and domineering, even arrogant, we become. That generates exactly what our enemies look for, and it makes their propaganda all the more effective. Arrogance, after all, is a substitute for the confidence of humility, and fear is fed by ignorance. The result is negativism: When you see the world first and foremost as a negative, then you act upon it negatively. It's karma, baby.

Perpetual warfare—not just social entitlements—has been the single greatest driver of our fiscal insolvency ever since 9/11, adding four to six trillion dollars to the national debt in fighting wars; defense spending wasteful orders of magnitude well beyond many other parts of the government; the costs of care of veterans and wounded warriors; and lost opportunity costs in infrastructure, public education, health, and other national investments. Along with homeland security and intelligence, the defense portion of what the Global Peace Index calls security spending remains at least 25 percent of the federal budget— more than what we spend on Social Security and about the same as we spend on Medicare and Medicaid together. Foreign aid? One penny from that same dollar.

Money's one thing, but freedom is another. Perpetual warfare predicated on the thin threat of terrorism has enabled not only the continuation but the expansion of a national security and intelligence apparatus that should have been pared back after the Cold War ended. What Benjamin Franklin would call our greatest existential threat is our decision to value security over freedom, and as James Madison, among others, phrased it, "No nation could preserve its freedom in the midst of continual warfare."

America cannot long remain the land of the free if it is no longer the home of the brave. When *national security* is the dominant narrative that ends debate, makes us all toe the political line, and makes everything else nice to do—and when a government, in a blanket sense, views its citizens as potential or suspected criminals or enemies of the state—then the United States can hardly hold claim to being the world's beacon of life, liberty, and the pursuit of happiness.

We are less liked not so much because of what we say we stand for. It's more because we don't stand for what we say. We make ourselves the exception to the rules we invented but expect everyone else to follow; we say we're special but don't always act that way. No one can stand a hypocrite for very long. When you lose your moral credibility, you lose the right to lead—and all the perks and bennies that go with it.

The other problem with all this pervasive negativism is that it generates an unwillingness to face the frontiers of change, to step outside our comfort zones and reach out to the other side of the aisle, let alone the other side of the ocean, in a real sense of human connectivity. When the world sees the large gap between what we say and what we do, and because fear overrules hope, then we are telegraphing our weaknesses rather than playing our strengths. Team America is playing not to lose, and playing not to lose is a strategy for losers. Name me one championship team that has won that way.

There's plenty of evidence that we're going under, but this is as much a psychological condition as it is a physical or virtual reality. Besides, we're doing better than advertised—we still have a lot more strengths to play than weaknesses to worry about. Huntington also noted that, in these cycles of declinism, fear plays a catalyzing role in national renewal. "Declinism is a theory that has to be believed to be invalidated," he wrote. Otherwise, that fear of decline becomes a self-fulfilling prophecy. Americans have also made a living out of being "misunderestimated"—if not by our adversaries, then by ourselves. We set ourselves up for failure because we love rooting for the underdog and casting ourselves as the comeback kids. It's in our DNA—hence Churchill's remark about doing the right thing at the last moment.

The larger point is that most of our sense of decline is an emotional response to something we perceive, rightly or wrongly. If it were a person, the United States of America would probably be diagnosed as borderline manic-depressive. If the country really is going to hell in a handbasket, it's because its citizens have finally convinced themselves to believe it is this time.

Our inherent strengths go beyond the blessings of geography, our demographic diversity, and our capacity for self-reinvention. Among them is an integrated immigration–assimilation culture centered on the simple yet sophisticated principle of E pluribus unum. This is, in fact, our greatest comparative advantage in the twenty-first century—a societal software the Russians or Chinese can neither hack into nor pirate. From a demographic perspective, we are becoming more the country we were set up to be in the first place. Our national formula of identity is a complex fractional equation, and although those fractions feature many numerators of human multiplicity, there is always one common denominator—personal freedom and human dignity.

But with every form of freedom comes an equal and concomitant responsibility—we have to walk our talk and live our values, here even more than there. Value-basing is essential to applied personal, organizational, or national strategy. Values, played out in space and time, provide impetus for identity as well as interests, which in turn inform strategy and policy, and then the actions of organizations and individuals—within as well as beyond our shores.

If we're honest with ourselves, what we're really uncomfortable, angry, and even fearful about is that, in many ways all at once, we have to get out of our comfort zones and change some of our ways. Individually as well as collectively, we now have to take the harder rights over the easier wrongs. For two centuries we didn't have to care much about the world beyond ourselves, at home or abroad, because it didn't affect us on a personal level all that much. Many of the strengths derived from geographic insularity and self-sufficiency have now become liabilities. Fear and ignorance do neither a great people nor a great nation make.

The painful moment of truth has arrived. If we don't like what's going on in or with our country, the first place to look is in the mirror. We say we don't like our government, but when so few of us show up to vote or sit in on a town hall meeting, we're getting exactly what we deserve. We say we hate all the mudslinging in Washington and the media, but our own dialogue seems to start off with how bad the government is rather than what should be made good about it. We don't want to pay taxes but want all the entitlements, including the national security complex, while expecting to reduce the national debt. We want it all our way but can't have it all our way. We and our elected leaders can no longer afford our supersized self-indulgence and willful ignorance. Washington is not going to fix itself, no matter what the polls or the pols say. We got away with absentee citizenship for much of our national life, but we can't anymore. The world beyond our doors and shores just won't let us anymore.

Not all the answers are in Washington, anyway. It's our communities that make our country great. The good news is that networks of metropolitan and municipal leaders—mayors, business and labor leaders, educators, and philanthropists—are stepping up to move the nation forward, in a demonstration of cooperation among organizations that once competed with each other. "Our potholes are neither Republican nor Democrat," one Texas town council member told me.

The key is in collaboration and engagement, which the latest generations seem to understand better than my own. Millennials are coming of age at a time when America is being humbled at home as well as on the world stage. More cognizant of the limits of American power and disenchanted with American exceptionalism as it has been practiced, they seem to care more about what happens beyond our borders. They tend toward multilateralism and a more cautious use of military force. More reluctant to think of their country as fundamentally superior to others, they are less likely than other generations have been to agree that foreign cultures are inferior. They like (soccer) football—the world's game—much more. In some rejection of the consumerism and materialism of their elders, they are learning to identify themselves more through their networks than their possessions.

Not long after I came back from my cross-country trip, I was attending a seminar at the National Defense University where, once again, discussion was focused on the issue of the rules of engagement in places like Afghanistan being too complex and restrictive for soldiers on the ground. Having heard this one too many times, I piped up.

"To say the American soldier is unable to grasp complexity in the heat of combat is to sell that young person short. These young people understand complexity and nuance far better than we do. Just look at their family situations. Half their parents are divorced. They have stepmothers, stepfathers, stepsisters, and stepbrothers. They didn't grow up in our Ozzie-and-Harriet, *Leave It to Beaver* world of white picket fences, and they have less of a problem with ethical as well as social diversity. Besides," I said, "try explaining to non-Americans what 'Three strikes and you're out' means."

People have multiple identities—in their professions, family lives, social circles, and so on. What makes you the same person in your various personal manifestations is your character—what you believe in enough to live out in all of them.

"So what they need are a handful of core principles to adopt and adapt, not a laundry list of rules," I went on. "Give them more credit than that. What they really need is a greater understanding of the political and cultural contexts of where they are and what they're doing there—and a clear communication from their chain of command on what's important. If the punishment for losing a weapon is still far greater than for burning a Koran, then you shouldn't be surprised at what you get. It's called command intent. American service personnel are always at their best when they understand not what they're doing as much as why they're doing it. They don't need training as much as they need education—to understand how the principles they are being taught work in their day-to-day duties."

In the same respect, Jefferson's informed and active citizenry is an idea whose time has finally come. As I told Joey back in Jersey City, the governance we need comes from citizenship as responsible to our neighbors as it is to our nation. And for those whose attitudes toward government, politics, and civic duty range from apathy to enmity—when you go bad on the system, the system goes bad on you. Our leaders won't rise to the occasion any more than we do. If you don't know who you are and what you're about, events control you more than you control them. Learning that takes a journey. The world we inhabit is often a cold, hard, and unfair place. It always has been. But you can't find the goodness in it unless you find the goodness in yourself. They are one and the same.

It begins and ends with us—what is good about America is all our doing; what is not is all our fault. That's why our behavior, big and small, should strive to reflect more what we're for and not what we're against. "The key to the future of the world," Pete Seeger said, "is finding the optimistic stories and letting them be known." What the heroes in our personal and collective consciousness have been teaching us is not just to keep the big picture and the long run in mind while living in the moment—but also to think globally and act locally.

"I think life is always dangerous," Nobel Peace Prize winner Malala Yousafzai told us. "Some people get afraid of it. Some people don't go forward. But some people, if they want to achieve their goal, they have to go. They have to move. Some people only ask others to do something. I believe that, why should I wait for someone else? Why don't I take a step and move forward?"

In a world of uncertainty, there's one thing we can be sure of: What we refuse to experience positively we will most assuredly experience negatively. Motorcycling is again an appropriate metaphor. Like people and nations, you can only stay upright when moving forward— there's no reverse gear. Neither is there any robo-drive. You have to actually attend to it, constantly, like freedom and democracy. Not too fast and not too slow for the conditions. Riding safely and successfully requires balance, anticipation, and understanding those conditions— and looking ahead and thinking about the future. What keeps you on track is your moral GPS—identifying yourself through values validated in action.

In terms of both personal and public senses of identity, what I learned most from this trip is that you have to learn from but let go of the journeys of the past to be ready for the journeys of the future. "Our consciousness is very spread out, and as a result it's hard to stay present," the actor Chris Evans said in an interview. "And if you can kind of stay present and know that's all you have in life—life is just a series of nows—if you can kind of surrender to that, you can never lose."

Somehow I knew that before I got rolling, but I had to do it anyway to revalidate it in my own life. That takes moral more than physical courage. I came to learn through my many journeys that, as Nelson Mandela said, "courage was not the absence of fear, but the triumph over it. The brave man is not he who does not feel afraid, but he who conquers that fear." Besides, moving on doesn't mean you have to leave everything behind you.

My mother is the most courageous person I know. She had a miserable childhood in wartime and postwar England, living in poverty and abandonment. Even though she had plenty of reasons to be, she was never mean-spirited toward us. She conscientiously broke her own cycle of negativity, and her children—and their children—are the better for it. It's the hardest thing for each and every one of us. Yet the power that enables us to say yes to the world, with all the good and bad, is the greatest of gifts. "The Eternal Feminine," Goethe ended *Faust*, "draws us on." It helped me summon the courage to be the rare officer of my rank to call Army OneSource to find out whether I had PTSD after I came back from Iraq. After a few sessions, it turned out I didn't—I was just angry—but having reached out helped me to move beyond that anger.

At the center of everything in our public lives is citizenship. Citizenship is ultimately a form of service to others—and by serving others, you serve (and save) yourself. That doesn't require a uniform. "I don't know what your destiny will be," said Albert Schweitzer, "but one thing I know: the only ones among you who will be really happy are those who will have sought and found how to serve."

By answering the constant call to citizenship—local, national, and global—we embrace and renew the strength and promise of American reinvention and renewal. Greatness is a lot of small things done well. Every one of us, in every generation, must take our own journey to learn what it means to be a citizen not only of our country but of a larger world that technology and trade are hooking us up with, within and beyond the horizons of our lifetimes. The choices we make along the way reveal our true character. By taking that personal journey, we change ourselves. When we change ourselves, we change our communities. By changing our communities, we change America. When we change America, we change the world.

Because the new frontiers are more psychological than physical, more internal than external, the path to a more perfect union and a more peaceful world lies within us. The big idea we seek has been with us all along: It is America itself. We need not look very far for that narrative. It's in our pockets and purses, on the back of a dollar bill. Look where the eagle's looking. How lucky, indeed, we are as a people—especially when we're good.

Both good leadership and citizenship require humility—an act of strength rather than a sign of weakness. Both reflect confidence in the future more than a fear imprisoned in the past. Isn't that, after all, what America should be most about? As I learned from my years abroad, Americans are no better than anyone else, but they are luckier. So when bad things happen, the best way to deal with it is to start with a positive and recall first what you know you've still got before obsessing about what you think you might have lost: Remember how lucky you are.

The present is a gift—that's why it's called a present. You cannot live in either the past or the future, but you can learn from one to look to the other. "Wisdom isn't a body of information," David Brooks noted in *The Road to Character*. "It's the moral quality of knowing what you don't know and figuring out a way to handle your ignorance, uncertainty, and limitation."

Eventually, you have to leave home in order to find home. The reason you take a trip, or do anything for that matter, is to validate in the heart what the head already knows. This usually results in the discovery of a new truth or a new understanding of it relevant to your time and place. "You've always had the power to go back to Kansas," the Good Witch told Dorothy—but she wouldn't have realized the strength and power she had if she hadn't gone to Oz to begin with. You learn by living, and when you stop learning, you stop living.

Even though I did not accomplish all the things I wanted to, either on my cross-country tour around America or during my thirty years of civil–military service, I am grateful to have been able to do both, for the places I've seen and the people I've come to know, for the experiences I've had, and for the things I've learned and the insights I've gained from them. In thought or in deed, greater engagement away makes us better persons at home. One thing I can tell you is that my life of service and sacrifice has made me a better American, because it has made me a more compassionate human being.

I have taken many journeys and will no doubt take many more—and what I've learned more than any other thing is not to fear the journey just because you're not sure how it will turn out. At the War College, I received a gift from someone helping me through a personal crisis—Dr. Seuss's *Oh, the Places You'll Go!* It has some great lines for anyone at any age on any journey:

You have brains in your head. You have feet in your shoes. You can steer yourself any direction you choose. You're on your own. And you know what you know. And YOU are the guy who'll decide where to go.... And while Bang-ups and Hang-ups can happen to you.... Today is your day! Your mountain is waiting. So ... get on your way!

America is in and of itself a journey—more than three hundred million of them—whose signposts are frontiers and whose ultimate destination is the world's and thus uncertain. It is the greatest collective adventure the world has ever seen. The arc of that collective journey is often a slow, imperfect, tortuous, violent, but inexorable march toward freedom and a more perfect union. But whether America is a family to which we are bound as much as a club to be joined is up to us.

I can't tell you what it should mean to you to be an American. You must go and find out for yourself. That journey, at first glance, is fraught with risks and dangers—but also opportunities. If past is prologue, then Americans should have little to fear other than their own unwillingness to embrace and navigate this future. We fear what we do not know, so we must learn more about the world around us, and thus ourselves—it's that engagement that frees us.

Peace out!

"Follow your bliss," Joseph Campbell advised his students, but bliss, like freedom, is not just doing what we want. As for anyone who finds art in his or her life, it's doing what you're compelled to do as an individual to find your place in the world. It's taking responsibility for your destiny. It's answering a call to a personal voyage in the public realm. We must all grab and pass the baton and run the human relay race, if only to enable others to do the same, as those who went before us did for us.

Get out and ride.

NOTES

INTRODUCTION

West Point professor Elizabeth D. Samet gives a fascinating account of how fellow veterans process their experiences in combat through motorcycling in *No Man's Land: Preparing for War and Peace in Post-9/11 America*, Farrar, Straus and Giroux, 2014. The reference to Robert Frost is from his poem "*The Road Not Taken.*" Of course, this book is heavily inspired by John Steinbeck's *Travels with Charley: In Search of America*, Penguin Books (reprint), 1980 (originally published in 1962). The quote from John Lennon can be found in numerous places, among them in his song "Beautiful Boy (Darling Boy)" in the *Double Fantasy* album released just before his death. The quote from Johann Wolfgang von Goethe, Germany's greatest literary figure, comes from www. brainyquote.com. This book was also inspired by Robert M. Pirsig's *Zen and the Art of Motorcycle Maintenance: An Inquiry into Values*, HarperTorch (reprint), 2006 (originally published in 1974). The Will Rogers quote comes from www.brainyquote.com. The reference to the "Skinner box," otherwise known as an "operant conditioning chamber," is a laboratory tool developed by the psychologist B. F. Skinner to study the behavior of mice in order to offer proof that most human behavior is conditioned. The Merton quote is from the Trappist monk Thomas Merton's *No Man Is an Island*, Mariner Books (reprint), 2002 (originally published in 1955). The quotes in this book from Pope Francis are from *Pope Francis: Conversations with Jorge Bergoglio: His Life in His Own Words*, written by Francesca Ambrogetti and Sergio Rubin, NAL, (reprint) 2014 (originally published in 2010). The Thomas Szasz quote can be found in www.brainyquote.com. The quote from David Brooks comes from *The Road to Character*, Random House, 2015.

CHAPTER 1—SOUTH CAROLINA

Al Santoli's book is *Everything We Had: An Oral History of the Vietnam War*, Ballantine Books, 1985. You can find out more about his Asia America Initiative at www.asiaamerica.org. John Keegan's book is *The Face of Battle: A Study of Agincourt, Waterloo, and the Somme*, Penguin Books, 1983. An excellent book I read much later on the issue of killing is West Point professor Lt. Col. Dave Grossman's *On Killing: The Psychological Cost of Learning to Kill in War and Society*, Back Bay Books, 1995. Walter Wintle's "Thinking" can be found in *Wikipedia*. Throughout this book, I quote from Khalil Gibran's *The Prophet*, Alfred A. Knopf, 1923. The General Social Survey is conducted by researchers at the University of Chicago. The quote from Larry Prusak comes from a March 4, 2010, interview he had with *Business Process Magazine*, which can be viewed on YouTube. The quote from Robert Putnam comes from *Bowling Alone: The Collapse and Revival of American Community*, Simon & Schuster, 2000. The interview with Malcolm Gladwell took place on April 12, 2015, on Fareed Zakaria's *GPS—Global Public Square* on CNN; a transcript is available at transcripts.cnn.com/transcripts. The quote from Army Chief of Staff General Raymond Odierno can be found in his article "The U.S. Army: Trusted Professionals for the Nation," *Army 2014-2015 Green Book*, October 2014. The reference to Don Quixote comes from Miguel De Cervantes's *Don Quixote*, translated by Edith Grossman, Harper Perennial (reprint), 2005 (originally published in two parts, in 1605 and 1615).

CHAPTER 2—MISSISSIPPI

Keep America Beautiful is a US-based nonprofit organization. Founded in 1953, it is the country's largest community improvement organization, with over one thousand affiliate and participating organizations participating in its programs. For more, go to www.kab.org. Much of the discussion about the geostrategic development of the United States is found in George Friedman's *The Next 100 Years: A Forecast for the 21st Century*, Anchor Books, 2010. Friedman also summarizes much of this discussion for his strategic intelligence corporation, Stratfor, in a series of articles called *The Geopolitics of the United States*, which can be obtained through www.stratfor.com. The renowned historian Stephen Ambrose explains the motivations leading to the exploration of the West in *Undaunted Courage: Meriwether Lewis, Thomas Jefferson, and the Opening of the American West*, Simon & Schuster, 1997. George Washington's Farewell Address of 1796 can be sourced from numerous places, most notably the Yale Law School Lillian Goldman Law Library. Alfred Thayer Mahan was among America's foremost historians and strategic thinkers, who argued in his seminal work, *The Influence of Sea Power Upon History, 1660–1783* (1890), that the power that dominates the seas would dominate the world. Dr. Ajit Maan succinctly explains the difference between Eastern and Western values and the meaning of *narrative* in *Counter-Terrorism: Narrative Strategies*, University Press of America, 2014. Shelby Foote's quote comes from "Episode I: The Cause" of Ken Burns's iconic documentary *The Civil War*, aired for the first time by the Public Broadcasting Service (PBS) in September 1990. The James Madison quote comes from "The Federalist #55—The Total Number of the House of Representatives," in a February 13, 1788, letter "To the People of the State of New York." All *The Federalist* Papers can be viewed at the Federalist Papers Project website, www. thefederalistpapers.org. Alexis de Tocqueville quotes are from the 2003 Penguin Books version of his classic *Democracy in America*, published in two volumes, the first in 1835 and the second in 1840, and written originally in French. The quotes throughout this book from Joseph Campbell's *The Power of Myth* are from the 1991 Anchor version of the book, written with Bill Moyers, who interviews him in the PBS series of the same name. Churchill quotes in this book are from www.brainyquote.com. The idea of balancing structure and chaos in organizational success is discussed by Shona L. Brown and Kathleen L. Eisenhardt in *Competing on the Edge: Strategy as Structured Chaos*, Harvard Business Review Press, 1998. *The Century of the Self* is a 2002 British television documentary series by Adam Curtis. It focuses on how the work of Sigmund Freud, Anna Freud, and Edward Bernays influenced the way corporations and governments have analyzed, dealt with, and controlled people. More can be found at *Wikipedia* and the film can be viewed on YouTube. The Institute for Propaganda Analysis is discussed and propaganda techniques are laid out at www.propagandacritic.com. I read the Randy Bernard quote in the May 16, 2010, edition of *USA Today*. The John Gardner quote can be found at www.brainyquote.com.

CHAPTER 3—TEXAS

Figures and analysis on US foreign aid can be found at the US State Department website (www.state.gov) under "Foreign Assistance Budget" as well as on *Wikipedia* and the website of the US Global Leadership Coalition (www.usglc.org). The quote from Joseph Campbell comes this time from *An Open Life*, Larson Publications, 1989. The Jefferson quote comes from www.brainyquote.com. Facts and analysis of US demographic developments are available from the Census Bureau at www.census.gov. The quote from Mark Twain comes from Ken Burns's documentary film *Mark Twain*. *History of the Second World War* by Marshall Cavendish was first published by BPC Publishing in 1966 and again in 1972, in 96 volumes, later expanded to 128 as the original series came to an end. Information on the Generalized Inequality Index, or Gini coefficient, can be found in many places, including *Wikipedia*. The Fragile States Index (formerly the Failed States Index) is an annual report on the relative stability of states around the world published by the Fund for Peace (www.fundforpeace.org) and *Foreign Policy* magazine since 2005. The Global Peace Index, produced by the Institute for Economics and Peace (www.visionofhumanity.org), ranks the nations of the world by their peacefulness. The Churchill quote is from www.brainyquote. com. The figures on foreign-born persons living in Germany and the United States can be found in *Wikipedia*. Joseph Campbell talks about the United States as a model for the world in *The Power of Myth*, published by Anchor in 1991. Information on the Alamo and Daniel Cloud is available from *Wikipedia* and www.history.com.

CHAPTER 4—NEW MEXICO

The Elizabeth Samet quotes come from her August 2, 2011, *BloombergView* op-ed, "On War, Guilt, and 'Thank You for Your Service.'" Both pictures posted in this part of the chapter can be downloaded from numerous sites. The term *Decade of War* is used in a 2012 Department of Defense study under the same title and can be downloaded from numerous sites, among them the *National Journal* (www.nationaljournal.com). All of the organizations cited in this chapter have their own websites. The Bernie Sanders quote can be found at multiple sources. The quotes from Admiral Mike Mullen are from an October 1, 2014, appearance on *The Colbert Report.* The Stephen Biddle observation comes from his article "Democracy and Military Effectiveness: A Deeper Look," written with Stephen Long, in the *Journal of Conflict Resolution*, vol. 48, no. 4, August 2004. Claude S. Fischer's "American Volunteer Spirit" can be found in the January/February edition of the *Saturday Evening Post.* The George H. W. Bush quote comes from www.notable-quotes.com. *Time* magazine's August 30, 2007, edition on "The Case for National Service" features numerous articles arguing for a broader concept of national service. ServiceNation's mission is to rekindle an ethic of civic responsibility in America through universal national service and to expand opportunities for young Americans to spend a year in nonmilitary national service in the organizations listed in the same paragraph in this chapter. For more, go to www.servicenation.org. United We Serve does likewise, but as a government-led nationwide service initiative that helps meet growing social needs resulting from the economic downturn. For more, go to www.serve.gov. Rolling Thunder and the LawRide each have their own websites. The Lincoln quotes can be found at *Wikiquote. SNAFU* is a term coined in the Army during World War II, meaning "Situation Normal—All Fucked Up."

CHAPTER 5—THE SOUTHWEST

The Khalil Gibran quote comes from *The Prophet.* Former Navy SEAL J. Robert DuBois inscribed my copy of *Powerful Peace*, Morgan James

Publishing, 2013, with "Here's to denting the universe!" Robert M.
Pirsig's quote is also from *Zen and the Art of Motorcycle Maintenance:
An Inquiry into Values*, HarperTorch (reprint), 2006 (originally published in 1974). The Oppenheimer quote is from www.brainyquote.
com. Russell Weigley's classic *The American Way of War: A History
of United States Military Strategy and Policy* was first published in
1973 by Indiana University Press. The quote attributed to Napoleon
is unverifiable; according to www.Bartleby.com: "A handwritten note
in Congressional Research Service files says that the War Department
Library had searched many times without success for a different version: 'Morale is to material as is the ratio of three to one.'" The quotes by
Anthony H. Cordesman come from his essay "The Real Revolution in
Military Affairs," *Commentary*, Center for Strategic and International
Studies, August 5, 2014. Stephen Ambrose is quoted here from *Citizen
Soldiers: The U.S. Army from the Normandy Beaches to the Bulge to the
Surrender of Germany*, Simon & Schuster, 1998. Colonel (ret.) Charlie
A. Beckwith, the founder of Delta Force, gave me an inscribed copy
of his book *Delta Force*, written with Donald Knox, Harcourt Brace
Jovanovich, 1983, just months before I left the *Armed Forces Journal
International* and reported to active duty in Germany. Max Boot's *The
Savage Wars of Peace: Small Wars and the Rise of American Power*, was
published by Basic Books in 2002. The Mitt Romney quote is from his
debate with President Barack Obama on October 22, 2012, which can
be pulled from most major media websites. George W. Bush first called
the Iraq War a "catastrophic success" at the end of August 2004, and the
quote is referenced on www.foxnews.com. The Ricks citation is from
Thomas E. Ricks's *The Generals: American Military Command from
World War II to Today*, Penguin Press, 2012. The "learning organization" reference is from John A. Nagl's *Learning to Eat Soup with a Knife:
Counterinsurgency Lessons from Malaya and Vietnam*, University of
Chicago Press, 2002. My copy of the *Truppenführung* was a reprint
given to me by a German army military attaché in 1984. The US Army
classified the document until 2000. However, it has been recently pub-
lished as *On the German Art of War: Truppenführung: German Army
Manual for Unit Command in World War II*, translated and edited by
Bruce Condell and David T. Zabecki, Stackpole Books, 2008. *The US*

Army Operations Field Manual, FM 100-5, of 1986 is considered the definitive "AirLand Battle" doctrine. The references to von Clausewitz all come from his classic *On War* (*Vom Kriege*), edited and translated by Michael Howard and Peter Paret, Princeton University Press, 1976. The book was originally published after his death by his wife between 1832 and 1835. Muhammad Ali's famous aphorism can be found through multiple sources online, including www.brainyquote.com.

CHAPTER 6—SIMI VALLEY

The Mark Twain quote is from *Wikiquote*. Nye coined the term *soft power* in a 1990 book, *Bound to Lead: The Changing Nature of American Power*, then further developed it in his 2004 treatise *Soft Power: The Means to Success in World Politics*. "The Tweet Is Mightier Than the Sword" is the title of an article by Max Boot in *Commentary* magazine, February 11, 2011. "NSC 68: United States Objectives and Programs for National Security," April 14, 1950, is available for download on numerous sites, including the US Department of State (www .state.gov), and discussed in *Wikipedia*. The Stalin quote was posted at the Reagan Library. The Steinbeck quote was likewise posted at the Steinbeck museum. Francis Fukuyama's *The End of History and the Last Man* made quite a splash when Simon & Schuster published it in 1992. Its more pessimistic retort was Samuel P. Huntington's *The Clash of Civilizations and the Remaking of World Order*, published by the same book company a few years later in 1996. The Pope Francis quote is from his book *His Life in His Own Words*, cited earlier. Daniel Schorr tells this story in his article "Perspective on the Next Big Threat" in the *Christian Science Monitor*, March 26, 1999. David Rothkopf's article "The Enemy Within" appears in *Foreign Policy* online, April 23, 2012. Tip O'Neill's famous phrase can be found at numerous sources online. *Soviet Military Power* is discussed in *Wikipedia*, and copies can be found online through numerous sources. *Pogo* is the title and central character of a long-running daily American comic strip, created by cartoonist Walt Kelly. The quote was a parody of a message sent in 1813 from US Navy Commodore Oliver Hazard Perry to Army General William Henry Harrison after his victory in the Battle of Lake Erie. The version you see appeared in time for Earth Day in 1970. For more, go to *Wikipedia*. The quote from Lincoln comes from Lincoln's address delivered to the Young Men's Lyceum of Springfield, Illinois, on January 27, 1838, titled "The Perpetuation of Our Political Institutions." The Alexis de Tocqueville quote is from *Democracy in America*, translated by J. P. Mayer, Harper & Row Publishers, 1969. Zakaria's "the democratization of violence" comes from his book *The Future of Freedom: Illiberal Democracy at Home and Abroad*, W. W. Norton & Company, 2007.

CHAPTER 7 — LIBERIA

The counterinsurgency doctrine Petraeus and Mattis developed is in Army Field Manual FM 3-24, *Tactics in Counterinsurgency*, April 2009. To find out more about international student exchanges, go to the US Department of State's Bureau of Educational and Cultural Affairs website. For information on the economic benefits of international students to the US economy, read the reports prepared by NAFSA: Association of International Educators, the Institute of International Education, and the State Department, available through their websites. For more on the Veterans for Smart Power program, go to the US Global Leadership Coalition's website. The reference to the quote by the French philosopher Henri Bergson is available at *Wikiquote*. The behavioral scientist Abraham Maslow proffered his idea of a hierarchy of needs in his 1943 paper on human motivational factors, "A Theory of Human Motivation," published in *Psychological Review*. Maslow used the terms *physiological, safety, belongingness, love, esteem, self-actualization*, and *self-transcendence* to describe the pattern that human motivations generally move through, in ascending order. T. E. Lawrence is more famously known as "Lawrence of Arabia." An archaeologist and British army officer renowned especially for his liaison role during the Sinai and Palestine campaigns, and the Arab Revolt against Ottoman Turkish rule of 1916–18, his lessons on insurgency and counterinsurgency are summed up in his book *Seven Pillars of Wisdom*. He is portrayed in the 1962 British film *Lawrence of Arabia*, starring Peter O'Toole. The reference to Jesus can be found in Matthew

13:8 and Mark 4:8. The Chinese proverb "Give a man a fish and you feed him for a day; teach a man to fish, and you feed him for a lifetime" can be found at numerous online sources. The Marshall Plan (officially the European Recovery Program) was the American initiative to aid Europe, in which the United States gave $13 billion (approximately $160 billion today) in economic support to help rebuild European economies after the end of World War II. See *Wikipedia* for more. The well-known Theodore Roosevelt quote came from www.brainyquote. com. Pope Francis is again sourced from his book *His Life in His Own Words*, cited earlier.

CHAPTER 8—THE PACIFIC COAST

A good book to read on Hearst Castle is Victoria Kastner's *Hearst Castle: The Biography of a Country House*, Harry N. Abrams, 2000. The Monuments Men were curators and archivists, artists and art historians brought into uniform during World War II to save and preserve art and cultural treasures from Nazi, and later Soviet, pillaging. The story is explained in Robert M. Edsel's book *The Monuments Men: Allied Heroes, Nazi Thieves and the Greatest Treasure Hunt in History*, Center Street, 2010, as well as in the movie of the same name starring George Clooney and the documentary film *The Rape of Europa*. Navy Chaplain Walter Colton's phrase is quoted on display at the Colton Hall Museum in Monterey, California. Guttieri's *Masters of Peace* had not yet been published as this book went to print. Jeffrey Record's op-ed "'Lessons' of Desert Storm" appeared in the May 16, 1991, edition of the *Baltimore Sun*. The Powell Doctrine can be found online at www. foreignpolicy.com, among other sources. *Black Hawk Down: A Story of Modern War* is a book published in 1999 by Mark Bowden, from which the movie was made. Thorwald Dethlefsen's *The Challenge of Fate* (*Schicksal als Chance*) is difficult to find in the United States. There is an English version by Coventure LTD, 1984, but it is expensive. General Odierno's remark is quoted in numerous places, including an October 23, 2013, online article by C. Todd Lopez, "Odierno: Those Who Doubt Relevance of Ground Forces Naïve," available through www.army.mil. His reference is to what the Army has been calling the human domain or human dimension of war, discussed in detail in "The U.S. Army Operating Concept (TRADOC Pamphlet 525-3-1)" of October 2014. The *Army Times* article on zero defects is by Patrick Pexton, "You Will Not Fail," in the February 12, 1996, edition. John Steinbeck's *America and Americans and Selected Nonfiction*, a collection of writings published by Penguin Classics in 1966, was his last book. The Michael Stipe induction of Nirvana in the Rock and Roll Hall of Fame can be viewed on the museum's website. Kennedy's October 26, 1963, speech at Amherst can be read on the National Endowment for the Arts and Kennedy Library websites.

CHAPTER 9 — THE NATIONAL PARKS

The term *Santa Claus* is largely an American invention, the concept going back as far as the anonymous publication of the poem "A Visit from St. Nicholas" (better known today as "The Night Before Christmas") in the *Troy Sentinel*, New York, on December 23, 1823. The Genesis text comes from Genesis 1:26. The text from President Theodore Roosevelt's seventh annual message to Congress on December 3, 1907, can be found at numerous online sources. Information on the national parks can be found on the National Park Service website and on *Wikipedia*. In addition, many insights are drawn from the Ken Burns documentary series *The National Parks*, broadcast by the Public Broadcasting Service in 2009. Information on UNTAES can be found on the UN website as well as *Wikipedia*. The Army Civil Affairs manual specifically in mind here is FM 41-10, *Civil Affairs Operations*, January 1993.

CHAPTER 10 — FROM WEST TO EAST

I read Stephen E. Ambrose's *Nothing Like It in the World: The Men Who Built the Transcontinental Railroad 1863–1869*, Simon & Schuster, 2001, while in Kuwait waiting to go to war in Iraq. The information and descriptions of the building of the Transcontinental Railroad are from this book as well as from *Wikipedia*. Kennedy's "New Frontier" is available through the John F. Kennedy Presidential Library and

Museum website (www.jfklibrary.org). The quote from Goethe comes from www.brainyquote.com.

CHAPTER 11—THE GREAT PLAINS

Much of the information and description of the Battle of the Little Bighorn comes from notes from the monument docent's presentation as well as Nathaniel Philbrick's *The Last Stand: Custer, Sitting Bull, and the Battle of the Little Bighorn*, Penguin Books, 2011, and *Wikipedia*. Mark Twain is quoted in this chapter from *Mark Twain*, the 2002 Ken Burns series for the Public Broadcasting Service. Barbara Tuchman's *The Guns of August*, Presidio Press, 2004 edition, was originally published in the summer of 1962. President Kennedy had just read it when the Cuban Missile Crisis began and leaned on it very heavily for its lessons on how not to inadvertently lead nations into war. General Tommy Franks talks about the rolling start and other considerations attributable to him in his *American Soldier*, written with Malcolm McConnell, Regan Books/Harper Collins, 2004. War correspondent Rob Schultheis, in *Waging Peace: A Special Operations Team's Battle to Rebuild Iraq*, Gotham, 2005, gives a good description of the work of Civil Affairs in Iraq from the ground perspective. Colin Powell's references to NGOs as "force multipliers," starting in late 2001 after the invasion of Afghanistan in a speech as secretary of state to NGO representatives, raised the ire of many humanitarian organizations, eventually leading Doctors Without Borders to publish an "MSF Statement on Humanitarian Aid in Iraq" on October 31, 2003, on ReliefWeb. The Chief Seattle letter is cited in Joseph Campbell's *The Power or Myth*; however, a copy of the purported 1855 letter to President Franklin Pierce has never been found. My encounters with Hogg in Iraq are also depicted in Thomas E. Ricks's *Fiasco: The American Military Adventure in Iraq*, Penguin Press, 2006. The citation and reference to polls of Iraqis are from my paper, "Integrated Civil-Military and Information Operations: Finding Success in Synergy," *Cornwallis Group IX: Analysis for Stabilization and Counter-Terrorist Operations*, George Mason University–Pearson Peacekeeping Centre, 2005. The quote by Stephen

Ambrose is found on many quote sites and is attributed as a "personal quote."

CHAPTER 12—THE HEARTLAND

The Cronkite quote was transcribed from the 2014 CNN series *The Sixties*. The accomplishments and quotes from President Kennedy are from the Kennedy Presidential Library and Museum website. The quote by Randy Pausch can be found on *Wikiquote*. Edward A. Corcoran's *Threats and Challenges: Strategies in a New Century* was self-published in 2012.

CHAPTER 13—THE HOMESTRETCH

The quote of Churchill's last words can be found on numerous websites, but there is no official record of him saying this. Samuel P. Huntington's views on American declinism are mainly found in an article he wrote in the Winter 1988–89 issue of Foreign Affairs: "The U.S.—Decline or Renewal?" Carl Sagan's "celebration of ignorance" is referenced at www.goodreads.com. The Jonathon Gatehouse citation is from his May 15, 2014, article, "America Dumbs Down," in Maclean's online magazine. Fareed Zakaria's idea of "the rise of the rest" is discussed in numerous articles and appearances, but they essentially source from his book *The Post-American World*, W. W. Norton & Company, 2009. William Butler Yeats's "The Second Coming" was written in 1919, just after the end of the First World War. The book *The Metropolitan Revolution: How Cities and Metros Are Fixing Our Broken Politics and Fragile Economy*, Brookings Institution Press, 2013, was written by Bruce Katz and Jennifer Bradley. James Madison's "passion never fails to wrest the sceptre from reason," cited earlier, is used for the second time here. Carlin's discussion of airport security and terrorism is in his 1999 performance on HBO, "You Are All Diseased"—which means it preceded 9/11. The national-security-related contribution to the national debt is made with reference to a March 2013 paper by Linda J. Bilmes of the Harvard John F. Kennedy School of Government, "The Financial Legacy of Iraq and Afghanistan:

How Wartime Spending Decisions Will Constrain Future National Security Budgets." The proportion of security spending and foreign aid are from the same sources on the Foreign Assistance Budget and Global Peace Index cited in Chapter 3. The Madison quote is from *Wikiquote*. Peter Seeger is quoted in www.brainyquote.com. Malala Yousafzai is quoted extensively in www.brainyquote.com and in *Wikiquote*. Chris Evans is quoted in the article, "All-American Hero," by Christy LeMire, in the May 2015 edition of *American Way* magazine. The Nelson Mandela quote is from *Wikiquote*, whereas Albert Schweitzer's is from www.brainyquote.com.

ABOUT THE AUTHOR

Christopher Holshek, colonel (retired), US Army Civil Affairs, is on the Leadership Council of the US Global Leadership Coalition's Veterans for Smart Power program, a senior fellow at the Alliance for Peacebuilding, and a senior associate at Protect the People. His three decades of military service included command of the first Army Civil Affairs battalion to deploy to Iraq, from which he was featured on *60 Minutes*, *PBS NewsHour*, and France's Arte TV. An international consultant on civil–military relations and operations, he is among the few Americans to have served in United Nations field missions in civilian and military capacities. He writes extensively on peace and security matters, with articles appearing regularly in *Foreign Policy*, the *Huffington Post*, and numerous other publications worldwide.

ACKNOWLEDGMENTS

During my last promotion, to colonel, I told people that "what stands before you is the sum of the work of those who helped me along the way on my journeys." With respect to the first two journeys this book describes, my eternal and profound thanks go to the far many more unnamed as well as the named who have helped me along the way.

With respect to the third journey, journalist, writer, editor, author, ghostwriter, and producer Matthew Hall provided sage advice and counsel in navigating the publishing world and helping me take the first steps. Sincere gratitude also goes out to my friends and colleagues who have shared their insights and ideas, especially the alumni of the Project on National Security Reform—Jim Locher, Nancy Bearg, Margaret Cope, Ed Corcoran, Priscilla Enner, Jack Gatesy, Dale Pfeifer, Nate Olson, Bob Polk, Rei Tang, Wally Walters, and the many others who set me on the path to this book in the creation of *Two Wheels and Two Questions*.

A special *danke vielmals!* to Hilda Nighswander, who helped me edit not only *Two Wheels and Two Questions* but also the first series of drafts of *Travels with Harley*.

My heartfelt appreciation goes to Jaimee Garbacik, of Footnote Editorial, developmental editor extraordinaire and author whisperer, whose candor and courage (and 984 comments) helped me find balance and voice to smooth the manuscript's many rough edges.

Immense thanks go out to the tremendous team at Inkshares led by Larry Levitsky, Thad Woodman, and Jeremy Thomas and including Tess Klingenstein, Angela Melamud, and Matt Kaye, as well as Holly McGuire and Devon Fredericksen at Girl Friday Productions, all of whom patiently helped this tenderfoot tread the crowdfunding, publication, and production labyrinths to produce the best (97,000+) words I could. And thanks to Marc Cohen of MJC Design for capturing the spirit of *Travels with Harley* on the cover, as well as to Rebecca Jaynes for her thorough copyedit and whose attention to detail in checking of every fact, figure, map reference, and quote left even this old soldier impressed!

To the multitude of backers and endorsers—among them Sarah Williamson and Protect the People, which sponsored my first public book introduction and reading—thank you!

To the Freedoms Foundation, ServiceNation, the Alliance for Peacebuilding, the Civil Affairs and Foreign Area Officers Associations, the Reserve Officers Association, the United Nations Association, the International Fellowship of Motorcycling Rotarians, the Harley Owners Group, and so many other organizations and individuals—thank you for helping to spread the message and pass the baton.

And most of all, I am eternally grateful for the perfect kindness of my wife, Rosa, who has helped me understand that the pathways to success are traveled by those who believe in themselves and the good that life can bring.

LIST OF PATRONS

Travels with Harley was made possible in part by the following grand patrons who preordered the book on Inkshares.com.

Thank you.

Albert M. Santoli
Alois Kuntz
Angela R. Dickey
Brad Gutierrez
Coulter D. Tillett
Dolores R. Goble
Edward J. McDonnell
Franz Kuntz
Gregory J. D'Emma
Harvey J. Langholtz
Hilda Nighswander
Hughes S. Turner
James R. Locher III
John R. Lytle
John R. Monahan
Jonathan Andrews
Jordan D. Ryan
Joseph P. Kirlin
Justin T. Arrington

Karen M. Walsh
Kevin A. Kaufman
Lance R. Hartwich
Lincoln S. Farish
Lucy Turner
Margaret D. Hayes
Michael M. Goble
Patricia DeGennaro
Rosa Zorzo
Sarah Williamson
Sean A. Porter
Stephen Vincent Sass
Vanessa Dornhoefer
Victoria Cartagena
William F. Smith

ABOUT INKSHARES

Inkshares is a crowdfunded book publisher. We democratize publishing by having readers select the books we publish—we edit, design, print, distribute, and market any book that meets a preorder threshold.

Interested in making a book idea come to life? Visit inkshares.com to find new projects or start your own.